EMORY UNIVERSITY STUDIES IN LAW AND RELIGION

John Witte Jr., General Editor

Power over the Body, Equality in the Family:
Rights and Domestic Relations in Medieval Canon Law
Charles J. Reid Jr.

Religious Liberty in Western Thought
Noel B. Reynolds and W. Cole Durham Jr., eds.

Hopes for Better Spouses: Protestant Marriage and Church Renewal in Early
Modern Europe, India, and North America
A. G. Roeber

Political Order and the Plural Structure of Society
James W. Skillen and Rockne M. McCarthy, eds.

The Idea of Natural Rights:
Studies on Natural Rights, Natural Law, and Church Law, 1150-1625
Brian Tierney

The Fabric of Hope: An Essay
Glenn Tinder

Liberty: Rethinking an Imperiled Ideal
Glenn Tinder

Religious Human Rights in Global Perspective: Legal Perspectives
Johan D. van der Vyver and John Witte Jr., eds.

Divine Covenants and Moral Order: A Biblical Theology of Natural Law
David VanDrunen

Natural Law and the Two Kingdoms:
A Study in the Development of Reformed Social Thought
David VanDrunen

Early New England: A Covenanted Society
David A. Weir

God's Joust, God's Justice
John Witte Jr.

Religious Human Rights in Global Perspective: Religious Perspectives
John Witte Jr. and Johan D. van der Vyver, eds.

Justice in Love
Nicholas Wolterstorff

Secular Government, Religious People

Ira C. Lupu *&* Robert W. Tuttle

WILLIAM B. EERDMANS PUBLISHING COMPANY

GRAND RAPIDS, MICHIGAN / CAMBRIDGE, U.K.

Published 2014 by
Wm. B. Eerdmans Publishing Co.
2140 Oak Industrial Drive N.E., Grand Rapids, Michigan 49505 /
P.O. Box 163, Cambridge CB3 9PU U.K.

Printed in the United States of America

20 19 18 17 16 15 14   7 6 5 4 3 2 1

Library of Congress Cataloging-in-Publication Data

Secular government, religious people / Ira C. Lupu & Robert W. Tuttle.
      pages   cm.   — (Emory University studies in law and religion)
   ISBN 978-0-8028-7079-7 (pbk.: alk. paper)
   1. Church and state — United States.
   2. Christianity and politics — United States.
   I. Lupu, Ira C.   II. Tuttle, Robert W., 1963-

   BR516.S38   2014
   322'.10973 — dc23

                    2014012159

www.eerdmans.com

Contents

Acknowledgments

This project was supported by a generous grant from the Alonzo L. McDonald Family Agape Foundation to the Center for the Study of Law and Religion at Emory University, and was prepared by the authors as Senior Fellows of the Center. The authors wish to thank especially Ambassador Alonzo L. McDonald, Peter McDonald, and the other McDonald Agape Foundation Trustees for their support and encouragement. The opinions in this publication are those of the authors and do not necessarily reflect the views of the Foundation or the Center.

Many others have urged us onward in this project, and they too deserve our gratitude. Our spouses, LeeAnn Schray (Bob's spouse) and Nancy Altman (Chip's spouse), have been infinitely supportive of and patient with us. Our extended families have gotten to know us and each other, and have been wonderful cheerleaders for the enterprise. Bob and Lee's dog, Agnus, has been our canine muse as we circled the Palisades neighborhood of D.C. and talked through the various chapters. Our deans and faculty colleagues at George Washington University have likewise been in our corner — providing research support, grilling us at workshops on various chapters, engaging us in helpful conversation, and generally being encouraging at all the right moments. We thank them all. We also thank the Pew Charitable Trusts and the Pew Forum on Religion & Public Life for supporting earlier work that fueled ideas carried forward in this book. In particular, we very much appreciate the support of Julie Sulc, who was our grant officer at the Pew Charitable Trusts, and the efforts of Luis Lugo, Sandy Stencel, Alan Cooperman, and David Masci at the Pew Forum.

For years, we have been studying and learning from the work of many others in the field. Our footnotes cannot and do not reflect all of that, but the book surely does. Several scholars in the field have been unusually important to us, both in their written work and in the moral support they have provided. John Witte may be *primus inter pares* in this regard; his model of scholarly excellence, personal integrity, and intellectual seriousness as the leader of Emory University's Center for the Study of Law and Religion has inspired us, and his patience with us in regard to this work gave us the time and space we needed to bring it to fruition. Others have also played a special role, as both scholars to emulate and friends who would tell us when we seemed on the right or wrong track. These include Fred Gedicks, Sally Gordon, Kent Greenawalt, Barbara Bradley Hagerty, Marty Lederman, Bill Marshall, Melissa Rogers, and Steve Smith.

Many, many others in the field have produced scholarship that taught and provoked us. At the inevitable risk of omitting some who should be included, we thank Frank Alexander, the late Milner Ball, Bob Benne, Tom Berg, Kathleen Brady, Alan Brownstein, Angela Carmella, Jesse Choper, Dan Conkle, Caroline Corbin, Chris Eisgruber, Carl Esbeck, Rick Garnett, John Garvey, the late Steven Gey, Steve Green, Abner Greene, Philip Hamburger, Marci Hamilton, B. Jesse Hill, Russell Hittinger, Cathy Kaveney, Andy Koppelman, Kurt Lash, Doug Laycock, Chris Lund, Michael McConnell, Jim Oleske, Michael Paulsen, Michael Perry, Jean Porter, Frank Ravitch, Larry Sager, Richard Schragger, Micah Schwartzman, John Stumme, and Nelson Tebbe. We apologize to anyone whose work we have studied and whose name we have inadvertently omitted.

We also want to express our deep appreciation for the many excellent lawyers in this field who have been our constant interlocutors over the past decade. One of the greatest benefits of working in Washington, D.C., is the rich professional community of practitioners devoted to advocacy at the intersection of religion and civil government. Through innumerable conversations about cases and pending legislation, moots in preparation for appellate arguments, and lunches just for the joy of talking about these issues, we have learned much that is reflected in this book. In these lawyers, we have also experienced firsthand the combination of intellect, skill, and passion that reflects the best of the bar. We thank Mark Chopko, Kyle Duncan, Maggie Garrett, Luke Goodrich, Phil Harris, Holly Holman, Richard Katskee, Ayesha Khan, Alex Luchenitser, Dan Mach, Eric Rassbach, David Saperstein, Eric Treene, David Ullrich, Walter Weber, Bill Wildhack, and Lori Windham.

A great number of former students and research assistants have aided our work over the past decade, and their contributions are noted in each of those works. As we brought this book from idea to completion, Marc Bohn, Sheldon Gilbert, Andrea Goplerud, Ben Hazelwood, and Jesse Merriam added considerably to our insights, and we are especially grateful to them. Josh Violanti helped substantially in preparation of the index.

The project has had a lengthy period of gestation. In our more reflective moments, we see that it has been developing for as long as we have been serious students of the subject of religion and the Constitution. For Bob, that includes his studies in religious ethics as well as law, subjects that have occupied his energy since the mid-1980s. Bob's teachers in religious ethics — especially Jim Childress, David Novak, and Hans Tiefel — deserve special thanks, for sharing with Bob their deep learning and passion for studying and teaching, and also for their continued conversations with both of us as we worked on this and other projects at the intersection of law and religion. For Chip, the relevant period goes back to about the same time, when he began teaching a course on the First Amendment. When the two of us first met, as teacher and student at George Washington University Law School in 1990, the first inklings of the ideas that appear in this book had begun to form.

Since that time, we have worked together on many other projects related to religion and law, and all of them have contributed to the learning and analysis contained in this book. We know we have been guided by the efforts of many others, but we never forget to appreciate and thank each other for the patience, the determination, the learning, the willingness to struggle with ideas, and, most profoundly, the friendship that we hope this book reflects.

Note to readers: The documentation of legal sources uses the form of "volume number, then name of series or journal, then relevant page number within the work, then date." For example, the citation *Van Orden v. Perry,* 545 U.S. 677 (2005), means that the U.S. Supreme Court's decision in the case of *Van Orden v. Perry,* decided in 2005, can be found in Volume 545 of the U.S. Reports (Supreme Court decisions), beginning at p. 677.

The manuscript for this book was completed prior to the Supreme Court's decisions in *Town of Greece v. Galloway,* a case discussed in chapter 5, and the contraceptive mandate cases, the issues in which are discussed in chapter 7. At the end of the book, we have added an Authors' Note on the Court's decision in *Town of Greece v. Galloway.* Time did not permit preparation of a similar note on the contraceptive mandate cases.

Introduction

CHAPTER 1

A Secular Government for a Religious People

Justice William O. Douglas famously said that "We are a religious people whose institutions presuppose a Supreme Being."[1] The justice was half-right. We are a religious people. Although studies show increasing rates of those who identify as atheist or agnostic, we still have rates of religious belief and observance that consistently rank the United States among the most religious countries in the developed world.[2] Religious movements have played central roles throughout American history, from the first European settlements through abolitionism to the contemporary debates over abortion and same-sex marriage. Indeed, many people believe deeply that the nation itself, including its government, has special religious significance.

But Justice Douglas was also half-wrong. Our political institutions do not "presuppose" a Supreme Being. The Constitution does not mention a deity,[3] and the institutions described in that founding document are not logically dependent on the idea or existence of a deity. The authority of law does not rest on revealed truth or even the idea of a Supreme Being. Moreover, the Constitution specifically bars any religious test for federal office,[4] so government service may not be conditioned on belief in a deity. Although many see a Supreme Being actively at work in the nation, the government

1. *Zorach v. Clauson*, 343 U.S. 306, 313 (1952).

2. The richest collection of data on this subject can be found at the U.S. Religious Landscape Survey of the Pew Forum on Religion and Public Life, available here: http://religions.pewforum.org/.

3. The signing statement, issued by those who drafted the Constitution in Philadelphia during the summer of 1787, included the phrase "year of our Lord," but that statement is not part of the Constitution itself.

4. U.S. Const., Art. VI, §3.

may not make that claim. We are a religious people, but we have a secular government.

This book explores the idea of secular government for a religious people. The idea rests on a foundational claim that is often overlooked or rejected — the distinction between the government and the people. The government, in Abraham Lincoln's words, is "of the people, by the people, and for the people,"[5] but the two are distinct. The people have diverse and robust views about religion, and display an impressive range of religious beliefs and practices. The government respects and recognizes those commitments by acknowledging that they exist, by accommodating many of the religious needs of communities and individuals, by providing various forms of assistance to religious entities, and by guaranteeing rights related to religious exercise. But the government does not have a religious identity of its own. Whatever the current religious demography of America, we do not have a Christian state — or a Jewish, Islamic, theist, or atheist state, for that matter.

Some people argue, however, that the idea of secular government is hostile to religion, and effectively establishes an official "religion" of secularism.[6] Those concerns are misplaced. Properly understood, the idea of secular government is not hostile or even indifferent to religion. Instead, it simply reflects the limited authority of civil government. The genius of our political system is the distribution of power and responsibilities — some matters lie within the jurisdiction of federal authorities, others belong to the states, and still others belong only to the people. Within the federal government, the executive, legislative, and judicial branches occupy distinct spheres of competence. At their best, these structures and relationships reflect mutual respect among the various institutions, and an awareness that usurpation of another institution's authority undermines the welfare of the whole.

We believe that the relationship between civil government and religion is similar in important, though certainly not all, respects to the Constitution's allocation of powers among various political institutions. In the late eighteenth century, most European states — and several states of the United States

5. President Lincoln used this phrase near the end of the Gettysburg Address. The full text is here: http://en.wikipedia.org/wiki/Gettysburg_Address. The last lines include "that we here highly resolve that these dead shall not have died in vain — that this nation, under God, shall have a new birth of freedom — and that government of the people, by the people, for the people, shall not perish from the earth."

6. See, e.g., *Sechler v. State College Area Sch. Dist.*, 121 F. Supp. 439 (M.D. Pa.) (rejecting plaintiff's argument that cultural and secular celebration of Christmas by public school district was "hostile to Christianity").

— assigned the government responsibility to care for the religious welfare of the people. Through various kinds of religious establishments, governments declared and enforced orthodox beliefs, imposed taxes to support ministers and churches, and compelled attendance at worship. The nonestablishment principle withdraws that responsibility from civil government. Under the nonestablishment principle, the government does not promote religious worship, oversee religious indoctrination, or exercise religious authority. Instead, that responsibility belongs solely to the people and their voluntary religious communities.

It may seem unusual to think of nonestablishment in terms of the character and structure of civil government, because most Americans tend to view the relationship between government and religion through the language of rights. In conflicts over that relationship, some emphasize the right to be free from unwanted religious experience, while others assert the right to freely exercise their faith in all dimensions of life, including public institutions. Although their differences are sharp, these rival claims both focus on religious liberty — the right of individuals and communities in religious matters.

In this book, however, we ask how the interaction between religion and government shapes the character of civil authority. By examining the relationship in terms of the character of civil government, we reach a quite different understanding of the nonestablishment principle. As we explain, the nonestablishment principle defines a government that receives its authority from the people, not from revealed or transcendent sources, and that recognizes the limited scope of its authority over the people.

This chapter, which sketches the broad outlines of this approach, begins by looking at why current conflicts over the relationship between government and religion are typically expressed in the language of rights. Then it briefly discusses structural approaches in other legal contexts, most notably federalism and the separation of powers, but also in relations between government and nongovernmental entities such as families. The chapter then moves to the core of our approach, which turns on the idea that religion constitutes a jurisdictional limit on civil government. That limit, we argue, arises from the distinctive relationship between religion and the quality of government authority. Under the nonestablishment principle, the state may not invoke religion as a source of civil authority; must disclaim the comprehensive sweep of religion as a subject within the scope of civil authority; and may not invoke the concept of worship as the character of citizens' response to civil authority.

As we elaborate later in the book, our understanding of nonestablishment also has striking implications for the government's role in preserving

5

the religious liberties of the people. Those liberties are protected by a variety of constitutional provisions, including the Free Exercise Clause, as well as through discretionary decisions by government to accommodate religious objections to general laws. Through these mechanisms, the government protects the right of individuals and religious communities to believe, gather for worship, express their faith both within and without their own religious communities, and pursue religiously motivated social practices. Facilitating this collection of rights to religious freedom, however, is not the primary objective of nonestablishment. Nor does the language of rights offer the proper vocabulary or conceptual apparatus within which to frame or analyze nonestablishment.

Indeed, as later chapters emphasize, the principle of nonestablishment carries two important limits on a robust approach to religious liberty. First, the principle limits the state's power to privilege religion over analogous nonreligious beliefs and practices. Second, the principle constrains government decisions to exempt religious adherents from general laws that burden their exercise of religion, where the exemptions require government officials to make substantive judgments about the religious meaning or importance of the burdened activity.

In the remainder of this introductory chapter we ask whether our approach is consistent with the history of the religion clauses, and whether it finds any support in recent doctrine. The chapter concludes with an overview of the rest of the book, where we explore the jurisdictional understanding of secular government by giving close attention to a number of the most challenging and complex interactions between government and religion.

Nonestablishment and Rights Talk

In this era of the "culture wars," each day seems to bring another conflict over religion's place in the political community. The news is thick with stories: about a fight over official prayer at a city council meeting, the expansion of a synagogue, the presence of an evangelical club in a public school's extracurricular program, and the public funding of an Islamic charter school, to name only a few.[7] Although the settings of conflict vary, the basic arguments in the dispute remain essentially the same. One side asserts a right to be free

7. Howard Friedman's Religion Clause blog, http://religionclause.blogspot.com/, includes an excellent daily digest of these conflicts, running back over many years.

of government-backed religion. This side argues that government endorsement or support of religion violates the rights of those who don't share the favored beliefs. The other side asserts a countervailing right to full involvement of religious individuals in public life, including the opportunity to express religious views in public spaces, equal access to public funding of religious education and causes, and an equal entitlement to government promotion of religious messages. The conflicts thus involve mutually incompatible claims of rights.

By asserting these rival and incompatible rights, each side ignores half of the Constitution's distinctive way of connecting secular government and religious people. One group exalts the secularity of the state but dismisses the religious character of the people, and the government's legitimate responsiveness to that character. The other group denies the distinction between the government and the people, and expects the government to mirror and celebrate the community's (usually the majority's) religious identity.

The rhetoric and results of Supreme Court decisions in Establishment Clause cases have tended to reinforce the two sides' understandings of the conflict. As a vivid and important example, the Supreme Court decided a pair of legal challenges to government-sponsored displays of the Ten Commandments.[8] Plaintiffs in the two cases argued that the displays violated the Establishment Clause. Although the texts of the displays were nearly identical, the Court — by 5-4 votes — upheld one and invalidated the other. The difference between the outcomes is attributable solely to Justice Breyer, who alone was willing to uphold one display and strike down the other.

The other eight justices divided equally, and each side's reasoning illustrates the broader conflict of rights. The side that voted against the displays focused on the injury to observers. The government's support for religious views expressed in the displays caused those who did not share those views to experience a sense of alienation or exclusion. In this understanding, the Establishment Clause protects observers against government practices that endorse or promote religion, and official displays of the Ten Commandments do just that. In contrast, the justices who voted to uphold the displays argued that the Establishment Clause does not bar political majorities from using the government to express their shared religious beliefs.

The evolution of rights talk as a mode of Establishment Clause discourse can be traced to at least four causes. First, as a matter of both English

---

8. *McCreary County v. ACLU of Kentucky,* 545 U.S. 844 (2005); *Van Orden v. Perry,* 545 U.S. 677 (2005).

and colonial history, establishments of religion frequently involved suppression of rights of religious liberty. Second, the structure of adjudication, especially in the federal courts, demands the presence of a plaintiff who can show that his or her own personal interests have been adversely affected. Third, Establishment Clause principles came of age in American constitutional law primarily during the rights revolution brought on by the work of the Warren and Burger Courts. Fourth, the current contours of Establishment Clause law have been strongly shaped by arguments that robust enforcement of non-establishment principles violates the equality-based rights of religious individuals, messages, and institutions.

Disestablishment and Religious Liberty

Rights talk seems natural in this conversation because we tend to see non-establishment as an aspect of religious liberty. Limits on the state's involvement with religion promote the freedom of individuals and communities to practice religion as they see fit. The link between religious liberty and non-establishment has strong historical roots. Indeed, the characteristic marks of a state-established church — reflected in the mid-eighteenth-century Church of England — include a variety of forms of oppression.

- Compulsory attendance: under threat of criminal penalty, all people were required to attend worship. Stricter forms of establishment mandated worship only in the official church, while looser forms permitted people to choose from a list of acceptable places of worship.
- State-prescribed worship: public officials defined the content of orthodox beliefs and forms of worship. For example, the Church of England's 1662 *Book of Common Prayer* gained its authority in that church through a formal act of Parliament.
- State-controlled ministry: the government selected, paid the salaries of, and exercised control over religious leaders. In effect, ministers were themselves public officials, subject to removal when they failed to comply with government direction in matters of faith. So, for example, more than a thousand Anglican priests lost their positions ("livings") when they objected to official adoption of the 1662 *Book of Common Prayer.*
- Required support for the official faith: as a state institution, the official church received public support, often in the form of taxes imposed on the locality specifically for the purpose of funding the church.

- Suppression of other faiths: the government's promotion of an official church was often accompanied by prohibition or other legal restrictions on rival faiths. Laws prohibited publication of unapproved religious texts, public preaching by those who did not have an official license, and unauthorized assembly for worship.[9]

Many of these features of religious establishment appeared in the English colonies during the seventeenth and eighteenth centuries. In mid-seventeenth-century Massachusetts, religious dissenters could face harsh punishments; for example, Quakers who returned to that colony after being exiled for unlawfully proclaiming their faith could be executed. A number of colonies routinely punished unlicensed itinerant preachers, especially those active during the religious ferment of the First Great Awakening. And, in the years before the Revolution, Baptists were prosecuted in Virginia for failure to attend state-approved worship.[10]

A robust principle of nonestablishment directly addresses all those limits on religious liberty. If the government lacks jurisdiction over the religious welfare of its people, the state loses its power to define orthodox belief and worship, compel observance or financial support of religion, or control the personnel of a faith community. Nonestablishment thus protects voluntarism in religious matters — that is, the right of individuals and associations of individuals to choose their own faith commitments. In this historical light, nonestablishment seems to be focused on the protection of rights.

Standing to Sue — Injuries and Rights

The tendency to view nonestablishment principles through a prism of rights has been strenuously reinforced by the structure of adjudication in the federal courts, where most Establishment Clause cases are litigated. Article III of the Constitution extends the judicial power of the United States only to the de-

9. See generally Harold Berman, *Law and Revolution II: The Impact of the Protestant Reformations on the Western Legal Tradition* (Harvard University Press, 2003) (describing the legal relationships between church and state that emerged in the wake of the Protestant Reformation). For a succinct summary of the features of sixteenth-to-eighteenth-century religious establishments, see Michael W. McConnell, John H. Garvey, and Thomas C. Berg, *Religion and the Constitution* (Wolters Kluwer, 2nd ed., 2011), at 15-17, and sources cited therein.

10. James H. Hutson, *Church and State in America: The First Two Centuries* 83-89 (Cambridge University Press, 2008).

cision of cases and controversies, a limitation requiring a party who invokes judicial power to have "standing" to sue. To demonstrate such standing, a plaintiff in the federal courts must show (among other things) that he or she has been personally "injured in fact."

The requirement that a plaintiff demonstrate a personal injury has been particularly problematic in Establishment Clause cases. Most Establishment Clause claims involve, at base, government support of religious ideas or activities. When government is acting in a supportive way — for example, by subsidizing an activity, or speaking in its favor — it is sometimes difficult to identify anyone who is personally injured. Some people are displeased, offended, or even outraged when the United States declares a National Day of Prayer, for example, but it's not simple to identify anyone who is personally and materially hurt by that declaration or by the activities it may generate.

When Establishment Clause cases first began to appear at the Supreme Court, doctrines of standing seemed to be an impediment to the possibility of adjudication.[11] To facilitate the possibility of judicial enforcement of the Establishment Clause, the Supreme Court eventually relaxed the law of standing in several significant ways. The leading examples of this tendency appear in the doctrines of taxpayer standing and "observer" standing. For the former, the Supreme Court has created a special Establishment Clause exception to the general rule forbidding federal and state taxpayers from bringing suit in the federal courts to challenge the legality of government expenditures. The exception first appeared in 1968,[12] and it has come under recent fire,[13] but current law still permits state and federal taxpayers to challenge in the federal courts the constitutionality of at least some expenditures to promote religion. This kind of taxpayer standing is anomalous. Such taxpayers could not similarly complain, for example, about expenditures made to administer allegedly cruel and unusual punishments.

---

11. See. e.g., *Doremus v. Board of Education,* 342 U.S. 429 (1952) (taxpayer may not mount a suit in federal court against practice of Bible reading in public schools). The earliest Supreme Court decisions in school-funding cases came out of appeals from state courts, where the doctrines of taxpayer standing are more generous. See *Everson v. Bd. of Educ.,* 330 U.S. 1 (1947).

12. *Flast v. Cohen,* 392 U.S. 83 (1968).

13. *Hein v. Freedom from Religion Foundation,* 551 U.S. 587 (2007). For more discussion of these developments, see Ira C. Lupu and Robert W. Tuttle, *Ball on a Needle:* Hein v. Freedom from Religion Foundation, Inc. *and the Future of Establishment Clause Adjudication,* 2008 BYU L. Rev. 115. See also *Arizona Christian School Tuition Organization v. Winn,* 131 S. Ct. 1436 (2011).

Similarly, the Supreme Court and the lower federal courts routinely permit observers of government-sponsored religious displays to bring suit, complaining that the displays endorse religion in violation of the nonestablishment clause. The anomaly here is equally stark. It is unimaginable that the federal courts would recognize as plaintiffs anyone who simply observes other constitutional violations, such as an unreasonable search or an unfair trial. Whether or not the standing rules in Establishment Clause cases are viewed as defensible anomalies, they have unquestionably helped to frame Establishment Clause norms in the language of rights.

The Rights Revolution and the Establishment Clause

The Supreme Court's earliest efforts to shape the law of the Establishment Clause appeared in the late 1940s and early 1950s.[14] Virtually all of what became the core of the relevant doctrine, however, first appeared during the time of the Warren Court and the Burger Court. In retrospect, it is apparent that concerns of individual rights rather than government structure dominated the constitutional zeitgeist of that era, and strongly influenced the content of nonestablishment norms.

Many of the rights-focused themes that emerged in the three decades of the Warren-Burger era made their way into religion clause adjudication. The most liberty-protective interpretations of the Free Exercise Clause in the Court's entire history appeared in *Sherbert v. Verner* (1963) and *Wisconsin v. Yoder* (1971). In both decisions, the Supreme Court ruled that free exercise protection extended to religiously motivated conduct, not merely belief, expression, and association. When civil laws significantly burden religiously motivated conduct, the Court held, believers should be accommodated unless the government has exceptionally good reasons for refusing to do so. The Court relied heavily on doctrines aimed at intentional efforts by the government to limit speech or discriminate against racial minorities. In *Sherbert* and *Yoder*, however, the challenged laws were not intended to burden religious liberty. They simply had that effect. Extending such strict, rights-protective review to laws that imposed an incidental burden on religious experience thus elevated religious freedom to a preferred position among First Amendment rights, rather than assimilating the Free Exercise Clause with its coun-

---

14. Earlier decisions by the Supreme Court had said very little about the clause. See *Bradfield v. Roberts,* 175 U.S. 291 (1899); *Quick Bear v. Leupp,* 201 U.S. 50 (1908).

terpart rights of speech and press. For reasons we will explain in detail in a later chapter, the expansion of Free Exercise Clause rights in this era set the stage for a dramatic reevaluation of religious liberty law in the late twentieth century.

The Court's Establishment Clause principles also reflected rights-based concerns, though such concerns were often subordinated to structural considerations. Rights-based concerns played an important role in the most controversial of the Court's Establishment Clause decisions, the school prayer cases.[15] Those decisions, which involved state-mandated prayer and Bible reading in public schools, arose in a context that made the emphasis on individual injury seem obvious. Because mandatory attendance laws require children to attend school, religious exercises at public school have the character of state-compelled worship. This is especially true for children, who are vulnerable to such indoctrination, and very likely to feel peer pressure against opting out of the religious exercises. With those considerations in mind, many people see the school prayer cases as a guarantee of protection of students and parents against state-imposed religious experience.

These rights-based concerns may seem obvious in the context of school-sponsored worship, but they were more strained when the Court took up the question of public aid for religious entities. In *Lemon v. Kurtzman* and a wave of decisions that followed during the 1970s, the Court struck down efforts to fund or otherwise support religious schools.[16] Unlike the school prayer cases, the school aid decisions do not fit comfortably into the model of individual injury. The law requires no one to attend religious schools, and as long as all religious schools are equally eligible for aid, the government has not preferred one faith over others. As we explain later, the Court's school aid decisions generally focus on the problems of church-state entanglement and interreligious conflict, neither of which maps easily onto a model of individual injury. Nonetheless, rights-based concerns arise in the school aid decisions, chiefly through the argument that taxpayers have a right not to have tax funds spent for religious indoctrination. In this narrative, spending violates the consciences of taxpayers who do not share the government-supported faith.

The cleanest connection between concerns of personal injury and a

15. *Engel v. Vitale*, 370 U.S. 421 (1962); *Abington Sch. Dist. v. Schempp*, 374 U.S. 203 (1963).

16. For detailed discussion of the decisions about state funding of religious schools, see chapter 3.

rights-based theory of the Establishment Clause appears in litigation challenging government-sponsored religious messages. In this context, the concept of "observer" standing dovetails perfectly with the rights-based norm that government may not endorse religious messages that a hypothetical reasonable observer would perceive as creating classes of political insiders and outsiders on religious lines.[17] As reflected in cases about religious holiday displays, the Ten Commandments, and war memorials, concepts of personal offense and alienation control both standing to bring suit and the ultimate outcome of the dispute.[18]

Well after the rights revolution had run its course, a rights-based theory of nonestablishment still retained much of its rhetorical force. The Supreme Court's decision in *Lee v. Weisman* (1992), which invalidated government-sponsored prayer at a public school commencement, provides the best example. The school district had argued the case on the rights-focused theory that the Establishment Clause barred only coercive practices, and that prayer at commencement was not coercive. Justice Kennedy's opinion showed the influence of that framing, though he concluded that the prayer practice was sufficiently coercive to violate the clause. Kennedy described the case as one in which "[t]he sole question presented is whether a religious exercise may be conducted at a graduation ceremony in circumstances where, as we have found, young graduates who object are induced to conform."[19]

The Court's nonestablishment decisions in this period may have been framed in the language of rights, but themes of structure and jurisdiction persisted, even if occasionally relegated to the margins.

Countervailing Rights Claims: Nonestablishment as Discrimination

Opponents of robust church-state separation have further strengthened the tendency to understand nonestablishment in rights language. Against separationists' asserted right to be free of government-sponsored religion, these

17. The fullest elaboration of this norm can be found in Christopher L. Eisgruber and Lawrence G. Sager, *Religious Freedom and the Constitution* ch. 4 (Harvard University Press, 2007).

18. See for examples the Ten Commandments cases, cited n. 8 above; *Lynch v. Donnelly*, 465 U.S. 668 (1984) (display of Christmas nativity scene); *Allegheny County v. ACLU*, 492 U.S. 573 (1989) (displays involving Christmas nativity scene, Hanukkah menorah, and Christmas tree); *Salazar v. Buono*, 559 U.S. 700 (2010).

19. *Lee v. Weisman*, 505 U.S. 577, 599 (1992).

opponents claim a right to public funding of religious activities, equal access to speech forums, and official recognition of widely held religious sentiments. Indeed, they argue that separationism discriminates against religious people and religious messages, and thus violates core principles of equality.[20]

In *Everson*, the decision that first applied the Establishment Clause to state and local governments, Justice Black outlined a very broad principle of nonestablishment, justified as a protection for religious liberty. But he also said that limits on government aid for religion must be balanced against the state's obligation to provide equal "benefits to all its citizens without regard to their religious beliefs."[21] At the time *Everson* was decided, the claim of equal rights to public benefits had special resonance because many public schools retained a distinctly Protestant character. Roman Catholic parents faced the choice of sending their children to public schools and exposing them to Protestant-influenced prayers and readings from the King James Version of the Bible, or paying to send them to Catholic parochial schools.

However, when the Court took up the question of prayer and Bible reading in public schools, supporters of the practice raised rights-based claims of their own. They argued that a ban on religious practices in public schools infringed on the rights of parents who want their children exposed to religious influences, and of children who want to pray at the opening of the school day. More recently, a similar argument has been raised in disputes over prayers at public school graduation ceremonies. Those who defend the practice argue that the majority has a right to commemorate significant events with an invocation that reflects widely shared religious beliefs.[22]

Although courts have refused to recognize a right to have the government sponsor prayer in the school context, those who claim a right to greater scope for religion in public have achieved significant success in gaining equal access of religious viewpoints to "public forums" — state-provided opportunities for debate and expression. By the late 1970s, some public administrators had overenthusiastically embraced the principle of church-state separation, and barred religious groups from reserving meeting space

20. See generally Michael Paulsen, *Religion, Equality, and the Constitution: An Equal Protection Approach to Establishment Clause Adjudication*, 61 Notre Dame L. Rev. 311 (1986).

21. *Everson v. Bd. of Educ.*, 330 U.S. 1, 16 (1947).

22. Justice Scalia, dissenting in the graduation prayer decision, made precisely this argument. *Lee v. Weisman*, 505 U.S. 577, 646: "[I]it is a bold step for this Court to seek to banish from [public school graduations], and from thousands of similar celebrations throughout this land, the expression of gratitude to God that a majority of the community wishes to make."

available to secular groups. Religious groups argued that they were being discriminated against, and the Supreme Court agreed, finding that religious associations have an equal right to participate in public forums.[23] Over the past three decades, litigation over equal access has extended the right of religious groups to a wide variety of settings, including the right to post displays on public property and to offer after-school religious programs in public schools.[24]

Litigants' success in gaining equal access to public forums has revitalized efforts to claim an equal right to public funding of religious activities. Starting in the mid-1980s, the Supreme Court gradually opened the door to public funding of religious schools, as long as the funding comes in the form of vouchers or other indirect aid. The Court reasoned that if a beneficiary decides to use the voucher for religious schooling, the government is not responsible for any religious instruction financed by the voucher, and thus the aid does not violate the Establishment Clause.[25] Indirect aid programs thus promote individual choice. This reasoning has opened significant opportunities for government funding of religious activities, both in the context of education and in social welfare.[26]

Finally, those who defend public displays of religious messages have also grounded that defense in rights language. Against those who claim that public displays of a nativity scene, Ten Commandments monument, or memorial cross violate the rights of observers to be free from government-endorsed religious messages, defenders invoke the rights of the majority who favor such displays. Dissenting in *McCreary County v. ACLU of Kentucky,* which held unconstitutional a display of the Ten Commandments in a courthouse, Justice Scalia argued that the interests of the minority in avoiding re-

23. *Widmar v. Vincent,* 454 U.S. 263 (1981); *Lamb's Chapel v. Center Moriches Union Free School Dist.,* 508 U.S. 384 (1993); *Board of Educ. v. Mergens,* 496 U.S. 226 (1990); *Rosenberger v. Rector & Visitors of the Univ. of Virginia,* 515 U.S. 819 (1995).

24. *Capitol Square Review and Advisory Board v. Pinette,* 515 U.S. 753 (1995) (private religious display on grounds outside Ohio statehouse); *Good News Club v. Milford Central School,* 533 U.S. 98 (2001) (right of evangelical program to equal access to after-school instruction opportunities in public school).

25. The leading decision is the Cleveland school voucher case, *Zelman v. Simmons-Harris,* 536 U.S. 639 (2002). For more detailed discussion, see chapter 3.

26. The Faith-Based and Community Initiative, initiated by President George W. Bush, is the most comprehensive effort in this direction. For full analysis of the issues raised by the initiative, now operating in the Obama administration under the program name Faith Based and Neighborhood Partnerships, see Ira C. Lupu and Robert W. Tuttle, *The Faith-Based Initiative and the Constitution,* 55 DePaul L. Rev. 1 (2005).

ligious messages must give way to "the interest of the overwhelming majority of religious believers in being able to give God thanks and supplication as a people, and with respect to our national endeavors."[27]

Sovereignty, Structure, and Jurisdiction

As the preceding discussion shows, the concept of nonestablishment is now understood primarily through the language of rights. But that understanding has led only to irreconcilable claims — freedom from unwanted religious experience set against freedom of religious exercise in all areas of life, including political institutions. In this section, we begin our description of an alternative account of nonestablishment, one framed as a jurisdictional limit on civil authority.

Sovereignty

What do we mean when we say that the Establishment Clause is primarily about structural limitations and an allocation of jurisdictional authority, rather than a source of individual rights? It may help to clear away one potential misunderstanding. Our argument does not treat religion, whether a Supreme Being or a particular faith community, as sovereign in a political sense — that is, capable of legitimately exercising coercive force. Important strands of Western thought about church-state interaction have framed that relationship in jurisdictional terms, but have done so by attributing coequal or even paramount political sovereignty to religious authority.[28] The concept of nonestablishment, as we understand it, breaks with that tradition and attributes political sovereignty solely to civil government.

One quite prominent strand emphasizes the sovereignty of God and subordinates the state to divine authority. This subordination can take a variety of forms — as a limit on government authority over individual consciences, which are bound to a separate and higher power; through the explicit integration of divine law into the state's positive law; or through a claim

27. *McCreary County v. ACLU of Kentucky*, 545 U.S. 844, 900 (2005) (Scalia, J., dissenting).

28. See Harold Berman, *Law and Revolution: Formation of the Western Legal Tradition* 94-99 (1983); Brian Tierney, *The Crisis of Church and State* 45-52 (1988).

that the authority of the state rests on a theological foundation. However, a government limited to secular jurisdiction neither recognizes divine sovereignty nor denies the ultimate universal governance of God. Civil government simply takes no position on the issue. Individual believers are free to assert divine supremacy over all institutions, and indeed the state's limited jurisdiction protects the freedom of believers to hold such commitments, subject only to the state's claim to their loyalty in secular matters. But the state makes no claim about divine authority.

Another strand of Western thought attributes a kind of sovereignty to specific religious institutions. The Roman Catholic Church in England, for example, once exercised broad legal jurisdiction over certain subjects, including family law and the transfer of personal property by will, and claimed exclusive jurisdiction over all legal matters affecting those in Holy Orders.[29] That legal jurisdiction reflected a claim of sovereignty, modeled partly on the immunity of diplomats and embassies from local law, and partly on an idea of temporal governance shared by religious and civil authorities. Our jurisdictional account of nonestablishment makes no such claims for the political autonomy of religious entities. Except for the Holy See in its relation to Vatican City, religious authorities do not possess the classical features of sovereignty — control over territory and the power to govern that territory. Instead, religious entities are subject to the positive law of the political jurisdiction in which they are located.

Structural and Jurisdictional Limitations

National sovereignty is a face presented to the world, but nested behind that external face are the structures chosen by nation-states to govern their territory and look out for their interests. Our own system of government is designed to channel democratic input, promote accountability, prevent abuses of power, and protect liberty through a complex regime of divided and separated powers. The most basic building blocks of this arrangement include federalism, a system for allocating power between nation and states, and, within both national and state governments, the separation of powers among legislative, executive, and judicial branches. Some powers are exclusive, while

29. See, generally, R. H. Helmholz, *Roman Canon Law in Reformation England* (Cambridge University Press, 2004); R. B. Outhwaite, *The Rise and Fall of the English Ecclesiastical Courts, 1500-1860* (Cambridge University Press, 2007).

many are shared. As a matter of federalism, for example, only the national government may speak for the United States in foreign affairs, but the nation and states may have overlapping domains over matters of violent crime.[30]

Less prominent and visible in the American regime are structural arrangements that divide power between government and private parties. The most obvious of these involve questions of familial and other intimate association. In constitutional terms, we frequently conceive of these questions as matters of individual rights, most commonly pulled together under the right of privacy. And many of the relevant doctrines fit the model of rights. For example, decisions like *Roe v. Wade* and *Lawrence v. Texas* protect individuals from state coercion with respect to matters of reproduction and sexuality.[31]

In addition to the rights-bearing character of this sort of activity, however, the separation between public and private activity can be fruitfully conceptualized in structural or jurisdictional terms. For example, ever since the decisions in *Pierce v. Society of Sisters* (1925) and *Meyer v. Nebraska* (1923), it has been understood that parents and guardians of children have the primary authority to decide how to educate their children, as well as to decide other basic questions of child-rearing practice.[32] This division of power between state and family over the upbringing of children can be understood as a familial right to be free from a certain degree of state coercion in such matters, but it can also be understood as a structural allocation, in which families and not government are given primary decision-making authority.

Viewed in jurisdictional terms, these kinds of arrangements shape our understanding of the state as nontotalitarian. The state sets broad boundaries of affirmative duty toward children and limitations on acts of abuse and neglect of children, and remits to private hands the particular decisions to be made with respect to these responsibilities. This separation of powers between the machinery of state, which establishes minimum standards, and private authorities, who implement these standards for the children or other wards under their care, has broad and vital implications for understanding

---

30. See, e.g., *Crosby v. National Foreign Trade Council,* 530 U.S. 363 (2000) (Massachusetts law requiring state agencies to boycott products manufactured in Burma is inconsistent with the constitutional requirement of a uniform national voice in foreign affairs).

31. See *Roe v. Wade,* 410 U.S. 113 (1973) (freedom of reproductive choice); *Lawrence v. Texas,* 539 U.S. 558 (2003) (sexual freedom of consenting adults).

32. See *Pierce v. Society of Sisters,* 268 U.S. 510 (1925) (parental freedom to choose private education for children); *Meyer v. Nebraska,* 262 U.S. 390 (1923) (right of parents to obtain instruction for their children in a foreign language); see also *Troxel v. Granville,* 530 U.S. 57 (2000) (right of parent to exclude grandparent from visitation with child).

the character and identity of the state. The political philosophy of the United States has made us quite consciously and structurally non-Spartan. We trust structures of private authority to raise each succeeding generation. Of course, this set of arrangements risks the creation of behavioral spheres within which domestic violence and abuse can go unchecked, so we quite appropriately bound the freedom of those within these structures. The existence of such boundaries, however, does not erase the significance of the long-standing idea that the zones of family life and intimate relationship lie primarily outside the area of state competence.

In ways that reflect and transcend the structural arrangements that characterize the interaction between the state and intimate or familial associations, the regime of nonestablishment also displays a structural character. In many respects, the state and religious communities have overlapping concerns. Both may be concerned about human suffering, for example, or questions of civil rights, character formation, and equal respect for all humans. Yet, in limited but profound ways, religious communities have an exclusive jurisdiction, akin to the exclusive jurisdiction of the national government in foreign affairs. Religious communities have an exclusive power to define the terms of worship, and to select their own leaders and teachers. Constitutional law fiercely protects these powers by excluding the state from composing prayers for its people, and from the enterprise of clergy selection and discipline.

Thus, nonestablishment of religion reflects a difference in kind from other structural ideas that animate the private-public divide in American law. In family law and elsewhere, the state leaves most decisions in private hands, but nevertheless retains a regulatory potential, a capacity to expend resources, and a voice of its own. Similarly, for reasons of both liberty and efficiency, the government does not own most means of production, but it retains the authority to surround those means of production with regulatory policies, subsidies for state-favored activities, and state messages of approval or disapproval. More broadly, with respect to art, science, secular morality, and human flourishing in the physical and psychological realms, government has the power both to subsidize private choices and to speak for itself, even if its regulatory powers are sometimes circumscribed by considerations of free expression or privacy.[33]

What, then, is distinctive about religious welfare? Why is that alone

---

33. *NEA v. Finley*, 524 U.S. 569 (1998) (subsidy of artistic expression); *Harris v. McRae*, 448 U.S. 297 (1980) (funding of abortions).

excluded from the government's jurisdictional competence, not only with respect to coercive regulation but also with respect to direct government subsidy and governmental recommendation of a preferred life? Why can't the same government that uses its resources to press its people to "just say no" to drugs similarly give funds and encouragement to a life of devotion to faith, perhaps even to a particular god?

What Makes Religion Special?

Contrary to the persistent contemporary tendency to treat religion as equivalent to its secular counterparts, the nonestablishment principle treats religion as constitutionally distinctive. As we describe in this book, government is often disabled from supporting or regulating religious ideas or institutions even though it would be free to support or regulate analogous secular ideas or institutions. This unequal treatment of religion requires explanation, but the task is complicated because it involves the relationship between two concepts, religion and nonestablishment, both of which have highly contested meanings.

The explanation, of course, must start with a definition of religion. But some accounts of religion resist identification of any special character. This is especially true where religion is defined in highly subjective terms — as the individual's "ultimate concern," however that concern (and ultimacy itself) is understood.[34] Someone may find ultimate meaning in the enjoyment of art or music, another through solitary walks in nature, and yet another through scientific inquiry. Apart from the individual's assignment of ultimate significance, these activities are perfectly legitimate candidates for government support. The possibility that someone may experience God while hiking through Yosemite is not a reason to question public funding of the park. The same can be said with understandings, quite widely held, that attribute religious significance to virtually all aspects of human life. For example, Martin Luther, John Calvin, and other Protestant reformers asserted that all believers — not just priests — receive "callings" from God, which transform ordinary occupations into religious vocations.[35] Indeed, even the quintessential gov-

---

34. See *United States v. Seeger*, 380 U.S. 163 (1965) (citing Paul Tillich, *Systematic Theology* [1957]).

35. See Douglas J. Schuurman, *Vocation: Discerning Our Callings in Life* (Eerdmans, 2004).

ernment careers of military service or political office-holding can be considered religious callings. Such an expansive conception conflicts with any claim that religion marks off a category of experience that is sharply distinct from nonreligious experience.

The nonestablishment principle, however, is informed by an understanding of religion that is driven by a particularized concern for constitutional structure, rather than from the spiritual experiences or theological commitments of believers. This shift in perspective — from bottom-up to top-down — is not intended to disparage believers' experience or commitments, but instead reflects the nonestablishment principle's character as legal artifact. Religion, for purposes of the nonestablishment principle, has a functional meaning, one that is different from — and likely much narrower than — the meaning assigned by religious communities. Our focus on specialized meaning is hardly novel as a legal device. Statutes and regulations typically define terms in ways that diverge, sometimes markedly, from ordinary usage. For example, "family" may be defined in quite different ways for rules governing rental housing, zoning law, welfare benefits, or hospital visitation.[36]

The same is true of "religion." In its interpretation of tax law, the Internal Revenue Service defines religion by focusing on the tangible elements of a faith tradition — regular and distinct worship community, shared creed and scriptures, identifiable and trained leadership, ecclesiastical governance.[37] By contrast, courts have used a much more capacious definition of religion when considering free exercise or statutory claims made by employees who seek unemployment benefits or protection against discrimination. In such cases, courts emphasize subjective characteristics — the depth and duration of the claimant's attachment to particular beliefs or practices — rather than objective features such as the doctrinal basis of the claim.[38]

These varying definitions of religion represent the overriding importance of context. Just as the definition of "family" may depend on whether

---

36. The legal definition of family differs widely among contexts. See, e.g., *Moore v. East Cleveland,* 431 U.S. 794 (1977) (in defining family for zoning purposes, constitution requires inclusion of extended family members sharing a household); *Braschi v. Stahl Associates Co.,* 543 N.E. 2d 549 (N.Y., 1989) (two men cohabiting in an apartment in New York City constituted a "family" for purposes of the city's rent and eviction regulations).

37. See *Lutheran Social Serv. of Minnesota v. U.S.,* 758 F. 2d 1283, 1286-1287 (8th Cir. 1985).

38. *Thomas v. Review Board,* 450 U.S. 707 (1981) (free exercise claimant decides content of religion for himself, and courts may not second-guess the credibility of those beliefs in light of the beliefs of others in the same denomination).

the rule in question is designed to protect settled patterns of cohabitation (in housing law) or the public purse (in welfare benefits law), the legal meaning of "religion" also depends on the term's function within the relevant legal norm. The IRS's understanding of religion reflects serious concerns about fraud, as well as having a policy that promotes bona fide voluntary organizations. If a group does not have a tangible common life, it falls outside the intended scope of protection. By contrast, the more subjective and individualized understanding of religion in the employment context, under religious liberty statutes or the Free Exercise Clause, signifies the law's concern for the vulnerability of individual conscience, even when the believer is not connected to a particular community and does not appeal to authoritative texts.

The same is true of the nonestablishment principle, within which the meaning and distinctive character of religion arise from the purposes served by that principle. But courts and commentators sharply disagree about the relevance and relative importance of purposes offered to justify nonestablishment. At the risk of oversimplifying a rich and complex debate, we begin that discussion with two broad justifications typically offered for the nonestablishment principle.

One prominent approach, which owes much to Protestant evangelicalism, views nonestablishment as an instrument for protecting religious liberty. For this approach, religion is special because of its constitutive role in human identity and well-being. But religious experience and commitment can be authentic only if they are freely chosen.[39] Nonestablishment safeguards the possibility of authentic faith in a variety of ways. Most obviously, it prohibits official coercion in religious matters — no one can be compelled to engage, or not to engage, in religious experience. Nonestablishment also protects against more subtle threats to authentic choice of faith. By prohibiting state sponsorship or funding of particular faiths, nonestablishment prevents the government from encouraging participation in the favored groups, discouraging membership in groups not favored, or inducing religious groups to change their beliefs in order to attract official favor.

The second prominent account of nonestablishment has its roots in the early modern history of religious wars. The fragmentation of western Christianity during the Reformation, coupled with the emergence of nation-states

---

39. John J. Witte Jr., *Religion and the American Constitutional Experiment*, 28 and notes thereto (Westview Press, 2nd ed., 2005) (citing the writings of Rhode Island founder Roger Williams and eighteenth-century Baptist theologian Isaac Backus on church, state, and Calvinism).

in Europe, led to more than a century of conflicts between Protestants and Roman Catholics, and among a wide array of Protestant groups. Drawing from this history, the second approach views religion as special because of its capacity to generate violent conflict. This capacity arises both from the intensity of believers' attachments and from the nonrational character of faith. Those two features make it more likely that religious conflicts will not be resolved by ordinary civil compromise, but will instead lead to violence or other politically destabilizing conflict.[40]

Against this backdrop, nonestablishment serves as an instrument for securing civil peace. By insulating government from religion, nonestablishment operates both directly and indirectly to limit interreligious conflict. The prohibition on government suppression of disfavored faiths eliminates the original source of interreligious violence. But nonestablishment also reduces religious groups' incentive to compete for political supremacy. If the machinery of government may not be used to support or promote any faith, religious groups will find control of government significantly less valuable.

The two approaches, which we label "authentic choice" and "civil peace," have important similarities. Both call for restrictions on state support for religion as well as bans on state coercion in matters of faith, and both link nonestablishment to the depth and intensity of religious beliefs. But the differences between the two are equally important. At the most basic level, the two operate with quite different understandings of religion. The first tends toward an expansive and individualistic definition of religion, because it focuses on the subjective quality of authentic choice. The second tends toward a narrower definition of religion as a communal system of belief, and focuses on the points of doctrinal conflict among those belief systems. With civil peace as the relevant objective, widely shared beliefs would not fit within the definition of religion because they do not tend to generate conflict. The two approaches also differ in their evaluation of religion. The focus on authentic choice sees religion as intrinsically good and deserving of significant protection. The focus on civil peace sees religion in more mixed terms — intensely important to individuals and communities but capable of provoking discord because of that intensity.

We do not mean to overstate either the differences between the two positions or the degree of unanimity among those who hold them. We recognize that the two approaches are often invoked in support of the same side

---

40. William P. Marshall, *Religion as Ideas: Religion as Identity,* 7 J. Contemp. Legal Issues 385 (1996).

on a disputed question. The differences between the two are likely to emerge only at the margins, not over the core elements of nonestablishment. Moreover, we also recognize the likelihood of practical disagreements among those who share either of the approaches. For example, those who see nonestablishment as an instrument for protecting authentic religious choice may not have the same understanding of inappropriate influence on that choice. One might regard a government voucher for private school tuition as an inappropriate inducement to receive religious education, while another might see the voucher as neutralizing the prior policy that steered students away from religious schools and toward free secular public education.

Concerns for authentic religious choice and civil peace have played important roles in the development of contemporary Establishment Clause doctrine, and continue to produce useful insights in disputes over government's relationship with religion. But neither approach offers a fully convincing explanation of why the concept of nonestablishment should treat religion as distinctive. The concern for authentic choice fails to explain why religious commitments deserve greater protection than nonreligious commitments, which may play an equally constitutive role in personal identity. Of course, some identity-constituting choices will be protected by the rights of privacy, speech, or association, but the relevant question is why the government should be disabled from materially influencing such choices. For example, we allow the government to use speech or subsidy to influence reproductive choices, which certainly have an identity-constituting character.

Some advocates of this approach have responded by expanding the scope of concern to include nonreligious commitments that play a similar role in individual identity.[41] That response may be appropriate when considering protection of individual liberty against coercion, such as the right to a conscientious exemption from military conscription. But the move to expand the scope of concern is implausible when applied to the concept of nonestablishment. It seems dysfunctional, at times absurd, to disable the government from promoting or discouraging commitments just because someone believes such commitments have a self-constituting character.

41. This is the primary strategy of Eisgruber and Sager, *supra* note 17 (advocating equal liberty for the important concerns and projects of the people); see also William P. Marshall, *What Is the Matter with Equality? An Assessment of the Equal Treatment of Religion and Nonreligion in First Amendment Jurisprudence*, 75 Ind. L. J. 193 (2000); Gregory P. Magarian, *How to Apply the Religious Freedom Restoration Act to Federal Law without Violating the Constitution*, 99 Mich. L. Rev. 1903 (2001) (advocating extending the act to analogous, nonreligious moral commitments).

Likewise, the "civil peace" approach fails to explain why religious conflicts pose a greater threat to order than nonreligious conflicts. Although the Civil War, our greatest national conflict, had religious overtones, it involved secular moral and political questions of chattel slavery and federal-state relations. In more recent times, interreligious conflict has been an important concern of our foreign policy, with a focus on radicalized Islamic groups, but domestic politics have been marked far more by interreligious harmony than by strife. The United States occasionally experiences threats to civil peace — antiwar protests, race riots, and militia movements come to mind — but they rarely are defined in terms of rivalries between religious groups. Of course, one might argue that the absence of widespread interreligious conflict proves that nonestablishment has been a success. The causal link is weak, however, because American religious peace preceded robust enforcement of nonestablishment.

Seen in terms of either subjective commitments or disputed doctrines, religion is not particularly distinctive. Individuals have important nonreligious commitments, and factions engage in intense disputes over nonreligious ideas. The distinctiveness of religion becomes evident only when it is seen as an attribute of political authority. From this perspective, three characteristics of religion present the problem to which nonestablishment responds. First, religion locates the source of its authority in a transcendent and eternal being or order, to which all temporal beings and orders are subject. Second, religion asserts comprehensive jurisdiction; its competence and authority extend to all dimensions of human life. And third, the subjects of religious authority respond to it by worship and submission.

In historical terms, most governments have asserted a religious source for their authority. Some, such as the pharaohs of Egypt, have simply proclaimed their own divinity. More commonly, rulers or states have claimed a special relationship with God that gives them political authority. This authority may be direct, such as a belief that God has chosen a particular person, family, or party. Or the authority may be indirect, mediated through religious leaders, as when the pope anointed the Holy Roman Emperor. Or the government may claim that it deserves political authority because of its fidelity to religious doctrine and norms. Although the claims are quite different, they share a common feature — the government locates its authority in a transcendent source.

The second characteristic, a comprehensive scope of political authority, was also the historical norm. Religion was the legitimate concern of civil government. This concern might arise because the ruler bore responsibility for the spiritual welfare of citizens, protecting them through laws against heresy, blasphemy, or Sabbath breaking, and requiring faithful attendance at worship. Or the concern might be instrumental, with the government promoting religion in order to achieve secular purposes such as civil peace and moral rectitude.[42] Whether the government's interest in religion is intrinsic or instrumental, the concern implies that civil authority is competent to determine the true or best faith, and that the state's responsibility extends to all dimensions of human life.

Accompanying the first two characteristics of religious authority is a third: rulers have frequently claimed the worship and submission of their subjects. In the modern West, examples of overt worship of government have been rare (Nazism is one of the few), but more subtle claims have been common. Indeed, the respect owed to a divinely appointed ruler is hardly distinguishable from worship. Those who trace their authority to a transcendent source tend to claim the reverence and submission owed to that source.

Nonestablishment marks a radical break with previous links between government and all three characteristics of religion. First, on the source of legitimacy, nonestablishment signals the government's disclaimer of any basis for its authority apart from that granted by the people, through and subject to the terms of the Constitution. This authority is contingent, not eternal. Every aspect of government is subject to revision. Individuals and religious communities are free to believe and claim that civil government has a transcendent source, but the government may not make any such claim about itself.

Government can breach this limitation in a variety of ways. For example, the national motto, In God We Trust, could be read as a claim about the piety of civil government, just as the phrase "one Nation under God" in the Pledge of Allegiance seems to indicate a special relationship between God and the state. Similarly, some who defended state-sponsored displays of the Ten Commandments argued that the biblical texts served as the foundation for civil laws. If those defenders mean that biblical texts provided the historical source for norms of civil law, the claim would not directly conflict with the nonestablishment principle.[43] But proponents have often made the foun-

42. Witte, *Religion and the American Constitutional Experiment* ch. 2, "The Theology and Politics of the Religion Clauses," *supra* note 39 (identifying a typology of spiritual and material concern that informed early American views on the relationship between religion and government).

43. Such a claim about biblical texts as a source of American law is, however, most likely false. See Steven K. Green, *The Fount of Everything Just and Right? The Ten Commandments as a Source of American Law,* 13 Journal of Law and Religion 101 (2000) (arguing that

dational claim in terms of authority — that Scripture provides the normative basis for civil laws — and this claim, if made by the government, does violate the nonestablishment principle.

Second, nonestablishment limits the scope of the state's authority in religious matters. This limitation means that the government is not responsible for the religious welfare of its citizens. That responsibility belongs solely to individuals and voluntary associations. By denying responsibility, the government does not signal hostility to religion. Instead, the disclaimer reflects the government's recognition of its own boundary, and is fully consistent with respect for activities that lie outside that boundary.

This disclaimer necessarily bars the state's exercise of authority to decide religious questions. As chapter 2 explains in detail, government is not competent to determine which doctrines represent the true faith of a religious community, how those doctrines should be interpreted, or who is fit to be recognized as a leader or member within such a community. These decisional limits come to the fore in legal disputes between factions of a congregation, in employment law claims brought by terminated ministers, or in challenges by individuals to exclusion from participation in worship or religious community life.

Less obviously, however, the decisional limits also have important implications for the interpretation of laws designed to promote religious liberty. As we explain in chapter 7, the government's incompetence to decide religious questions makes it extremely difficult to design or administer a regime that will accommodate objections to laws that indirectly burden religiously motivated conduct. If the government cannot evaluate the significance of a particular practice within a believer's faith, it will effectively lack the ability to identify — in a principled way — meritorious claims for accommodation. And if such laws then amount to a presumptive exemption of religiously motivated conduct from exercises of the state's regulatory power, the resulting privilege for religious over analogous nonreligious conduct demands justification that secular reason cannot provide.

The state's disclaimer of authority in religious matters applies whether its purported interest in religion is an end in itself — encouraging individuals to embrace and practice the true faith — or a means to some secular end.

---

the Ten Commandments are not a direct source of anything in American law). If the historical claim is false, it may just be a pretext, designed to mask the idea that Scripture is a source of divine authority for our laws. If government acts on the intention to promote that idea, the government violates the nonestablishment principle. See chapter 5 for further discussion of the Ten Commandments cases, where the issue of such pretexts is prominent.

As a limit on the state's intrinsic concern for religion, the nonestablishment principle requires that the state act for legitimate secular purposes. Some actions undoubtedly fall short of that standard. For example, if a public school's science curriculum includes religious teachings, such as the account of human origins from the book of Genesis, it would violate the nonestablishment principle because the only plausible purpose of including that teaching would be religious indoctrination.[44]

Other state practices are more difficult to assess. For instance, the government employs military chaplains to meet the religious needs of service members and their families. At first glance, the military seems to have assumed responsibility for religious welfare — an act that would exceed the limited scope of government authority. Seen from another perspective, however, the military chaplaincy is consistent with that limitation because the chaplaincy does no more than offer service members an opportunity to practice their chosen faith, in circumstances that might make other religious leaders inaccessible. As we describe in chapter 8, the validity of a chaplaincy program depends on quite specific details about how the program is structured.

The nonestablishment principle also bars the government from using religious means to achieve secular ends. This limitation has been far more controversial than the secular purpose requirement, in part because its consequences reach more broadly and deeply into civil government. Those who favor greater government involvement with religion invariably claim that the partnership furthers secular ends. Defenders of prayer in public school have asserted that the practice promotes morality and improves students' ability to concentrate. More recently, some have argued that faith-intensive substance abuse treatment programs are more effective than comparable nonreligious programs, so government should be free to fund and promote the religious services.[45] Assume that these religious activities confer significant secular benefits. Why should the government not avail itself of those benefits?

---

44. See *Edwards v. Aguillard,* 482 U.S. 578 (1987) (state may not require teaching of creation science by public schools that choose to teach Darwinian evolution); *Kitzmiller v. Dover Area Sch. Dist.,* 400 F. Supp. 2d 707 (M.D. Pa. 2005). For commentary on these problems, see Frank Ravitch, *Marketing Intelligent Design: Law and the Creationist Agenda* (Cambridge University Press, 2010); Jay D. Wexler, *Darwin, Design and Disestablishment: Teaching the Evolution Controversy in Public Schools,* 56 Vand. L. Rev. 751 (2003).

45. See generally John DiIulio, *Godly Republic: A Centrist Blueprint for America's Faith-Based Future* (University of California Press, 2007); Stephen V. Monsma, *When Sacred and Secular Mix: Religious Non-profit Organizations and Public Money* (Rowman and Littlefield, 2000).

The nonestablishment principle applies to government use of religious means because it is always difficult, and sometimes impossible, to separate means from ends. At times, the assertion of a secular justification seems little more than a sham, as illustrated by the claims about school prayer. Even when the secular purpose is legitimate, however, the government's choice of or support for religious means raises a number of complicated issues, which we identify and discuss in chapter 3.

Third, the nonestablishment principle prohibits the government from demanding the worship and reverence of its citizens. The relationship between government and people is not one of master and servant, but quite the reverse. Government is an agent of the people, created by consent and limited to its delegated powers. The state may demand loyalty and obedience to law, but the relationship is always one of political equals. This limitation conflicts with the powerful inclination, especially in times of crisis, to see the nation in mystical terms. The mystical union may be comforting and inspiring, but it can also tempt officials to manipulate and exploit religious imagery for political ends. For example, at the peak of the Cold War, Congress added the phrase "one Nation under God" to the Pledge of Allegiance. The phrase certainly highlighted our nation's distance from the official atheism of the Soviet Union. But some argue that it also changed the loyalty oath into a prayer, in which submission to God and to country are intertwined. Chapter 5 addresses these issues in detail.

The Character of Government and the Interpretation of the Establishment Clause

History

Is the structural account that we offer consistent with the relevant historical materials that inform the meaning of the Establishment Clause? Some scholars, like Professor Michael McConnell, insist that those materials lead inexorably to the conclusion that coercion of individuals is a necessary element of any unconstitutional "establishment of religion."[46] McConnell and others frequently point to events in the early life of the republic, such as Thanksgiving proclamations and the appointment of a congressional chaplain, to

---

46. Michael W. McConnell, *Coercion: The Lost Element of Establishment,* 27 Wm. & Mary L. Rev. 933 (1986).

demonstrate that the Framers intended to permit the federal government to interact with and support voluntary religious experience.

The history of religious oppression associated with religious establishments indeed suggests that the primary evils associated with such arrangements involve the coercion of individuals. We believe, however, that a focus on coercion does not exhaust the meaning of the Establishment Clause.[47] Moreover, as religious coercion by governments in America has abated over time, other concerns about the role of government in relation to religion have become more visible. Nevertheless, concerns about the character of government have been immanent in the subject right from the start.

Let's begin with the structural character of the entire project in which the religion clauses appear. While the language of much of the Bill of Rights refers to protection of individual liberties, significant parts of the Bill are not framed in such terms. The Tenth Amendment explicitly focuses on the structural question of power distribution between nation and states. Moreover, the Bill recognizes a number of the rights enumerated, including those of peaceable assembly, bearing of arms, and security against unreasonable searches and seizures, as belonging to the people — this in marked contrast to "the person" protected by a number of provisions in Amendment 5 and "the accused" protected throughout Amendment 6. These choices suggest that parts of the Bill protect characteristics of the polity, including federalism, institutions of self-defense (militias), and sources of deliberation (juries and assemblies).[48]

Second, the role of James Madison as principal architect of the Bill as a whole, and what became the religion clauses of the First Amendment in particular, reinforces a structural account of the Establishment Clause. Whether or not the clause should be read to fully reflect the rich and varied themes of Madison's "Memorial and Remonstrance," which includes both anticoercive and structural elements, there can be little doubt that Madison was the structurally oriented genius of our constitutional design. For prominent examples, Federalist Paper 10, on the role of factions in an extended republic, Federalist Paper 39, on the combined federal-national character of the government, and Federalist Paper 51, on separation of powers in the federal government,

---

47. For sharp judicial rebuttals of a litigant's argument that coercion is a necessary element of an Establishment Clause violation, see *Lee v. Weisman*, 505 U.S. 577, 604-609 (1992) (Blackmun, J., concurring, joined by O'Connor and Stevens, JJ.); *id.* at 618-626 (Souter, J., concurring).

48. Akhil Reed Amar, *The Bill of Rights: Creation and Reconstruction* (Yale University Press, 1998).

are Madisonian elaborations of what our governmental institutions really do presuppose. Indeed, Federalist 51 specifically alludes to the multiplicity of religious sects in the United States, and not to any constitutional promises of religious liberty, as the primary guarantor of such freedom. Madison believed in the value of competition, and he knew that a government-supported church was a source of unfair competition for the allegiance of the citizenry.

Nor is there anything idiosyncratically Madisonian about a structural account of the Establishment Clause. Like so many other matters that received attention in the Bill of Rights, the drafters were writing on a tablet already thick with prior notations. They knew the shape, history, and vices of the Anglican establishment in England, and they were even more familiar with the various colonial and state establishments, many of which had faded away by 1791, in America. Accordingly, they had many reasons to understand a nonestablishment principle in structural as well as rights-oriented terms. Achieving religious pluralism simultaneously with civil peace, and separating ecclesiastical from secular power, were eighteenth-century themes quite as prominent as individual freedom from religious coercion.[49]

Nothing in the final drafting choices for the clause, which reads "Congress shall make no law respecting an establishment of religion,"[50] precludes this sort of structural interpretation. Moreover, the language of the Free Exercise Clause seems quite squarely aimed at protecting an individual right to be free from religious coercion, and therefore buttresses the case that additional, structural themes animated the Establishment Clause. The Free Exercise Clause is about the free character of the people's faith. The Establishment Clause is about the limited character of the government created by those people.

Those who resist this account of nonestablishment frequently point to references in the founding era to the idea that America owes its existence to some version of divine Providence. The Jefferson-drafted Declaration of Independence, for example, invokes the Creator as the source of inalienable rights. Thus, despite the Framers' wariness of partnerships between ecclesiastical institutions and government, they at times spoke in a generically mono-

---

49. See Adam Smith, *Wealth of Nations,* bk. 5, ch. 1, pt. 3, art. 3 (1776). James Madison's famous "Memorial and Remonstrance against Religious Assessments" (1785), discussed further in chapter 3, drew heavily from this work of Adam Smith. See also Carl H. Esbeck, *The Establishment Clause as a Structural Restraint on Governmental Power,* 84 Iowa L. Rev. 1 (1998).

50. This language emerged without explanation from the House-Senate conference committee that produced the entire Bill of Rights. McConnell, Garvey, and Berg, *supra* note 9, at 61.

theistic voice on behalf of a developing American political ethos. But an ethos is a dynamic reflection of popular understandings, rather than a definitive declaration of government's character.[51]

From a different angle, defenders of a narrow, coercion-focused Establishment Clause point to the text and historical context of the clause as an affirmation of the independent power of state governments, as distinguished from the federal government, to maintain religious establishments. State establishments were commonplace in the early eighteenth century, but most of them had been abandoned as a consequence of the anti-Anglican sentiment unleashed by the American Revolution. When the First Amendment was drafted, a few New England states still retained a system of local establishments, under which a majority within each community might choose a Protestant Christian church that all local taxpayers were obliged to support.[52] The continued existence of these local establishments, combined with the ultimate choice to prohibit federal laws "respecting an establishment of religion," has led some commentators and judges to assert that the clause had a dual purpose. In this interpretation, the clause simultaneously prevents coercive federal establishments while affirmatively protecting the authority of states to establish one or more faiths.[53] The latter purpose, were it to be conclusively demonstrated, might show that the Establishment Clause does not guarantee a secular government, but rather confirms that states — not the federal government — have political responsibility for the people's religious welfare.

The historical material necessary to demonstrate that sort of affirmative, state-protecting purpose in the First Amendment, however, is extremely sparse. Congress may indeed have been disabled from legislating with respect to state establishments, but that disability does not reflect a constitutional objective of insulating state establishments from federal interference.[54] The

---

51. In reading the Declaration of Independence, and its overt invocation of the Deity, it is important to remember that the document is self-consciously an expression of the people professing their release from allegiance to a particular political community, rather than an exercise of authority by an established government.

52. See *Barnes v. The Inhabitants of the First Parish in Falmouth*, 6 Mass. 401 (1810). For a general discussion of the New England establishments, see Leonard W. Levy, *The Establishment Clause: Religion and the First Amendment* 26-46 (Macmillan, 1986); Carl H. Esbeck, *Dissent and Disestablishment: The Church-State Settlement of the New American Republic*, 2004 BYU L. Rev. 1385 (2004).

53. Justice Thomas so argued in his concurring opinion in *Elk Grove Unified Sch. Dist. v. Newdow*, 542 U.S. 1, 49-52 (2004) (citing A. Amar, *The Bill of Rights* 36-39). See also *Cutter v. Wilkinson*, 544 U.S. 709, 726-731 (2005) (Thomas, J., concurring).

54. There is every reason to believe, for example, that the federal Constitution would

First Amendment may originally have tolerated state establishments, but it did not embrace them.

The Constitutional Evolution of Establishment Clause Norms

Even if there had been a universally understood meaning to the Establishment Clause in 1791, the evolution of religion-state relations in the nineteenth century set the groundwork for a changed understanding of the Establishment Clause. As other scholars have demonstrated, the relationship among Christianity, the state, and the law changed considerably between 1791 and the era of Reconstruction. The last remaining state-backed establishments disappeared by the 1830s. The common law had shed much of its explicitly Christian character, and blasphemy prosecutions had fallen into disrepute.[55] Even before the Civil War, Protestant-Catholic tensions arising from immigration patterns had begun to strain the notion that America reflected a unified Protestant culture, in which public education could reflect Protestant ideals of religious self-reliance and Protestant practices of Bible reading and prayer.[56] The most profound changes in our constitutional culture, however, emerged from the Civil War and the ensuing period of Reconstruction.

A number of historically and thematically linked phenomena coalesced during that period to expand the ethos of secular government. The Reconstruction amendments and the civil rights laws of the period thoroughly and forcefully repudiated the idea that the states could be trusted to have comprehensive control over the lives and liberties of their people. The emancipation of enslaved African Americans, who among other cruelties had been denied religious freedom in a regime of state-backed bondage, was the first and most dramatic manifestation of the states' loss of constitutional authority.

---

always have been a bar to a state-controlled church granting a title of nobility, U.S. Const., Art. I, §10, par. 1, cl. 7; acting in a way that impaired an obligation of contract, *id.*, Art. I, §10, par. 1, cl. 6; or refusing to return fleeing felons or fugitive slaves, *id.*, Art. IV, §2, cl. 2-3.

55. For discussion of these nineteenth-century developments, see Kurt T. Lash, *The Second Adoption of the Establishment Clause: The Rise of the Non-Establishment Principle,* 27 Ariz. St. L. J. 1085 (1995); Esbeck, *supra* note 52; Sarah Barringer Gordon, *Blasphemy and Religious Liberty in Antebellum America,* AM. Q. 52 (Dec. 2000).

56. For discussion of mid-nineteenth-century conflicts in New York and Massachusetts between Catholics and Protestants, and the rise of the nativist Know Nothing Party, see Philip Hamburger, *Separation of Church and State* pt. 3, ch. 8 (Harvard University Press, 2002); John C. Jeffries Jr. and James E. Ryan, *A Political History of the Establishment Clause,* 100 Mich. L. Rev. 279 (2001).

Simultaneously, however, national political elites were reacting along similar lines to the growth in America of both a new church and an old one. The overtly theocratic assertions of the Church of Jesus Christ of Latter-day Saints, and those of the Church of Rome, though by no means identical, presented threats to the supremacy of popular political authority and the separation of ecclesiastical and political institutions. Without question, religious ignorance and bigotry were the dominant elements in the American reaction to these churches. But the reaction also included impulses that were ideologically connected to the elimination of race slavery, and reaffirmation of an ethos of individual freedom, both political and religious. It is not an accident that Republicans at the time linked slavery and polygamy as the "twin relics of barbarism," and described Democrats as the party of "rum, Romanism, and rebellion."[57]

These political themes coalesced in the 1870s in a series of congressional efforts, ultimately successful, to force the Mormons to renounce plural marriage. Similar themes brought about the failed attempt, sponsored by House Speaker James Blaine, to amend the federal Constitution in ways that would explicitly preclude state establishments and state funding of religious institutions. Blaine and his Republican supporters lost that particular battle. Nevertheless, subsequent enactment of "Baby Blaine" amendments at the state level, and congressional requirements that new states entering the Union include such provisions in their state constitutions, moved the country toward a new constitutional settlement, in which states too would be restricted from organizing their governments in ways that manifested a religious character.[58] In a reconstructed nation of free and equal citizens, the absolute dominion of masters over slaves and centralized institutional churches over freethinking members of the political community became constitutionally unacceptable.

Incorporation of the Religion Clauses

The seismic impact of these tremors in the American regime of religion and government would not be thickly experienced until the middle of the twen-

---

57. For the reaction to theocratic claims of Mormons, see Sarah Barringer Gordon, *The Mormon Question: Polygamy and Constitutional Conflict in Nineteenth Century America* 55-83, 195-208 (University of North Carolina Press, 2002). With respect to reactions against official Roman Catholic attitudes toward liberal democracy, see Jeffries and Ryan, *supra* note 56.

58. See Kyle Duncan, *Secularism's Laws: State Blaine Amendments and Religious Persecution,* 72 Fordham L. Rev. 493 (2003).

tieth century, when the Supreme Court held for the first time that both the Free Exercise Clause (*Cantwell*, 1940) and the Establishment Clause (*Everson*, 1947) applied to the states. In those decisions, the Court reasoned that the Fourteenth Amendment incorporates the religion clauses of the First Amendment. Incorporation of these clauses meant far more than merely subjecting state and local government to the constraints of free exercise and nonestablishment. Extension of the clauses to the states meant they would reach, for the very first time, into public education and other day-to-day interactions between local government and the citizenry. At those earliest moments of incorporation, particularly in *Cantwell*, the Free Exercise Clause appeared to be entirely rights-oriented.

The earliest, pre–Warren Court Establishment Clause opinions in *Everson* and *McCollum* (1948), however, were thematically different from any prior decisions of the Court about religion and the Constitution. Both focused on the distinctive qualities of religion as a source of discord, and both emphasized structural themes of forbidden church-state alliances and of civil peace, threatened at that time by Protestant-Catholic feuds over public funding of education. The famous litany in *Everson* of what the Establishment Clause means (at the least) begins with one purely structural focus, "Neither a state nor the Federal Government can set up a church," and ends with another, "neither a state nor the Federal Government can, openly or secretly, participate in the affairs of any religious organization or groups or vice versa." These admonitions from *Everson* reinforce our central thesis: the state may not act as a religious community.

In the Warren and Burger Court years, the focus of Establishment Clause adjudication moved in the direction of rights-oriented theory. The school prayer cases represent a subtle shift toward the language of rights, because these decisions recognized the compulsory character of school attendance, and the inevitable peer pressure of the school environment. Doctrines of taxpayer standing, which emphasized rights to not have one's tax contributions put to religious use, also played an important role in that movement. And the nonendorsement test, with its accompanying focus on the subjective experience of believers and nonbelievers, brought rights orientation in Establishment Clause cases to its zenith, and helped fuel the backlash of counterrights of religious people to be heard in an amorphously defined public square.[59]

---

59. The foundations of the nonendorsement test in the Supreme Court appear in the opinions of Justice O'Connor. See *Lynch v. Donnelly*, 465 U.S. 668, 687-694 (1984) (O'Con-

In his last religion clause opinion, Chief Justice Rehnquist wrote that the Court's work on this subject remained Janus-like, looking in two directions.[60] The image is intriguing, but the faces can be described in ways quite different from the chief justice's distinction between the strong role of religion in our history and the threat to religious freedom associated with "governmental intervention in religious matters."[61] The two directions we would emphasize instead are the rights of the people, on one face, and government's jurisdictional limits on the other.

In addition to noting the danger of coercion, *Engel v. Vitale* highlighted the independent constitutional problem of government officials composing prayers for the people.[62] From a rights-based perspective, it is hard to see why authorship matters. The decision in *Lee v. Weisman,* invalidating school-sponsored prayer at public school commencements, likewise emphasized state authorship as well as coercive social pressure.[63] Similarly, the decision in *Lemon v. Kurtzman* depended deeply on the purely structural concern that government and religious institutions not be "excessively entangled."[64] Such a concern has nothing to do with the interests of taxpayers in not supporting religion. And, on a number of occasions, the Supreme Court has facilitated resolution of disputes within religious organizations by effectively declaring a judicial disability to decide a certain class of questions, as distinguished from a more sweeping right of religious organizations to be free from state interference.[65] All these developments reflect a steady narrative about the required constitutional distance between the state's exercise of authority and the nonstate enterprises of worship and religious teaching.

The meaning of nonestablishment has been essentially contested from the beginning, and remains so. Nevertheless, history, constitutional change, and the line of judicial development reveal ideas that have been with us from the beginning of the republic — a political community that is not restricted to a community of the believers and the saints, is focused on temporal common good, and is accountable only to the people, not to the authoritative revelation or experience of a God known only to some of the people.

---

nor, J., concurring); *Allegheny County v. ACLU,* 492 U.S. 573, 623-637 (1989) (O'Connor, J., concurring).

60. *Van Orden v. Perry,* 545 U.S. 677, 683 (2005).
61. *Id.*
62. *Engel v. Vitale,* 370 U.S. 421, 425-435 (1962).
63. *Lee v. Weisman,* 505 U.S. 577, 586-590 (1992).
64. *Lemon v. Kurtzman,* 403 U.S. 602, 615-622 (1971).
65. See discussion of these decisions in chapter 2.

Modern Establishment Clause Adjudication

In the consciousness of most American lawyers, and of the public more generally, the Establishment Clause protects rights, and courts are the primary guarantors of the rights so protected. In challenging the dominant narrative of rights, we are challenging both the institutional and normative content of that narrative. If the Establishment Clause is primarily about structures, enforcement of it will depend heavily on the behavior of political actors acting within the framework of those structures. Judicial elaboration may play a crucial role, but will never be a complete substitute for internalization, by other branches of government, of the relevant norms.

Perceiving these norms as structural provokes a useful comparison to the ways in which American constitutionalism has protected norms of power separation and federalism. Very little of the day-to-day operation of these systems of checks, balances, and divisions of power depends on judicially crafted standards or judicial decrees. Instead, these allocations of power operate around mutual understandings and evolving political norms. Of course, nation and states are continuously pushing at one another, as are the respective branches of the government. As Madison predicted, ambition is forever countering ambition.[66] Perhaps one can expect similar dynamics in the roles of religious communities and the state, which compete for the loyalty of citizens.

Nevertheless, we hope that by explaining the reasons underpinning the relevant boundaries, this book will help political institutions and religious communities to internalize religion clause norms and make judicial enforcement less necessary. Even now, for example, with all the uncertainty over Establishment Clause standards, we might fairly expect that legislatures would not choose a Latin cross to mark a newly created war memorial, as distinguished from taking steps to preserve such a cross in a preexisting and long-standing war memorial.[67] Political and religious pluralism, where they exist, are powerful checks against the government adopting and advancing a particularized religious account of the state's authority.

For reasons quite analogous to those that operate within the regimes of power separation and federalism, adjudications of Establishment Clause

66. Madison, Federalist #51, available at http://avalon.law.yale.edu/18th_century/fed51.asp (to control the different branches of government, "[a]mbition must be made to counteract ambition").

67. For a narrative of precisely this sort, see *Salazar v. Buono,* 130 S. Ct. 1803 (2010).

disputes will tend to present their own specialized forms and will confront a variety of limits. In several different ways, a structural focus matters deeply in judicial decisions about the scope of the Establishment Clause. First, Article III's specification of a "case" or "controversy" as a prerequisite to the power of the federal courts will continue to constrain who has standing to bring such actions. In some cases, perhaps egregious ones, there may be no one who can successfully bring a lawsuit. Second, the choice and consequence of remedies in Establishment Clause cases are a flash point for controversy. Indeed, much of the focus in recent disputes about religious displays revolves around the practical implications of ordering their removal. Third, as is true of other questions of constitutional structure, judges must be mindful that constitutional allocations of power may not be altered by agreement of the parties involved — neither the state, nor any religious believers, may consent to a swap of constitutionally separated functions.[68]

Overview of Subsequent Chapters

In what follows, this chapter's thematic exploration of the history, purposes, and limits of the First Amendment's religion clauses will reappear in a variety of particularized legal and political contexts. The rest of the book is divided into three parts. Part I (chapters 2–3) addresses the historical and conceptual root of our understanding of nonestablishment, which is found in the relationship between civil government and religious communities. Chapter 2 explores the regulation by government of religious institutions. We address Establishment Clause–based limits on adjudication of disputes about clergy, membership, and church property, and delegation of state power to religious entities. Chapter 3 focuses on issues of government funding of religious institutions, both historically and in connection with the modern welfare state. The ever-present questions of state financing of religiously affiliated schools and religion-based social welfare services are the primary concern of this chapter.

Part II (chapters 4–5) turns to the questions that arise when religious activity takes place inside of government. Chapter 4 addresses questions about religious activity, expression, and instruction in the context of public

---

68. For a comparable principle in the field of separation of powers within the national government, see *Immigration & Naturalization Service v. Chadha,* 462 U.S. 919 (1983) (Congress may not reserve to part of itself a veto over actions delegated to the executive branch).

schools. This is a subject with a deep history and a contentious present, ripe with possibilities of conflict between the public duties of secular governance and the private rights to engage in religious experience. Chapter 5 turns to the context in which the Supreme Court has been least helpful and most divided over the past twenty years — the permissibility of government-sponsored religious displays and messages. We address the problems of attributing public responsibility to expression with an arguably private character; the contours of a doctrine of ceremonial Deism; and the permissibility of both seasonal and permanent displays of religious sentiment.

Part III (chapters 6–7) explores the question of the secular state's duty or power, given our understanding of nonestablishment, to facilitate voluntary private religious exercise. Chapter 6 shows how the principle of religious liberty has come to be protected primarily through rights that encompass both religious and analogous nonreligious acts or associations. It then asks whether courts should ever treat religion-based exemptions from general laws as constitutionally mandatory. Chapter 7 turns to the issue of discretionary accommodation of religious believers and institutions. These discretionary accommodations include both specific exemptions from otherwise binding laws, such as the accommodation for peyote use by members of the Native American Church, and more sweeping provisions that allow claims of religious exemption from any government rule or practice that burdens free exercise. This chapter also discusses constitutional limits on discretionary accommodation, including limits that stem from the state's secular character.

The book's concluding chapter ties together our overarching themes in a particularly challenging context — the military chaplaincy. Using that context, we explore the extent to which the government may affirmatively accommodate the religious needs of individuals under its control. We also look at specific controversies that have arisen in that setting, including the asserted right of chaplains to pray in Jesus' name.

PART I

Civil Government and Religious Institutions

Comprehensive works on religion and government tend to start with questions that are at the forefront of the minds of contemporary readers. For questions commonly associated with the idea of a secular government, a series of relatively recent controversies fit that category. Should government be free to sponsor prayer at public events, including graduation ceremonies at schools? What about government display of Christmas symbols in that holiday season, or the congressional choice of In God We Trust as the national motto? The most intense recent controversies about the religious liberty of the people include the mandate that employers insure the cost of contraceptive services for their female employees. Do those who have religious reasons to avoid legal duties have a right under the Free Exercise Clause to exemption from obligations that others must respect?

We will address all those matters in due course. But the logic and chrono-logic of our approach to this subject lead us to begin exploring the details in a quite different place. One of the primary functions of government is the resolution of disputes between people. In its role as dispute resolver, the government is normally indifferent to the character of the private parties or institutions involved. Our courts can resolve multibillion-dollar controversies between high-tech giants like Google and Microsoft, as well as everyday matters concerning personal injuries, breaches of contract, employment relations, and the like.

However, some disputes that involve religious communities are constitutionally distinctive. Whether these conflicts involve employment matters, competing claims to real estate, the significance of membership in voluntary associations, or other matters, their resolution may turn on "ecclesiastical questions." When those questions appear — as they may in assertions of discrimination by a minister, or in claims by rival factions within a faith community for control of a valuable piece of property — the limited character of secular government imposes sharp restrictions on how courts may resolve them. These concerns are as old as the United States, and as recent as the Supreme Court's decision in 2012 in the *Hosanna-Tabor* case. Analysis of these problems highlights deep historical lessons, and sharply illuminates the concept of a government limited in its competence to secular concerns and excluded by its constitutional disability from ecclesiastical matters. Chapter 2 addresses the various ways that limited governmental competence in ecclesiastical affairs shapes the resolution of these kinds of controversies.

As one might expect, the constraints on government control of ecclesiastical matters have a reverse side — the limits on government financial support of religious institutions. Financial support almost always entails control. The history of our institutions and the logic of secular government combine to dictate that government not design, build, or maintain houses of worship. Likewise, government should not pay the salaries of those who lead others in prayer, or those who engage in religious indoctrination through teaching or proselytizing. When government supports religious entities for purely secular ends, however, the questions become considerably subtler, and courts have struggled with them for years. Chapter 3 confronts the development of the law on this subject. When government financially assists religiously affiliated schools, hospitals, or social service agencies, must or should it treat them identically with their secular counterparts? What appear over time are various devices, more or less successful, to permit some forms of financial support for secular ends while simultaneously maintaining the government's distance from subsidizing the ecclesiastical functions of religiously inspired institutions.

CHAPTER 2

Civil Authority and the Self-Government of Religious Communities

Our introductory chapter advanced a theory of disestablishment that emphasizes the limited competence of civil authority in religious matters. This idea reverberated through the Supreme Court's 2012 decision in *Hosanna-Tabor Evangelical Lutheran Church and School v. EEOC*,[1] which held that the Constitution significantly limits ministerial employees from pursuing antidiscrimination and other employment claims against religious institutions. In reaching its decision, the Supreme Court explicitly invoked the government's limited competence to determine who is fit to be a minister.

Some commentators, both before and after the decision in *Hosanna-Tabor*, argued for a far broader doctrine, rooted in the Free Exercise Clause, of church autonomy in matters of religious concern.[2] Either implicitly or ex-

---

1. *Hosanna-Tabor Evangelical Lutheran Church and School v. EEOC*, 565 U.S. ——— (2012); 132 S. Ct. 694 (2012); 2012 US LEXIS 578 (No. 10-553, Jan. 11, 2012).

2. Scholarly works arguing for free exercise doctrines of church autonomy, both before and after the decision in *Hosanna-Tabor*, include Christopher Lund, *Church Autonomy Reconceived: The Logic and Limits of Hosanna-Tabor*, 108 Northwestern U. L. Rev. ——— (forthcoming, 2014); Mark D. Rosen, *Religious Institutions, Liberal States, and the Political Architecture of Overlapping Spheres*, http://papers.ssrn.com/sol3/papers.cfm?abstract_id=22544089; Steven D. Smith, *Freedom of Religion or Freedom of the Church*, http://papers.ssrn.com/sol3/papers.cfm?abstract_id=1911412; Paul Horwitz, *Church as First Amendment Institutions: Of Sovereignty and Spheres*, 44 Harv. C.R.-C.L. L. Rev. 79 (2009); Richard W. Garnett, *The Freedom of the Church: (Towards) an Exposition, Translation, and Defense*, 21 J. Contemp. Legal Issues 33 (2013), available at http://papers.ssrn.com/sol3/papers.cfm?abstract_id=2297586; Richard W. Garnett, *Do Churches Matter? Towards an Institutional Understanding of the Religion Clauses*, 53 Vill. L. Rev. 273 (2008); Richard W. Garnett, *The Freedom of the Church*, 4 J. Cath. Soc. Thought 59 (2007). Much of the recent work on church autonomy builds upon the earlier writing of Professor Douglas Laycock. See Douglas Laycock, *Toward a General Theory*

plicitly, these scholars asserted the "freedom of the church" to determine its own affairs, subject to being overridden only for grave reasons of state. In response, other commentators denied entirely that the institutional or communitarian character of religion holds constitutional significance.[3] These opposing scholars argued that the First Amendment's protection of religious liberty applies exclusively to individuals.

In our view, both sets of scholars misperceive the relevant constitutional questions. Neither the Free Exercise Clause nor the Establishment Clause embraces or rejects a sweeping doctrine of church autonomy. As later chapters explain in detail, the Free Exercise Clause is not a source of religious privilege or special exemption for either individuals or institutions. And, as our first five chapters argue, the Establishment Clause is not a source of rights for any person or entity. The Establishment Clause does generate respect for religious communities, by deferring to their answers to ecclesiastical questions. This deference, however, is limited by the government's retained power to decide which questions are ecclesiastical and which religious bodies have the authority to resolve them.

As the Court's decision in *Hosanna-Tabor* explains, judicial deference to religious institutions in the formulation of answers to ecclesiastical questions has very deep and rich historical roots.[4] A core feature of religious establishments was the power of state officials to license clergy — that is, to determine who was eligible to serve. From the early years of the American republic, state and federal courts have rejected any such role for the government, and have thus consistently refused to decide who is fit to be a minister or teacher of religion. Significantly, they have demonstrated similar reticence about related questions, such as who is fit to be a member of a religious community or which faction of a congregation represents the "true church."

This chapter opens with a survey of that historical tradition. It then explores three areas in contemporary legal doctrine that reflect the government's limited competence in matters of religious disputes. The first of these

---

of the Establishment Clause: The Case of Church Labor Relations and the Right to Church Autonomy, 81 Colum. L. Rev. 1373 (1981). For Professor Laycock's later refinements of his thesis, see Douglas Laycock, *Church Autonomy Revisited*, 7 Georgetown J. L. & Pub. Pol'y 253 (2009).

3. See, e.g., Richard Schragger and Micah Schwartzman, *Against Religious Institutionalism*, 99 Va. L. Rev. 917 (2013), available at http://papers.ssrn.com/sol3/papers.cfm?abstract_id=2152060. See also Caroline Maia Corbin, *The Irony of* Hosanna-Tabor Evangelical Lutheran Church and School v. EEOC, 106 Northwestern U. L. Rev. 951 (2012), available at http://papers.ssrn.com/sol3/papers.cfm?abstract_id=2118167.

4. 132 S. Ct. at 702-705.

areas, which ultimately produced the *Hosanna-Tabor* decision, involves employment disputes between clergy and congregations. The second focuses on the frequently litigated question of property ownership in a congregation that is either dividing internally or withdrawing from a denominational body. The third involves claims by congregation members that they have been wrongfully excluded or harmed by leaders of a religious community. In all three contexts, courts have attempted to reconcile the Constitution's ban on religious decision making by the government with civil authority's crucial functions of peacefully resolving disputes and protecting individuals' rights.

Historical Background

During the nineteenth century, religious communities and their members brought hundreds of disputes before civil courts.[5] Some involved deep theological questions about the interpretation of Scripture or the need for individual religious rebirth. Others arose from more political or moral questions such as the abolition of slavery or abstinence from alcohol. Still others reflected the experience of immigrant communities settling into a new land, deciding whether to maintain old traditions and language in their worship. And some simply involved ordinary conflicts over personality and power.

With very few exceptions, these disputes played out in state rather than federal courts, and were resolved by common law doctrines instead of explicit appeal to constitutional rules or principles.[6] To a remarkable extent, courts throughout the nineteenth century were conscious of limitations on their competence to resolve certain kinds of religious questions. This can be best seen in cases involving membership in religious communities. Although many courts resolved these cases by declaring that members had no property right in their church membership, and thus no legal ground for complaint, that declaration frequently accompanied an observation about the limits of civil authority. An 1846 Pennsylvania decision, rejecting a member's challenge to his excommunication, offered an eloquent statement of these limits:

---

5. See Frank Way, *Religious Disputation and the Civil Courts: Quasi-Establishment and Secular Principles,* 42 Western Political Quarterly 523-543 (1989) (surveying all published church property disputes between the founding and 1982).

6. *Id.* at 536-537.

The decisions of ecclesiastical courts, like every other judicial tribunal, are final; as they are the best judges of what constitutes an offence against the word of God and the discipline of the church. Any other than those courts must be incompetent judges of matters of faith, discipline and doctrine; and civil courts, if they should be so unwise as to attempt to supervise their judgments on matters which come within their jurisdiction, would only involve themselves in a sea of uncertainty and doubt, which would do any thing but improve either religion or good morals.[7]

When ministers brought employment claims against their congregations, courts generally invoked the same principle of jurisdictional limit. If a minister challenged a religious body's decision to remove him from office on substantive grounds — such as conformity with church teaching or expectations for ministers' conduct — the court would deny that it had the authority to decide such questions. For example, in *Connitt v. The Reformed Protestant Dutch Church of New Prospect* (New York, 1874),[8] a minister complained that he had been wrongfully removed from his office. The court ruled that it could not review Rev. Connitt's assertion that he was fit to continue as pastor of his congregation. The court made clear that the limit on its jurisdiction encompassed more than questions of theology, and extended to any assessment of his job performance.

The only issue that courts could, and quite regularly did, resolve in such cases was whether the religious body — such as a congregation's governing board, a congregation acting as a whole, or a denominational officer, such as a bishop — that made the challenged employment decision had the legal authority to do so. Odd as it may seem to modern readers, courts routinely ordered congregations to accept ministers who had been appointed by denominational authorities, even when the congregation refused to admit them to the church. As in *Connitt,* these courts disclaimed any competence to decide who was fit to serve as minister, and instead asked only whether the challenged employment decision had been made by the authorized body. If the congregation's constitution entrusted decisions about pastoral leadership

---

7. *The German Reformed Church v. The Commonwealth Ex rel. Seibert,* 3 Pa. 282 (1846). Most courts reached the same conclusion as the Pennsylvania Supreme Court in *Siebert.* See, e.g., *State of Indiana, ex rel. Hatfield, v. Cummins,* 171 Ind. 112, 85 N.E. 359 (1908); *Landis v. Campbell,* 79 Mo. 33 (1883); *Sale v. The First Regular Baptist Church of Mason City,* 62 Iowa 26, 17 N.W. 143 (1883).

8. *George W. Connitt v. The Reformed Protestant Dutch Church of New Prospect,* 54 N.Y. 551 (1874).

to a bishop or other ecclesiastical leader, then the court would enforce those decisions.[9]

The distinction between decisions about fitness and decisions about legal authority to act stands on sound constitutional ground. In contrast to questions of a minister's fitness, questions of how a religious community allocates decision-making authority may be resolved using ordinary secular legal sources. A congregation's governing documents will typically assign certain powers to a board of trustees and others to the congregation as a whole, and recognize that yet others are held by the denomination to which the congregation belongs. By locating the appropriate decision maker for a particular question, such as the termination of a minister, the court respects and gives legal effect to the religious community's self-governance. A judicial refusal to intervene in the matter, or an unwillingness to consider the religious community's allocation of authority, would deny the community such respect.

Disputes over control of congregational property proved more difficult for courts than disputes involving membership or ministerial employment, because property disputes typically involved contested claims to decision-making authority within the church. An 1893 Indiana Supreme Court decision, *Smith v. Pedigo*,[10] provides a useful example. In 1889, Mount Tabor Regular Baptist Church split into two factions over the necessity of "means of grace" for salvation. The majority faction asserted that salvation depended upon the use of such means, including the church's preaching and teaching, but the minority faction claimed that the Holy Spirit requires no such instruments to save souls. Each faction claimed to be the true successor to the congregation founded in 1835, and therefore entitled to ownership of the church property.

Faced with these conflicting claims to control of the congregation and its property, the Indiana courts could have decided that the questions were inextricably linked with ecclesiastical matters outside the competence of civil courts, and thus refused to hear the case. Doing so, however, would have had

9. For an interesting example of such a case, see *Jacob Feizel v. The Trustees of the First German Society of the M.E. Church of Wyandotte City,* 9 Kan. 592 (1872). Rev. Feizel was appointed by the regional bishop to be pastor of a Methodist congregation in Wyandotte City. The lay trustees of the congregation refused to admit him to the church, and Feizel sought a judicial order to gain entry. The Kansas Supreme Court ruled in favor of Feizel and ordered the trustees to admit him. The court reasoned that the trustees were free to find another church if they disagreed with Feizel's teaching, but the congregation was governed according to Methodist doctrine, which gave the bishop power to appoint the minister.

10. *Smith v. Pedigo,* 145 Ind. 361; 33 N.E. 777 (1893).

intolerable consequences. Without the possibility of redress in civil courts, such disputes would leave property ownership uncertain and risk escalation of conflict into ever-greater discord.

With such considerations in mind, the Indiana Supreme Court — like courts in every state — agreed that civil tribunals have jurisdiction to decide which faction has the right to control church property. The court in *Smith*, again echoing decisions across the country, emphasized the limited reach of its decision. Civil courts must resolve disputed questions of property ownership, but they do not have the competence or power to decide whether the "means" or "antimeans" faction is theologically correct.

In resolving property disputes, however, courts frequently could not avoid the underlying theological controversy. Some disputes involved property that was given to the church subject to an express trust, under which the church held title to the property so long as it remained faithful to particular doctrines.[11] If the church departed from the doctrine specified in the trust, title to the property could be claimed either by an heir of the original donor or by church members who remained faithful to that doctrine. Of course, the congregation often disagreed with the assertion that it had violated the terms of the trust, and a court would have to decide whether the controlling faction of the congregation still adhered to the specified doctrine. Courts hearing such cases recognized the difficulty that civil tribunals had in parsing religious doctrines, but nonetheless decided such cases because donors clearly intended that their property be used for specific purposes. Use for other pur-

11. For examples of express trusts that limited use of the donated property to a particular denomination or set of beliefs, see *Cape v. Plymouth Congregational Church*, 130 Wis. 174 (1906); *Nance v. Busby*, 91 Tenn. 303 (Tenn 1892); *Beckwith v. Rector, Wardens and Vestrymen of St. Philip's Parish*, 69 Ga. 564 (1882); *App v. Lutheran Congregation*, 6 Pa. 201 (1847). Judicial interpretations of express trusts could take unexpected turns, as in *Attorney General Ex. rel. Abott v. The Town of Dublin*, 38 N.H. 459 (1859). The late Congregational minister of the town of Abbott, Rev. Sprague, left a very substantial sum in trust, to be used "for the sole purpose of supporting the Christian religion in the Congregational Society, so called, in said town; the interest thereof to be paid quarter-yearly to the minister of the Congregational persuasion who shall be regularly ordained and statedly preach in said Society." *Id.* at 512. Following Rev. Sprague's death, the church he had served elected a Unitarian minister, and continued to be served by a Unitarian minister at the time of the litigation. The local Trinitarian Congregationalist congregation claimed the proceeds of Rev. Sprague's trust, but the court held that they still could be used by the congregation he had served. The court reasoned that, at the time Sprague drafted the trust terms, the Congregationalist ministry included many Unitarians. Rev. Sprague did not specifically define "minister of the Congregational persuasion" to exclude Unitarians, so the court reasoned that his trust should not be interpreted to imply such a limitation. *Id.* at 536-554.

poses — that is, the support of religious precepts inconsistent with the terms of the trust — breached the church's promise to the donor.[12]

In deciding whether the congregation had breached that promise, courts used their standard methods for interpreting the original intent of the donor. They then measured that intent against the current beliefs of the controlling faction of the congregation. If that group had substantially departed from the donor's intent, and a rival faction was more faithful to that intent, the court would award control of the property to the rival faction. Courts hearing such cases invariably disclaimed any power or ability to decide the religious truth or moral superiority of the positions held by the rival factions.

Much more typically, however, churches did not hold property under an express trust. As in *Smith v. Pedigo,* the congregation used funds donated by many members over many years to purchase property. If the congregation then split over doctrinal matters, such as Mount Tabor's dispute over the means of grace, the court did not have the expressed intent of any donor to use in resolving rival claims to church property.

Courts developed two sharply divergent methods for responding to these circumstances. Under the first approach, seen in *Smith v. Pedigo,* courts reasoned that those who contributed money or land to support a church did so with the expectation that future leaders of the congregation would profess and practice the same beliefs as the founders. Even if those expectations were not reflected in an express condition on future use of the property, courts implied such a limit. The court in *Smith* offered the following rationale for the implied trust doctrine: "[T]he law allows every one to believe as he pleases, and practice that belief so long as that practice does not interfere with the equal rights of others. But that is a very different thing from the claim of a right of a church member to repudiate the faith and doctrine upon which his church was founded, and at the same time insist on his right to exercise and enjoy the benefits and privileges of a member of such church, contrary to the rules and laws upon which such church is established."[13] Members of the congregation certainly had the legal right to embrace different beliefs, but in doing so they ceased to be faithful members of Mount Tabor Baptist and thus lacked the authority to act in the name of the congregation. After assessing the beliefs of the rival factions and comparing them against the congregation founders' declaration of faith, the Indiana Supreme Court decided that the majority faction (the "means party") had substantially departed from the

12. See generally *Town of Dublin,* 38 N.H. 459 (1859).
13. *Smith v. Pedigo,* 145 Ind. 361, 365-366 (1893).

faith held by the congregation's founders, while the "antimeans party" continued to hold that faith. Applying the implied trust doctrine, the court awarded
control of the property to the minority faction.

The second approach arose from frequently expressed concerns about
the implied trust doctrine. The most basic objection was rooted in ordinary
property law norms. Common law courts strenuously opposed limitations on
the use or ownership of real property, because such restrictions impeded the
free development of communities. Implied limitations received even greater
disfavor because they lacked the certainty of written restrictions. Thus, the
implied trust doctrine placed a double burden on property owned by religious communities. Control of church property was perpetually subject to
challenge from dissenting members, who could object to any shift in doctrine
or practice on grounds that it departed from the founders' faith.

Moreover, the implied trust doctrine required civil courts to make
quintessentially theological judgments. Even if, as courts following that approach invariably asserted, the judge did not need to determine which of the
rival positions was "true," the judge still had to decide which was more consistent with the doctrine held at some point in the past. A cursory overview of
implied trust cases shows the difficulty of making such determinations.

Kniskern v. The Lutheran Churches of St. John's and St. Peter's (New York,
1844)[14] offers a particularly compelling illustration of this problem. The case
involved disputes over control of several Lutheran congregations in which
the leaders and a majority of members decided to sever ties with the General
Synod of the Evangelical Lutheran Church in America and join the Franckean
Evangelical Lutheran Synod. The minority claimed that the Franckean Synod
was not truly Lutheran because its declaration conflicted with the Augsburg
Confession — the traditional statement of Lutheran beliefs. To resolve the
dispute, the court undertook a lengthy examination of church history to determine whether adherence to the Augsburg Confession is necessary for one
to be considered authentically Lutheran, followed by an even more detailed
theological comparison of the Augsburg Confession and the Franckean Lutheran declaration. The court concluded that Franckean Lutherans were not
faithful Lutherans and awarded control of the congregations to the minority.

The concerns about restraint on property and theological competence
merge in the most important objection to the implied trust approach. By giving control of church property to those deemed by a civil court most "orthodox," the approach effectively imposed a civil penalty on the development of

14. *Kniskern v. The Lutheran Churches,* 1 Sanf. Ch. 439 (New York Chancery, 1844).

religious doctrine. The beliefs and practices of most, perhaps all, faith traditions evolve in subtle and sometimes quite dramatic ways. The implied trust approach allowed courts to intervene on behalf of those who would attempt to freeze that evolution. In other words, the approach effectively "established" the congregation founders' faith, as discerned by a civil court. More troubling, civil courts' power to interpret religious doctrine allowed the religious, moral, or even political preferences of judges to affect the outcome of cases.

In *Watson v. Jones*,[15] the U.S. Supreme Court explicitly rejected the implied trust approach, and set forth an alternative method for resolving internal church disputes. This method emphasizes judicial deference to the governance structure adopted by a religious organization. The method applies to all internal disputes, including those over membership, ministerial employment, and control of church property.

Watson involved a struggle for control of Walnut Street Presbyterian Church in Louisville, Kentucky. Immediately following the Civil War, the General Assembly of the Presbyterian Church in the United States required a statement of repentance from church leaders who had been sympathetic to the causes of slavery and secession. This led to a sharp division among Presbyterians in Kentucky, including those at the Walnut Street church. A majority of the Walnut Street congregation accepted the national church's requirement, but a determined minority rejected the demand for repentance. Extended litigation over control of the congregation's property wound up in the U.S. Supreme Court, which ruled in favor of the majority faction.

Although the Court's opinion in *Watson v. Jones* has constitutional overtones, the decision itself is based on common law principles and does not establish a constitutional rule governing church property disputes across the nation. The Court adopted a three-part classification for analyzing such disputes.[16] The first tracks the traditional method for enforcing express trusts. If a congregation holds property subject to an express trust that conditions ownership on continued adherence to particular doctrine, courts should enforce those conditions.

The second and third parts apply in the absence of an express trust, and focus on the form of governance embraced by the congregation involved in the dispute. If the congregation is independent of higher ecclesiastical authorities, courts should defer to decisions about control of church property made by that congregation's governing structure, which typically includes

15. *Watson v. Jones*, 80 U.S. (13 Wall.) 679 (1871).
16. 80 U.S. at 722-723.

election of officers by majority vote of members. If the congregation belongs to a denominational body that possesses supervisory power over the local church, then courts should defer to decisions about control of church property made by the highest authority within the denominational body.

Although parts two (independent) and three (denominational) were treated by the Court as distinct categories, they reflect the same analytic focus. As the opinion recognized, both categories arise from the voluntary character of American church governance. In the American legal tradition, congregations are free to adopt any lawful model of self-government, including models that place the congregation under the discipline of a denominational authority. This contrasted markedly with the status of congregations in Great Britain, where the established church operated under direct state regulation, and dissenting congregations had limited legal protections and were under extensive state oversight.

This difference between American and British arrangements undergirds the Court's rejection of the implied trust doctrine. The Court reasoned that the implied trust doctrine arose from a legal tradition in which civil authorities governed religious institutions, and civil courts routinely interpreted and enforced ecclesiastical laws. In such a tradition, courts would experience no discomfort "in grappling with the most abstruse problems of theological controversy, or in construing the instruments which those churches have adopted as their rules of government, or inquiring into their customs and usages."[17]

In contrast, America's tradition of nonestablishment, religious liberty, and wide diversity of faith groups renders courts especially unfit to apply the implied trust doctrine. As several state courts had previously explained, American judges lack adequate knowledge about the widely varying faiths that might come before the bench. The Court placed even more emphasis on religious voluntarism. Like the authority of American civil government, the legal authority of American churches and denominations arises solely from the consent of the governed. In joining a religious community, a member gives consent — express or implied — to that community's structure of governance. Courts respect that consent by deferring to the chosen structure of religious authority.

The Court stressed, however, that religious communities are not beyond the reach of civil government. For example, religious tribunals do not have jurisdiction over civil offenses such as theft or murder. Civil court def-

17. 80 U.S. at 727-728.

erence is limited to the resolution of specifically ecclesiastical questions. "[I]t is a very different thing where a subject-matter of dispute, strictly and purely ecclesiastical in its character, — a matter over which the civil courts exercise no jurisdiction, — a matter which concerns theological controversy, church discipline, ecclesiastical government, or the conformity of the members of the church to the standard of morals required of them, — becomes the subject of its action."[18]

With respect to questions that are "strictly and purely ecclesiastical in . . . character," *Watson* teaches that civil courts should defer to the religious body chosen by members to resolve such questions. The Court found that the contest for control of Walnut Street Presbyterian Church involved just such an ecclesiastical question. Because the congregation belonged to the Presbyterian Church in the United States, and the highest tribunal in that denomination had awarded control over the church property to the majority faction, the Court held that federal courts must respect that judgment and affirm the majority faction's ownership.

It would be another century before this principle embraced in *Watson v. Jones* would take on constitutional significance. Nevertheless, the principle exerted significant influence over the development of American law governing disputes within religious bodies, including controversies over clergy employment and church membership as well as fights over property ownership.

The principle of deference to religious institutions on matters that are "strictly and purely ecclesiastical" is not merely long-standing. The principle is constitutionally essential. Matters that fit this characterization are off-limits to the secular state. The language of "strict" and "pure" represents a boundary, not a rhetorical flourish. Many questions of empirical fact and moral concern have ecclesiastical counterparts. Whether capital punishment is cruel, and whether it is justifiable in some circumstances, offers one good example of a context that invites both secular and ecclesiastical judgments. The state is of course free to engage with and answer such questions in light of its own tools of inquiry and appraisal. Questions are "strictly and purely ecclesiastical" when they depend entirely upon judgments involving the word or will of the divine; or upon interpretation of works believed to be sacred by those who follow them; or upon the internal understandings of the structure and function of religious institutions, such as the appropriate criteria for salvation or ordination to ministry. These questions are never within the jurisdiction of a secular state, which is barred by the nonestablishment principle from pro-

18. 80 U.S. at 733.

viding official or authoritative answers to them. The state may decide if capital punishment is morally or unconstitutionally cruel, but it may not decide that administration of such a punishment is consistent with any faith tradition, or with the Bible, or with God's will.

Civil Courts and Clergy Employment

Armed with this understanding of the nonestablishment principle, we start our inquiry into modern developments in this area by returning to disputes over employment of clergy. Recall that in the nineteenth century courts sharply distinguished the substantive question of whether someone was fit to be a minister from the procedural question of whether a challenged decision was made by the proper authority within the church. This distinction echoes the approach to ecclesiastical disputes embraced by the Supreme Court in *Watson v. Jones.* Confronted with a controversy involving religious institutions, the court first determines whether the dispute involves "ecclesiastical issues." If it does, the court then asks whether the authoritative decision-maker has spoken on those issues. If the proper religious authority has decided the question, the court should defer to that decision. This approach assumes, of course, that deference is not warranted if the dispute involves only nonecclesiastical questions, or the challenged decision was made by an entity that lacked final decision-making authority within the community.

Recall also that the Court in *Watson* adopted that approach as an alternative to the implied trust doctrine. At the same time, the Court affirmed the competence of civil courts to resolve ecclesiastical disputes arising from express trusts — gifts of money or land to a religious body, made on condition that the proceeds of the gift be used for specified purposes. Fifty years after *Watson,* in *Gonzalez v. Roman Catholic Archbishop of Manila,*[19] the Court returned to the subject of ecclesiastical disputes over express trusts. The case involved an early-nineteenth-century trust, in which the donor provided funds for a "Father chaplain to say sixty masses annually"[20] on behalf of the donor and her family. The trust also specified that the chaplain's position funded by the trust should be occupied by a descendant of the donor. In 1922, Raul Rodrigo Gonzalez, a ten-year-old descendant of the donor, claimed the right to the chaplain's position or the income payable under the trust. The archbishop

---

19. *Gonzalez v. Roman Catholic Archbishop of Manila,* 280 U.S. 1 (1929).
20. 280 U.S. at 11.

of Manila refused, reasoning that, under the 1918 Code of Canon Law, Gonzalez was too young and lacked the formal education or training to exercise the office of chaplain.

Gonzalez filed suit in the Philippines, and the trial court ruled in his favor,[21] holding that the trust should be governed by canon law in effect when the trust was created. In the early nineteenth century, canon law would have permitted Gonzalez to exercise or otherwise enjoy the benefits of the chaplaincy. Because the Philippines was a U.S. territory at the time, the dispute eventually found its way to the Supreme Court, which ruled in favor of the archbishop. The Court held that "the appointment is a canonical act, [thus] it is the function of the church authorities to determine what the essential qualifications of a chaplain are and whether the candidate possesses them."[22] Nothing in the express terms of the trust overrode the archbishop's authority to assess the qualifications of candidates for ministry. Most famously, the *Gonzalez* opinion strenuously reaffirms the idea of judicial deference to ecclesiastical judgments, while reserving an uncertain scope for civil court review. "In the absence of fraud, collusion, or arbitrariness, the decisions of the proper church tribunals on matters purely ecclesiastical, although affecting civil rights, are accepted in litigation before the secular courts as conclusive."[23]

It was another half-century before the Supreme Court revisited the issue of clergy employment. During the interval, the Supreme Court ruled that the religion clauses of the First Amendment applied to the states.[24] The Court also held that the principles of *Watson* and *Gonzalez*, originally articulated as common law norms, rested on constitutional foundations. In 1976, the Court decided *Serbian Eastern Orthodox Diocese v. Milivojevich*,[25] in which the former bishop of that diocese challenged his removal from office, as well as the division of the diocese into three smaller units.

In a legal dispute that stretched back for more than a decade, Bishop Milivojevich claimed that the governing body of the Serbian Eastern Orthodox Church (the "Mother Church") failed to follow its own rules when it removed him and reorganized the North American diocese he had headed. Relying on the language in *Gonzalez* that seemed to permit civil court review of "arbitrary" ecclesiastical decisions, the Illinois state courts concluded that the Mother Church failed to follow its own rules in the proceedings against Milivojevich.

21. *Id.*
22. 280 U.S. at 16.
23. *Id.*
24. We discuss this very important move in chapter 3.
25. *Serbian Eastern Orthodox Diocese v. Milivojevich*, 426 U.S. 696 (1976).

The Illinois Supreme Court ordered the Mother Church to reinstate Milivoje-vich as bishop and invalidated the division of the North American diocese.[26]

Reversing the Illinois decision, the U.S. Supreme Court held that the First Amendment forbids civil courts from reviewing decisions on ecclesiastical matters made by the governing religious body. The Court explicitly rejected the suggestion, made in *Gonzalez*, that civil courts may review such decisions for "arbitrariness," either procedural or substantive.[27] *Watson* clearly establishes the principle that civil courts may not review substantive decisions by church authorities, and *Milivojevich* extends that principle to judicial review of procedural decisions by church authorities. Procedural decisions, the Court reasoned, are equally likely to involve ecclesiastical considerations as are substantive judgments.

In a dissenting opinion, Justice Rehnquist invoked *Watson* and *Gonzalez* to argue that religious bodies should be treated in exactly the same manner as analogous secular nonprofit organizations.[28] Because civil courts would have authority to examine whether a secular organization, such as a private club, followed its own rules in dismissing a leader or member, courts should have the same power with respect to churches. This objection misses the central point of *Watson* and *Gonzalez*. Although both decisions link treatment of religious and secular organizations, they also emphasize the distinctive quality of "purely ecclesiastical" questions. Civil courts may be competent to make judgments about the purposes of secular organizations or the qualifications of leaders of such organizations, but civil courts may not make judgments about matters that are quintessentially religious. That distinction lies at the heart of the Supreme Court's rejection of the implied trust doctrine in *Watson,* as well as the Court's refusal to require the archbishop of Manila to accept Gonzalez as a chaplain.

Moreover, *Milivojevich* correctly holds that at least some procedural issues have no less ecclesiastical significance than substantive matters. In *Milivojevich*, the Mother Church held final authority over the bishop's appointment to his position and the organization of dioceses. The procedures used by the Mother Church to assess the performance of bishops or subordinate bodies cannot easily be separated from the standards used in those evaluations. But *Milivojevich* should not be read to insulate all procedural issues from civil court review. Civil courts must defer to decisions, made by the governing religious

26. 60 Ill. 2d 477, 328 N.E. 2d 268 (1975).
27. 426 U.S. at 712-720.
28. 426 U.S. at 725-734.

body, on ecclesiastical matters. Accordingly, courts may appropriately decide whether the body that purports to act in the name of the church actually has the power to do so.[29] In this regard, *Milivojevich* gives constitutional weight to the principle we identified in nineteenth-century decisions about ministerial employment: courts do not have authority to second-guess judgments about the fitness of ministers, but courts do have power to decide whether the appropriate religious body has made the challenged judgment.

The 1976 decision in *Milivojevich* coincided with important developments in federal and state employment law. Title VII of the 1964 Civil Rights Act and many similar state laws bar employment discrimination on various grounds, including religion. Title VII exempts religious institutions from its ban on religious discrimination,[30] but applies to their employment practices in all other respects. The law raised an immediate question about its application to clergy. On its face, for example, the statute would require the Roman Catholic Church to open its priesthood to women.

Faced with a variety of antidiscrimination claims involving the employment of clergy, courts in the 1970s began to develop a "ministerial exception" to employment discrimination laws.[31] The exception immunizes religious entities from discrimination suits brought by employees with "ministerial" responsibilities such as teaching religious doctrine or leading worship. Courts rooted the exception in both religion clauses of the First Amendment, and emphasized in particular the limitations of civil court review developed in *Watson, Gonzalez,* and *Milivojevich.*[32]

By the time the Supreme Court decided *Hosanna-Tabor Evangelical Lutheran Church & School v. EEOC* in 2012, every federal circuit had embraced the ministerial exception.[33] The doctrine's widespread acceptance, however, masked

---

29. As far back as *Bouldin v. Alexander,* 82 U.S. 131 (1872), the Supreme Court had ruled that courts could evaluate the legal authority of the body purporting to act for a religious entity. Rehnquist's dissent conflates review of this constitutive procedural question with the more ordinary sort at issue in *Milivojevich.*

30. Civil Rights Act of 1964, sec. 702, codified at 42 U.S.C. sec. 2000e-1 (1982).

31. The first decision to adopt the ministerial exception to Title VII was *McClure v. Salvation Army,* 460 F. 2d 553 (5th Cir. 1972).

32. The decision that most carefully explicated the constitutional theories that help explain the exception is *Rayburn v. General Conference of Seventh Day Adventists,* 772 F. 2d 1164 (4th Cir. 1985), *cert. denied* 478 U.S. 1020 (1986).

33. *Hosanna-Tabor Evangelical Lutheran Church & School v. EEOC,* 132 S. Ct. 694, 705 n. 2 For further discussion of the law before the decision in *Hosanna-Tabor,* see Ira C. Lupu and Robert W. Tuttle, *Courts, Clergy, and Congregations: Disputes between Religious Institutions and Their Leaders,* 7 Georgetown J. L. & Pub. Pol'y 119, 123-128 (2009).

important uncertainties about its constitutional grounding and the range of positions covered by the exception. Both of those uncertainties surfaced in *Hosanna-Tabor.* The case involved an employment discrimination claim filed by teacher Cheryl Perich against her former employer, Hosanna-Tabor Evangelical Lutheran Church and School. Perich asserted that she had been fired in retaliation for filing a discrimination claim against Hosanna-Tabor, which had rejected Perich's attempt to return to work after a disability leave.

The Equal Employment Opportunity Commission agreed with Perich and filed suit against Hosanna-Tabor. Invoking the ministerial exception, the school contended that Perich fell within its scope because she taught a weekly religion course, led the class in daily prayers, and occasionally helped to lead worship for the students. In addition, the school argued, Perich was formally ordained as a teacher by the congregation's denomination and called by the congregation to serve in the school. At the trial and appellate stages of the litigation, the EEOC challenged only the school's designation of Perich as a ministerial employee. The agency argued that she taught predominantly secular subjects, that any religious duties were peripheral to her core duties, and that she held a position that could be filled by someone who was not ordained. The U.S. Court of Appeals for the Sixth Circuit agreed with the EEOC and found that Perich was not a ministerial employee because she spent less than one of her seven daily instructional hours involved in religious activities.[34] The appeals court also highlighted the fact that nonordained — and even non-Lutheran — teachers at the school performed the same tasks as Perich.

Hosanna-Tabor successfully sought review of the case in the Supreme Court. In reply, the EEOC challenged the constitutional foundation of the ministerial exception. It argued that neither the Free Exercise nor the Establishment Clause requires the ministerial exception's deference to religious employers. Echoing Justice Rehnquist's dissent in *Milivojevich,* the EEOC asserted that religious employers deserve no more or less protection than secular nonprofits for their employment relationships with organizational leaders.

The Supreme Court unanimously and emphatically rejected the EEOC's effort to dismantle the ministerial exception and declared that the ministerial exception arises from both religion clauses of the First Amendment.

> We agree that there is such a ministerial exception. The members of a religious group put their faith in the hands of their ministers. Requiring

34. *EEOC v. Hosanna-Tabor Evangelical Lutheran Church & School,* 597 F. 3d 769 (6th Cir. 2010).

a church to accept or retain an unwanted minister, or punishing a church for failing to do so, intrudes upon more than a mere employment decision. Such action interferes with the internal governance of the church, depriving the church of control over the selection of those who will personify its beliefs. By imposing an unwanted minister, the state infringes the Free Exercise Clause, which protects a religious group's right to shape its own faith and mission through its appointments. According the state the power to determine which individuals will minister to the faithful also violates the Establishment Clause, which prohibits government involvement in such ecclesiastical decisions.[35]

In exploring the historical foundations of the religion clauses, the Court emphasized the power government officials had over the appointment of clergy in established churches, first in England and then in several of the colonies. The Free Exercise and Establishment Clauses, the Court reasoned, "ensured that the new Federal Government — unlike the English Crown — would have no role in filling ecclesiastical offices."[36] The Court traced this denial of government power over clergy employment through its unbroken history of deference, reflected in *Watson* and *Milivojevich,* to religious organizations' decisions about ecclesiastical matters.

In *Hosanna-Tabor,* the parties sharply disagreed about the reasons for Perich's termination, with the school asserting a religious justification and the EEOC denying that assertion. As framed by the Court, however, the exemption does not depend on the employer's assertion of a religious reason for the challenged employment decision.[37] The constitutional constraint arises from the position, not the employer's reasons for any particular decision. In that respect, *Hosanna-Tabor* closely follows *Milivojevich.* If the subject of the dispute is ecclesiastical, civil courts have no power to second-guess a decision about that subject made by the appropriate religious authority.[38]

Having recognized the doctrine, the Court then considered whether Perich's duties fell within the scope of the ministerial exception. The Court rejected the test for that scope used by the Sixth Circuit, which focused pri-

---

35. 132 S. Ct. at 706.
36. 132 S. Ct. at 703.
37. 132 S. Ct. at 709.
38. Indeed, the long history of ministerial exception cases is dominated by claims of covert discrimination, rather than overt discrimination against women or others. In the vast majority of cases, the defendant religious entity offers no religious reason for the challenged job action. See Lupu and Tuttle, *supra* note 33, at 127-128.

marily on the quantitative proportions of religious and secular duties, and looked instead at all the circumstances of her employment. Those included "the formal title given Perich by the Church, the substance reflected in that title, her own use of that title, and the important religious functions she performed for the Church."[39] The four elements identified by the Court may not provide a bright-line rule, but they do indicate several important features of any constitutionally appropriate standard for the ministerial exception. Most importantly, the scope of the exception is determined by an objective standard, applied by courts based on the relevant parties' expectations as well as the employee's actual duties. Although courts should take seriously a religious employer's formal designation of an employee as a minister, that designation is only one consideration. Likewise, the employee's self-identification as a minister is neither necessary nor conclusive.

Because the ministerial exception is about judicial competence rather than the self-perception of employees or employers, a reviewing court must decide independently whether it is constitutionally capable of assessing the employee's job performance. In *Hosanna-Tabor,* such an assessment would have required the court to determine the congregation's standards and review process for called teachers, along with the school's expectations for those who teach the religion curriculum and lead worship. To borrow a phrase from *Watson* and *Milivojevich,* such determinations seem well within the bounds of ecclesiastical matters, which civil courts have no authority to decide.

The civil court, not the religious community, defines the scope of ecclesiastical matters. Once the court decides that the subject of a dispute falls within that definition, the court must defer to the governing religious body's judgment about that disputed subject. If, however, the court determines that the subject of a dispute falls outside that definition, the court should reject the ministerial exception defense and hear the case. Many aspects of the relationship between clergy and religious employers do not implicate ecclesiastical matters. For example, if a bishop physically assaults a priest, the ecclesiastical relationship among the church, bishop, and priest does not insulate the wrongdoer from civil or criminal liability.

Even disputes that are more directly related to clergy employment may still fall outside the ministerial exception. Consider, for example, a minister hired by a congregation under a two-year employment contract, which provides for review after the first year and termination only for good cause. Should the ministerial exception bar a suit by the minister for breach of that

39. 132 S. Ct. at 708.

contract? Any answer to that question depends on specific details of the minister's claim. If the congregation terminated the minister after the first year, and the minister asserts that the congregation used a defective review process and lacked good cause for ending the contract, then the ministerial exception should apply. As demonstrated in *Milivojevich,* judicial assessment of either the review process or the grounds for termination would involve constitutionally forbidden inquiry into ecclesiastical matters.

By contrast, if the minister claimed that the congregation refused to pay the minister for the final four months of the contract, even though the minister had fulfilled the terms of the agreement, the ministerial exception would not apply. Under ordinary employment law standards, an employee is entitled to wages for time worked even if the employee has performed poorly during that time. The minister only needs to prove actual performance of the duties expected under the contract, and that the agreed salary was not paid. The court can resolve any disputes about those two issues without inquiry into ecclesiastical matters.

Civil Courts and Church Property Ownership

Many disputes over the employment of clergy are entangled with struggles for control of a congregation or denomination. One faction supports a particular minister, and another challenges the minister's doctrinal fidelity or denominational affiliation. If the dispute leads to a split, the rival factions almost invariably claim ownership of the congregation's property. It should come as no surprise, then, that the legal norms governing ministerial employment disputes in civil court also apply to suits for control of church property. In both contexts, the First Amendment bars civil courts from deciding ecclesiastical questions, although civil courts retain the power to determine which questions are ecclesiastical and which entity within the religious body has ultimate decision-making authority.

Recall that in *Watson v. Jones* (1871) the U.S. Supreme Court adopted that principle as a matter of common law. Over the next eighty years, *Watson* proved increasingly influential with state courts, although far from all jurisdictions ultimately accepted its limitations on civil court jurisdiction.[40] Soon

40. Professor Way states that "The *Watson* case, however, had little immediate impact on the state courts. Indeed, in the years following the *Watson* decision state courts either ignored the court's admonition on congregational polities or misused the case." Way, *supra*

after the Supreme Court ruled that the religion clauses apply to the states, the Court returned to the principle articulated in *Watson* and placed it on constitutional footing. In *Kedroff v. St. Nicholas Cathedral of the Russian Orthodox Church in North America* (1952),[41] the Supreme Court considered a dispute over property, located in New York State and belonging to the Russian Orthodox Church. In response to concerns that Soviet authorities were exerting undue influence over the patriarch and ruling body of the Russian Orthodox Church in Moscow, a majority of Russian Orthodox church leaders in the United States met in 1924 and formed an independent ecclesiastical body. The U.S. body asserted its autonomy in matters of church governance, including control over property and the appointment of church leaders. New York adopted a statute that formally recognized the U.S. body's autonomy and gave legal effect to that body's claims over church property.

The lawsuit arose when the U.S. body attempted to wrest control of the Russian Orthodox cathedral in New York City from leaders faithful to the patriarch of Moscow. Citing the state statute, the New York courts ruled in favor of the U.S. body. The New York Court of Appeals held that the state legislature's concerns about Soviet domination of the Moscow church authorities "justified the State in enacting a law to free the American group from infiltration of such atheistic or subversive influences."[42]

The Supreme Court reversed. Under governing ecclesiastical norms, recognized not merely by the church in Moscow but across Eastern Orthodox communities, the patriarch of Moscow and the Holy Synod exercise ultimate

---

note 5, at 534-535. As he goes on to explain, a number of state courts did make dubious use of the Court's reasoning in *Watson*. Indiana's Supreme Court represents the most egregious example, as it routinely cited *Watson* in support of decisions — including *Smith v. Pedigo* — that use the implied trust doctrine to award property to the more faithful faction. See also *White Lick Quarterly Meeting of Friends v. White Lick Quarterly Meeting of Friends,* 89 Ind. 136 (Ind. 1883). Nonetheless, we think he understates the influence of *Watson's* argument for civil court avoidance of ecclesiastical questions. Most importantly, state courts regularly invoked *Watson's* rule of deference to established procedures within church bodies. See, e.g., *Horsman v. Allen,* 129 Cal. 131 (Cal. 1900); *Trustees of Trinity M.E. Church v. Harris,* 73 Conn. 216 (Conn. 1900); *Brayshaw v. Ridout,* 79 Md. 454 (Md. 1894). But even in congregational cases, a number of states followed *Watson's* emphasis on using settled principles that govern other voluntary organizations, and declining to consider doctrinal differences. See, e.g., *Bates v. Houston,* 66 Ga. 198 (1880); *Wilson v. Livingstone,* 99 Mich. 594 (Mich. 1894); *Fort v. First Baptist Church of Paris,* 55 S.W. 402 (Tex. Civ. App. 1899).

41. *Kedroff v. St. Nicholas Cathedral of the Russian Orthodox Church in North America,* 344 U.S. 94 (1952).

42. *St. Nicholas Cathedral of the Russian Orthodox Church in North America v. Kedroff,* 96 N.E. 2d 56, 62 (N.Y. Court of Appeals 1950).

decision-making authority in the Russian Orthodox Church. The New York statute substituted state-approved religious leaders for the authority recognized under those ecclesiastical norms.[43] Such state interference in ecclesiastical matters, the Court held, violates the Free Exercise Clause, which encompasses the principles announced in *Watson*. "[*Watson*] radiates . . . a spirit of freedom for religious organizations, an independence from secular control or manipulation — in short, power to decide for themselves, free from state interference, matters of church government as well as those of faith and doctrine."[44]

In a significant concurring opinion, Justice Frankfurter offered a subtly different justification for invalidating the New York statute. Like the majority, Frankfurter found that *Watson* stated a principle of constitutional law. He located that principle in a broader vision of limitations on the jurisdiction of civil government, not in the Free Exercise Clause alone. The New York state legislature exceeded its jurisdiction when it purported to strip the Moscow patriarch of authority over U.S. churches because of concerns about Soviet control. Frankfurter compared the New York legislation to other governmental assertions of control over religious bodies, including Nazi efforts to separate German Catholics from adherence to Rome. As we argued in the first chapter, such efforts reflect an attempt to use religion as an instrument of state power. "Under our Constitution," Frankfurter wrote, "it is not open to the governments of this Union to reinforce the loyalty of their citizens by deciding who is the true exponent of their religion."[45]

Kedroff explicitly stated that the First Amendment mandates *Watson's* principle of limited civil authority over ecclesiastical questions. Nonetheless, a number of states continued to enforce, either by statute or by common law rule, the implied trust doctrine under which courts resolve intracongregational property disputes by awarding title to the faction that has remained faithful to the church founders' beliefs and practices.

The Supreme Court returned its attention to this issue in *Presbyterian Church in the United States v. Mary Elizabeth Blue Hull Memorial Presbyterian Church* (1969).[46] The case involved two Georgia congregations that withdrew

---

43. In a follow-up decision, the Supreme Court held that the same principles apply to a common-law judgment in favor of the U.S. body. *Kreshik v. St. Nicholas Cathedral of the Russian Orthodox Church*, 363 U.S. 190 (1960). Courts, just like legislatures, lack authority to make ecclesiastical decisions.

44. 344 U.S. at 116.

45. 344 U.S. at 125 (Frankfurter, J., concurring).

46. *Presbyterian Church in the United States v. Mary Elizabeth Blue Hull Memorial Presbyterian Church*, 393 U.S. 440 (1969).

from the Presbyterian Church in the United States (PCUS) because of theological and political positions taken by the denomination. The two congregations objected to the national body's support for the civil rights movement, as well as its opposition to public school prayer and the Vietnam War. In addition, the congregations rejected the national body's decision to ordain women as ministers. When the national body asserted ownership of the withdrawing churches' property, the congregations filed suit in state court to confirm their title to the property.

Despite the Court's decision in *Kedroff*, Georgia courts still applied the implied trust doctrine to disputes over ownership of church property. Thus, the trial court asked the jury to decide whether the national denomination's political and doctrinal positions "amount to a fundamental or substantial abandonment of the original tenets and doctrines of the [general church], so that the new tenets and doctrines are utterly variant from the purposes for which the [general church] was founded."[47] The jury found that the national church had abandoned the faith of the church's founders, and awarded title to the local congregations. On appeal, the Georgia Supreme Court affirmed,[48] agreeing with the trial court that the PCUS had departed from Presbyterian doctrine by adopting liberal positions on political issues, encouraging civil disobedience, and ordaining women to the ministry.

The Supreme Court reversed. Invoking *Watson* and *Kedroff*, the Court restated the constitutional limitation on civil authority to decide ecclesiastical questions. Georgia's implied trust doctrine inevitably required such decisions, and thus violated the First Amendment. The majority opinion in *Hull Memorial Church*, written by Justice Brennan, is important for three reasons. First, the Court eliminated any uncertainty that might have remained after *Kedroff* about the limits of civil court intervention in religious disputes. *Kedroff* could have been read to bar only laws that were specifically intended to benefit a particular religious faction at the expense of another. *Hull Memorial Church* declared that the New York legislation at issue in *Kedroff* violated the First Amendment's religion clauses because the legislation asserted the competence of civil officials to decide which religious leaders represented the authentic faith of their group. The assertion of such competence, not merely the discriminatory design of a particular law, represented the core constitutional defect in New York's efforts against the patriarch of Moscow. The

47. 393 U.S. at 443-444.
48. *Presbyterian Church in United States v. Eastern Heights Presbyterian Church*, 159 S.E. 2d 690 (1968) (Georgia Supreme Court).

Court bluntly restated the principle adopted in *Watson* and made constitutional law in *Kedroff*. "The logic of this language leaves the civil courts no role in determining ecclesiastical questions in the process of resolving property disputes."[49]

Second, *Hull Memorial Church* broadened and enriched the constitutional justification for the principle of limited civil authority in ecclesiastical matters. The majority in *Kedroff* grounded that holding in the Free Exercise Clause, but *Hull Memorial Church* repeatedly turned to the Court's Establishment Clause decisions, including those prohibiting state-sponsored prayer and Bible reading in public schools. Citing one of those decisions, the Court reasoned that "the First Amendment enjoins the employment of organs of government for essentially religious purposes . . . ; the Amendment therefore commands civil courts to decide church property disputes without resolving underlying controversies over religious doctrine."[50] As in the school prayer cases, more is at stake than the religious liberty interests of individuals affected by the government's involvement in religious matters. The character of secular government demands this limitation on civil court decisions of ecclesiastical questions.

Third, although *Hull Memorial Church* is best known for its statement of what civil authorities may not do in response to church property disputes, the decision also makes an important, though often overlooked, statement of how jurisdictions should handle such cases. The Court suggested two approaches that would avoid the defects of the implied trust doctrine. In one, reflected in *Gonzalez* and *Watson,* the civil court defers to the governing religious body's resolution of a disputed ecclesiastical question. In the other, the civil court uses "neutral principles of law, developed for use in all property disputes,"[51] to decide which of the competing factions is entitled to ownership of the contested property. The Court treated both approaches as feasible alternatives but strongly urged interested parties to adopt some constitutionally appropriate method for resolving such disputes. "Hence, States, religious organizations, and individuals must structure relationships involving church property so as not to require the civil courts to resolve ecclesiastical questions."[52]

One year later, concurring in the Court's decision not to consider an appeal in *Maryland and Virginia Eldership of the Churches of God v. Church of*

---

49. 393 U.S. at 447.
50. 393 U.S. at 449, citing *Abington Sch. Dist. v. Schempp,* 374 U.S. 203 (1963).
51. 393 U.S. at 449.
52. *Id.*

God at Sharpsburg (1970), Justice Brennan offered an extended discussion of the two approaches.[53] Brennan explained that jurisdictions may adopt either of the two approaches, provided that a court in any given case is not required to decide ecclesiastical questions in order to use the preferred approach. For example, a state could prefer the deference approach, under which a civil court would resolve a church property case by looking to the governing religious body's decision on the matter, if the congregation is governed by any entity with authority to make that decision. If, however, the civil court was required to decide ecclesiastical questions in order to determine the identity or power of the governing body, then the court would need to use some other method for resolving that dispute.

Alternatively, a state could prefer the neutral principles approach, under which a court would look first to the standard legal documents that determine ownership of property. These would include the legal title or deed of trust, which describes the identity of the property's record ownership. They might also include the congregation's corporate documents or the details of any trust agreement, which would specify powers and limitations attaching to ownership of the property. The civil court would inspect those documents and, using traditional legal rules for resolving property, trust, or contract disputes, determine the prevailing party in the dispute. As with the deference approach, this method is limited by the fundamental constitutional constraint. "Again, however, general principles of property law may not be relied upon if their application requires civil courts to resolve doctrinal issues."[54] If application of neutral principles would require the court to decide ecclesiastical questions, the court would need to base its ruling on some other method.

The subsequent history of *Hull Memorial Church* provides a good example of this method in practice. After the Supreme Court held unconstitutional Georgia's implied trust doctrine, the state supreme court again ruled in favor of the local congregations.[55] It did so, however, through the use of "neutral principles." The PCUS argued that, as the superior ecclesiastical body, it was entitled to determine ownership of congregational property. But the Georgia court concluded that it could find no reference to PCUS's ownership of the property in the deeds or governing documents. To rule for the PCUS, the Georgia court said, it would need to imply a trust in favor of the denomi-

53. *Maryland and Virginia Eldership of the Churches of God v. Church of God at Sharpsburg*, 396 U.S. 367, 368-370 (1970) (Brennan, J., concurring in the dismissal of appeal).
54. 396 U.S. at 370.
55. *Presbyterian Church v. Eastern Heights Church*, 167 S.E. 2d 658 (Georgia Sup. Ct. 1969).

nation — precisely what the U.S. Supreme Court prohibited. Once again, the PCUS appealed to the U.S. Supreme Court, but it declined to hear the case.[56]

In *Jones v. Wolf* (1979),[57] the U.S. Supreme Court formally adopted Justice Brennan's two-track method. By a 5-4 vote, the Court ruled that Georgia was not required to adopt the deference approach, but could use neutral principles to resolve church property disputes. The decision emphatically reiterated what Justice Brennan, a decade earlier, had instructed church lawyers to do: make clear agreements for civil courts to enforce, provided that the agreements do not require courts to decide religious questions. "Through appropriate reversionary clauses and trust provisions, religious societies can specify what is to happen to church property in the event of a particular contingency, or what religious body will determine the ownership in the event of a schism or doctrinal controversy. In this manner, a religious organization can ensure that a dispute over the ownership of church property will be resolved in accord with the desires of the members."[58]

Many denominations followed the Court's direction. Just two months after the Court decided *Jones v. Wolf*, the Episcopal Church in the United States of America (ECUSA) amended its canons to include the following provision: "All real and personal property held by or for the benefit of any Parish, Mission or Congregation is held in trust for this Church and the Diocese thereof in which such Parish, Mission or Congregation is located."[59] Over the past decade, congregations, dioceses, and ECUSA have litigated numerous cases in which that canon has figured prominently. Tensions within ECUSA had been growing for decades, tracing back to the denomination's decisions to ordain women and change the liturgy. But strife intensified following the ordination of an openly gay bishop in 2003, along with ECUSA's increasing acceptance of same-sex intimacy. In response, dozens of congregations, along with several dioceses, have withdrawn from ECUSA and asserted ownership of property in their possession; ECUSA has challenged that assertion. As *Jones v. Wolf* permitted, state courts faced with these cases have adopted either the deference or the neutral principles approach. Whichever approach the courts used, the 1979 Trust Canon has played an important role in the decisions.

56. 396 U.S. 1041 (1970).

57. *Jones v. Wolf*, 443 U.S. 595 (1979).

58. 443 U.S. at 603-604.

59. *Rector v. Bishop of the Episcopal Diocese of Georgia*, 290 Ga. 95, 112 (Georgia Sup. Ct. 2011) (citing section 4 of the Dennis Canon, enacted by the House of Bishops at the 1979 General Convention of the ECUSA).

A majority of states, regardless of the approach preferred, have concluded that the 1979 Trust Canon creates a trust in favor of the national church. Although the local congregation or diocese enjoys possession and substantial control over the property, its possession and control are contingent on the holder's continued membership in ECUSA. A prominent decision from Georgia illustrates this outcome. In *Rector v. Bishop of the Episcopal Diocese of Georgia* (2011),[60] the congregation of historic Christ Church in Savannah voted to withdraw from ECUSA, although a minority faction wanted to retain membership in the denomination. The Georgia Diocese, joined by ECUSA, filed suit against the leaders of the majority faction. The national body and state diocese asserted title to the property of the congregation on behalf of the minority faction.

Applying the neutral principles approach, the Georgia courts ruled in favor of the diocese and ECUSA. The state supreme court reasoned that the 1979 Trust Canon formalized an understanding of the relationship between congregation and denomination that had been implicit since the founding of the Episcopal Church, just after the American Revolution. Moreover, the Georgia high court found, Christ Church made no effort to disavow the 1979 Trust Canon for more than two decades, during which the congregation engaged in numerous acts that confirmed its subordination to the canons of ECUSA. The congregation majority sought U.S. Supreme Court review of the Georgia Supreme Court's decision in favor of the diocese and ECUSA, but the Court declined to take the case.[61]

Other states have taken a different view of the 1979 Trust Canon. *All Saints Parish Waccamaw v. Episcopal Church* (2009)[62] involved another historic congregation that withdrew from ECUSA. Unlike the Georgia courts, the South Carolina Supreme Court ruled that the 1979 Trust Canon did not create a property interest in favor of ECUSA. Property interests, the court reasoned, require express consent by both parties. Examining the long history of the parish's property ownership, the court concluded that the parish held sole ownership of its property.[63] The 1979 Trust Canon unilaterally asserted ECUSA's interest, but because the congregation never formally recognized and accepted that assertion, ECUSA acquired no legal right to the property.

---

60. 290 Ga. 95 (Georgia Sup. Ct. 2011).

61. 132 Sup. Ct. 2439 (2012).

62. *All Saints Parish Waccamaw v. Episcopal Church,* 385 S.C. 428, 685 S.E. 2d 163 (S.C. Sup. Ct. 2009), *cert. dismissed* by *Green v. Campbell,* 2010 U.S. LEXIS 3113.

63. 385 S.C. at 448. The relevant facts included an express disclaimer of interest filed by the diocese in 1903. *Id.*

As in the Georgia case, the losing parties asked the U.S. Supreme Court to review the decision, but the Court denied their petition.[64]

These two rulings represent only a small fraction of the lawsuits over church property decided by courts since 1979. Although the losing parties in many of these lawsuits, like the ECUSA cases from Georgia and South Carolina, have sought Supreme Court review, the Court has invariably denied those petitions.[65] Although such denials of review do not have independent significance, the Court's refusal to intervene in any of these controversies since 1979 suggests that the alternative approaches recognized in *Blue Hull* and *Jones v. Wolf* have generated a constitutionally appropriate framework for resolving these disputes. Most importantly, no court at any level has decided one of these cases by asking which faction is the authentic representative of the faith. The Constitution removes that question from the authority of the state.

Civil Courts and the Rights of Congregation Members

As this chapter has illustrated, the principle that civil courts are constitutionally incompetent to decide ecclesiastical questions is long-standing, deep, and far-reaching. The Supreme Court and other courts have applied this principle to employment disputes between clergy and their congregations, as well as to disputes within congregations over control of church property. The principle also applies to disputes between congregations and their members. For example, if a congregation refuses to admit someone to communion, or excommunicates a member, the person excluded can find no relief in civil courts. Resolution of the person's claim would involve precisely the same kind of ecclesiastical question found in employment disputes with clergy: Who is fit to be a member?

This principle, however, does not bar all claims by members against their congregations. Here again it is important to understand the difference between assertions of institutional autonomy — the immunity of the church from civil jurisdiction — and the nonestablishment principle's much more

64. *Green v. Campbell*, 2010 U.S. LEXIS 3113.
65. See, e.g., *Presbytery of Ohio Valley, Inc. v. OPC, Inc.*, 973 N.E. 2d 1099 (Ind. 2012), *cert. denied*, 2013 U.S. LEXIS 3321 (U.S., Apr. 29, 2013); *Episcopal Church in the Diocese of Conn. v. Gauss*, 302 Conn. 408 (Conn. 2011), *cert. denied*, 2012 U.S. LEXIS 4624 (U.S., June 18, 2012); *Presbytery of Greater Atlanta, Inc. v. Timberridge Presbyterian Church, Inc.*, 290 Ga. 272 (Ga. 2011), *cert. denied*, 132 S. Ct. 2772 (2012); *Falls Church v. Protestant Episcopal Church*, 740 S.E. 2d 530 (2013), *cert. denied*, 2014 U.S. LEXIS 1901 (U.S., No. 13-449, March 10, 2014).

limited restriction on civil court competence to decide ecclesiastical questions. If a member's claim does not implicate ecclesiastical questions, courts are free to adjudicate it on precisely the same grounds as any other lawsuit. To take an example that has been far too frequent in the last decade: a member who claims sexual abuse by a minister should be free to sue the church for negligence in hiring, supervising, or retaining the minister, on exactly the same basis as if the abuse was caused by a public school teacher or athletic coach.[66] Adjudication of those tort claims does not typically raise ecclesiastical questions, so courts should be free to decide them.

Some lawsuits brought by members are more difficult to assess in these terms. In a variety of contexts, the law imposes civil liability on those whose speech injures others. For example, a speaker may be held liable for communications that invade someone's privacy, harm someone's reputation through falsehoods, or intentionally inflict emotional distress. Any of these claims might arise in the course of a member's relationship with a religious community, but civil court adjudication of those disputes can implicate the problem of state competence to decide ecclesiastical questions.

The decision of the Oklahoma Supreme Court in *Guinn v. The Church of Christ of Collinsville* (1989)[67] offers a richly illuminating example of how courts should treat a congregant's claim of harmful speech by congregational leaders. The elders of the Church of Christ confronted an unmarried congregant, Marian Guinn, with allegations that she was engaged in an improper sexual relationship. In several private meetings, the elders urged her to end that relationship. When she did not do so, the elders instituted a process of formal discipline, which could lead to her expulsion from the church. In that process, church leaders describe, during worship services, the offending member's sinful conduct. That public shaming is designed to encourage the member to repent and return to good standing in the community. Guinn, through her lawyer, sent letters to the elders asking them not to censure her publicly. When the elders refused, Guinn formally terminated her membership in the congregation. The elders replied that, under church doctrine, congregants may not unilaterally terminate their membership. The following Sunday, the elders read from the pulpit statements about Guinn's conduct. They also sent written statements about Guinn to several neighboring churches.

Guinn filed suit, alleging that the elders' acts of discipline invaded her

66. We collect and analyze many of these decisions in Ira C. Lupu and Robert W. Tuttle, *Sexual Misconduct and Ecclesiastical Immunity,* 2004 BYU L. Rev. 1789.

67. *Guinn v. The Church of Christ of Collinsville,* 775 P. 2d 766 (Sup. Ct. Okla. 1989).

privacy and intentionally inflicted emotional distress. A jury awarded Guinn substantial compensatory and punitive damages, and the congregation appealed. The Oklahoma Supreme Court ruled that the trial court should have drawn a line between the elders' acts of discipline before Guinn terminated her membership and those following that declaration, and accordingly remanded the case for a new trial.[68]

The elders' pretermination acts, the court held, deserved protection under the First Amendment. The court invoked both religion clauses of the First Amendment. Citing *Watson,* the court said that members voluntarily subject themselves to the governance of a religious body when they join it. Guinn knew, or should have known, that the church practices the biblical form of discipline reflected in the steps taken by the elders — private admonition by one member, and then by a group of members, followed by more public censure. Unless such discipline threatens public peace or safety, the court reasoned, civil authorities have no legitimate interest in intervening on behalf of a congregant. The court thus ruled in favor of the elders with respect to harms caused to Guinn by the elders' pretermination conduct.

About their conduct after Guinn ended her membership, however, the Oklahoma Supreme Court ruled that the trial court and jury could properly consider, in the retrial of the case, claims arising from it. The church had argued that it still viewed Guinn as a member, and that civil courts must defer to the church's conception of membership, because that is an ecclesiastical matter.[69] Any attempt by a court to second-guess the church's membership decision, the congregation claimed, would violate the religion clauses. The court disagreed, and its reasoning offers a helpful elaboration of our thesis. Although courts defer to the decisions of proper religious authority on purely ecclesiastical questions, civil courts must always have the power to decide whether a question is ecclesiastical and, if so, which religious body has authority to decide it. If that power were not reserved to civil courts, churches would be free to define the scope of their own civil immunity, and that liberty would present an intolerable risk of abuse. In this respect, churches are exactly like all other private institutions. They do not have the privilege of being judges in their own cause.

In *Guinn,* the Oklahoma Supreme Court ruled that the congregation's religious authority over the plaintiff ended when she formally notified the church of her withdrawal. Her voluntary withdrawal was certainly a religious

68. 775 P. 2d at 785-786.
69. 775 P. 2d at 777.

decision, but the legal power to make it belonged to Guinn, not to the church. Because she ended her relationship with the congregation, its civil immunity for harmful statements about her ended as well. From that point, the congregation was subject to ordinary legal rules for statements about others, including the duty to refrain from disclosing embarrassing private information about someone to those who have no legitimate interest in receiving it.

The court contrasted the congregation's posttermination statements about Guinn with other contexts in which courts have held churches immune from liability for statements about nonmembers. When a congregation instructs its members not to have dealings with a former member, the former member has no claim against the church.[70] The church's speech is directed to its members, and concerns their conduct; the speech is not focused on describing the conduct of the former member. Likewise, when a congregation informs other churches that a terminated pastor should not be hired, the former pastor has no claim.[71] In that case, the congregation's speech is directed to the conduct of the other congregation, and is not simply a statement about the former pastor. In these examples, civil courts have properly determined that the disputed matters are ecclesiastical, and fall within the legitimate authority of the congregation. Or, seen from a slightly different perspective, civil courts are not competent to second-guess the congregation's judgment about who should be a pastor, or with whom congregants may properly associate.

70. See, e.g., *Paul v. Watchtower Bible & Tract Society of N.Y.*, 819 F. 2d 875 (9th Cir. 1987), *cert. denied*, 484 U.S. 926 (1987); *Decker v. Tschetter Hutterian Brethren, Inc.*, 594 N.W. 2d 357 (S. Dak. 1999); *Anderson v. Watchtower Bible & Tract Soc'y of N.Y., Inc.*, 2007 Tenn. App. LEXIS 29 (Tenn. Ct. App., Jan. 19, 2007), *cert. denied*, 552 U.S. 891 (all rejecting tort claims based on denial of fellowship by church members). But see *Bear v. Reformed Mennonite Church*, 462 Pa. 330 (Pa. 1975) (holding that defendant church did not have absolute constitutional immunity from suit based on plaintiff's claim that he was shunned by church members, including his wife and children).

71. See generally Lupu and Tuttle, *supra* note 33, at 155-160 (discussing claims of defamation made by clergy, and the relationship between such claims and the ministerial exception). As the article explains, most defamation claims by clergy against their present or former congregations implicate concerns identical to those raised by ministers' employment actions. The facts at issue typically involve the pastor's character or performance. See, for example, *Hiles v. Episcopal Diocese*, 773 N.E. 2d 929 (Mass. 2002). Not all defamation claims, however, raise such concerns. For example, if members allegedly defame a pastor by speaking about the pastor with those outside the faith community, the statements will be subject to ordinary principles of tort law. See, e.g., *Ausley v. Shaw*, 193 S.W. 3d 892 (Tenn. App., 2005) (no privilege for defamatory statements about former pastor made by lay members "apart from any ecclesiastical undertaking").

Conclusion

As this chapter has demonstrated in quite different contexts, the constitutional limits of government competence shape the state's response to disputes involving religious communities. In cases concerning ministerial employment, disputes over property between competing groups within a faith community, and rights of members and former members of congregations, courts and other agents of the state are disabled from deciding ecclesiastical questions.

In some contexts, that disability has profound consequences for the ways in which controversies are resolved. To return to the example with which we began this chapter, the Supreme Court unanimously and properly ruled that Ms. Perich could not press her claims that Hosanna-Tabor Evangelical Lutheran Church and School had discriminated against her, and then retaliated against her for complaining about the discrimination. Because the Court found that her duties made her a ministerial employee, decision of her case involved questions of her fitness for ministry, and the Establishment Clause precludes the state from deciding these questions.

The deference to religious communities' decisions about fitness for ministry is a central feature of religious freedom in America. So is the comparable deference to the ways that religious organizations choose to structure ownership of property, or determine qualifications for membership. This posture of deference is not a narrow, technical, or specialized approach for arcane and unusual cases. Instead, the approach outlined in this chapter represents, in perhaps its purest form, the essence of our central thesis that the Constitution guarantees a government whose character must be secular.

As the next several chapters will further demonstrate, the secular character of government creates space within which individuals and institutions can flourish in their faith commitments. Such a regime is not the product of any sweeping theory of church autonomy or religious privilege. Instead, it is the inevitable consequence of a limited state.

CHAPTER 3

Government Funding of Religion

As analyzed in chapter 1 and elaborated in chapter 2, the concept of religious establishment has for centuries been closely connected to the relationship between the state and religious institutions. An established church is typically controlled, in theology and personnel, by the state and, just as typically, is financed by the state. Unsurprisingly, the financing and control go hand in hand. Chapter 2 focused on questions of state control of theology and church personnel, through a variety of mechanisms, including the resolution of disputes over property as well as the regulation of the employment relationship between faith communities and their leaders. That sort of control may involve assertion of religious identity or competence by the state, and inevitably threatens the religious freedom of the people.

Questions of state financing of religious institutions are just as old, important, and difficult as questions of state regulation of those institutions. Like issues of regulation, issues of financing are frequently translated into terms that resonate with notions of individual rights. Two standard rights-based arguments tend to recur against financial support of religious entities by the government. First, coercive taxation of individuals to support religious entities is frequently said to violate the right of each individual to religious voluntarism — that is, the right of the individual to decide freely whether or not to support a religious institution or community.

Second, state financing of religious entities is commonly thought to undermine rights of equality among such entities, because the dangers of state favoritism for approved sects are so great. This concern is especially grave when financing is coupled with a large degree of official discretion about which entities will receive public financing. Those who criticized the Faith-Based and Community Initiative, begun by President George W. Bush and continued by President Barack Obama, often invoked the specter of religious discrimination as a primary constitutional danger.

Concerns about official discrimination in the distribution of public funds are inescapable, and a prohibition on sectarian discrimination rightly has been part of our constitutional law for many years.[1] But, in a society in which the government distributes funds for a very wide variety of causes — many of which are opposed by at least some taxpayers — we think the concern about taxpayer voluntarism is overstated and misplaced. Such a concern cannot adequately explain where our law has been, or where it is headed. The state, for example, frequently expends funds both directly and indirectly to protect the physical security of houses of worship,[2] and virtually no one asserts that such expenditures are constitutionally forbidden.

Instead, we believe that questions of the permissibility of state funding of religious entities are far better understood through the lens of jurisdictional disability. Government financial support of religion may exceed the scope of public authority, but analysis of the permissible scope of that authority requires an inquiry into the legitimate purposes, competence, and identity of the state. When the state acts to facilitate its own religious identity, express its religious competence, or transform the religious identity of its people, the state has unequivocally exceeded its constitutional bounds. In contrast, when the state acts for legitimate public ends, such as educating its citizens or shaping their moral conceptions, the question of using religious means — including financial support of religious institutions — to those ends is far more complicated, as our history and constitutional law reveal. This chapter unpacks that history and the evolution of our law on funding religious institutions, with an eye to tracing the myriad ways that the jurisdictional principle repeatedly appears. To understand one of the central ways a secular government interacts with a religious people, one must watch the money.

Government Aid for Religion from the Colonial to the Modern Era

Although official establishments of religion vary in many details, all share the practice of government subsidy for the key features of religious life. Those

---

1. See, e.g., *Larson v. Valente,* 456 U.S. 228 (1982).
2. This would include long-standing protection of houses of worship by police officers and firefighters, as well as more direct and focused grants to houses of worship from the U.S. Department of Homeland Security.

features include public provision of places for worship as well as payment for ministers and teachers of the faith. Such support has persisted across parts of western Europe long after more repressive features of establishment have been replaced by full freedom of belief and worship.

The British North American colonies differed widely in the forms of aid they provided to churches. During the seventeenth century, some colonial governments provided no assistance, others promised aid but actually delivered little, and several — most notably Virginia, Massachusetts, and Connecticut — followed the traditional European models of establishment. Those colonial governments provided houses of worship, lands to be farmed or grazed for the benefit of the church, and tax-financed payments for clergy and religious teachers.[3] Following the reinvigoration of Anglican political power in late-seventeenth-century England, colonial governments actually increased their subsidy for the established church. In addition to more colonies providing aid in the early eighteenth century — the Carolinas, Maryland, New Jersey — the period is also notable for the changed rationale for support of the established church. Earlier justifications for state funding of religion focused on the theological benefits of government care for the spiritual welfare of its subjects. For a variety of reasons, defenders of state aid for religion in the early eighteenth century shifted their argument to a political footing. They claimed that support for an established faith was necessary to promote morality and good order.[4]

Following the American Revolution, the Church of England (reconstituted here as the Episcopal Church) had no plausible claim to continued status as the established church of the new nation or any of its states. Although prominent revolutionaries were Anglican, George Washington foremost among them, the clergy disproportionately sided with the Crown. But public hostility to the Church of England did not resolve the question of whether religion deserved public support. The belief that government aid for religion was politically necessary led several New England states to require local governments to support Protestant worship and religious instruction. The Massachusetts Constitution of 1780 offers a striking example: "Therefore, to promote their happiness, and secure the good order and preservation of their government, . . . the legislature shall from time to time authorize and require, the several towns, parishes, precincts, and other bodies politic, or religious

---

3. For a general history of education in the colonial era, see Lawrence A. Cremin, *American Education: The Colonial Experience, 1607-1783* (1970).

4. James H. Hutson, *Church and State in America: The First Two Centuries* 54-57 (2008).

societies, to make suitable provision, at their own expense, for the institution of the public worship of God, and for the support and maintenance of public Protestant teachers of piety, religion, and morality."[5] As a practical matter, the Massachusetts Constitution's command to subsidize faith benefited the Congregationalist Church, whose ministers were far more supportive of the Revolution than the Anglican clergy.

Matters were more complicated in states whose clergy had formerly supported the Church of England. The most famous such dispute involved Virginia, where in 1785 Patrick Henry introduced in the state legislature "A Bill Establishing a Provision for Teachers of the Christian Religion."[6] The bill would have permitted taxpayers to direct their tax to the Protestant denomination of their choice. Echoing the justification found in the Massachusetts Constitution, Henry's bill argued that "the general diffusion of Christian knowledge hath a natural tendency to correct the morals of men, restrain their vices, and preserve the peace of society."

James Madison led the opposition to Henry's bill with his most famous statement on religious liberty, "Memorial and Remonstrance against Religious Assessments."[7] Madison's arguments are quite diverse, and focus on the hazards to both religion and government that follow any scheme of government aid. First, he claimed that official support harms religion. Compulsory religious taxation deprives individuals of the opportunity to give voluntarily. Public support promotes indolence in the clergy and makes them dependent on the state. Second, Madison responded directly to Henry's key assertion and claimed that aid for religion damages the political order. By inducing religious groups to compete for public aid, it creates strife rather than civil peace. And by encouraging government to use religion as a tool for public policy, public aid invites government to exceed its limited mandate and become tyrannical. One paragraph offers an especially pointed indictment of Henry's proposed scheme. The bill "implies either that the Civil Magistrate is a competent Judge of Religious truth; or that he may employ Religion as an engine of Civil policy. The first is an arrogant pretension falsified by the contradictory opinions of Rulers in all

5. Constitution of Massachusetts (1780), Art. II, reprinted in Michael W. McConnell, John H. Garvey, and Thomas C. Berg, *Religion and the Constitution* 17-18 (Wolters Kluwer, 3rd ed., 2011).

6. The proposed bill is set out in the appendix to the dissenting opinion of Justice Rutledge in *Everson v. Bd. of Educ.*, 330 U.S. 1 (1947).

7. The "Memorial and Remonstrance" is also set out in the appendix to the Rutledge dissent in *Everson,* as well as in McConnell, Garvey, and Berg, *supra* note 5, at 51-55.

ages, and throughout the world: The second an unhallowed perversion of the means of salvation."[8]

Madison's view prevailed. The Virginia legislature rejected Henry's bill and soon thereafter adopted Thomas Jefferson's Statute of Religious Freedom.[9] That statute included robust nonestablishment language, which provided that "no man shall be compelled to frequent or support any religious worship, place or ministry whatsoever." Jefferson's language proved highly influential for other state constitutions in the late eighteenth and early nineteenth centuries.[10]

With such diverse and contested views among the states, the drafters of the federal Constitution settled on a brief and ambiguous statement of national policy. The First Amendment, proposed by the first Congress in 1789 and ratified by 1791, provided that "Congress shall make no law respecting an establishment of religion, or prohibiting the free exercise thereof."[11] The first part of that provision reflects widespread agreement that the federal government should not establish a particular faith as the church of the United States. Beyond that obvious limitation, however, the provision was open to a variety of interpretations. Most importantly, the provision is agnostic about state establishments of religion. It does not impede, affirm, or even acknowledge such arrangements. With respect to the powers of the federal government, early Congresses did pass laws that touched on religious experience. For example, both House and Senate continued the practice, initially adopted by the Continental Congress, of employing legislative chaplains.[12]

During the first half of the nineteenth century, debate over government aid for religion gradually shifted focus from places of worship to support of education. Importantly, virtually all this debate occurred at the state or local level. By the early 1830s, every state constitution barred government support for houses of worship or ministers' salaries. At the same time, however, the states and localities saw increased popular demand for government funding

---

8. "Memorial and Remonstrance," par. 5.

9. The original text of Jefferson's bill can be found at http://www.firstfreedom.org/PDF/Statute-original-language-pic.pdf. The operative section is now part of the Virginia Constitution, Art. I, §16, available here: http://constitution.legis.virginia.gov/.

10. Very similar language appears in the constitutions of New Hampshire (see N.H. Const., Art. I, pt. 5), New Jersey (see N.J. Const., Art. I, par. 3), and Vermont (see Vermont Const., Art. 3).

11. U.S. Const., Amendment I.

12. The history of the legislative chaplaincies in Congress is set out in *Marsh v. Chambers*, 463 U.S. 783 (1983).

of education. The crucial question, which would engender sharp — even violent — controversy throughout the nineteenth century, and remains hotly disputed today, is the place of religion in publicly financed education. In the colonial era and the early years of the republic, many jurisdictions funded schools with specific denominational character.[13]

Led by Horace Mann and other activists, supporters of universal free public education argued for government funding of common schools rather than a plurality of denominational schools.[14] In addition to teaching basic knowledge and learning skills, the common schools movement aimed to transform students, many of whom were immigrants or children of immigrants, into fellow citizens of a shared polity. Free citizens, the schools taught, required the capacity to make independent rational judgments about worldly affairs.[15] Thus, the common schools curriculum inculcated a set of substantive moral and political values. Sensitive to concerns that the common schools movement was hostile to religion, its leaders asserted that the curriculum taught students the basic moral values shared across Protestant denominations and reflected in the Bible. Because the curriculum avoided instruction in particular and disputed doctrines, advocates described the schools as "nonsectarian." Doctrinal matters belonged in the private sphere of home and church, not in the public schools.

Although initial disputes over funding involved claims by Protestant denominational schools, and the earliest no-aid provisions in state constitutions arose out of such disputes, public support for Roman Catholic schools generated the most intense, broadest, and longest-lasting controversies.[16] These fights were initially local, arising in the mid-Atlantic and northeastern cities that attracted Irish and other Catholic immigrants during the 1830s and 1840s. Catholic leaders criticized the overtly Protestant character of the common schools. They claimed that the nondenominational prayers and readings

13. See McConnell, Garvey, and Berg, *supra* note 5, at 382-383, and sources cited therein.

14. For a fuller exposition of the philosophy of Horace Mann and the common schools movement, see Rosemary C. Salamone, *Visions of Schooling* 14-18 (Yale University Press, 2000).

15. Lawrence A. Cremin, *American Education: The National Experience, 1783-1876* 107-147 (1980) (on the republican ideology of common schools).

16. For greater elaboration of the details of these controversies in a variety of Northeastern cities, see Salamone, *supra* note 14, at 18-23; Joan DelFattore, *The Fourth R: Conflicts over Religion in America's Public Schools* 15-51 (Yale University Press, 2004); John C. Jeffries Jr. and James E. Ryan, *A Political History of the Establishment Clause*, 100 Mich. L. Rev. 279 (2001).

from the King James Bible implicitly advanced Protestant understandings of piety and worship, and that the emphasis on independent rational judgment and personal liberty at the heart of the common schools' ethos was hostile to Catholic values of respect for traditional authority. Once it became clear to Catholic leaders that the common schools movement would not abandon those practices or values, they committed to developing a system of parochial schools and began advocating for public support of those schools.[17]

They met with little or no success. To make matters worse, opponents in many states enacted constitutional provisions to explicitly prohibit public funding of schools controlled by religious denominations. During the pre–Civil War years, the strong rejection of public aid for religious schools became a central tenet of the nascent Republican Party in the northeastern states. After the war, that opposition held a central place in the national agenda, energetically supported by President Ulysses S. Grant. House Speaker James Blaine proposed a federal constitutional amendment that would have clearly imposed nonestablishment and free exercise norms on the states, and categorically barred states from supporting religious schools: "No State shall make any law respecting an establishment of religion, or prohibiting the free exercise thereof; and no money raised by taxation in any State for the support of public schools, or derived from any public fund therefor, nor any public lands devoted thereto, shall ever be under the control of any religious sect; nor shall any money so raised or lands so devoted be divided between religious sects or denominations."[18] Although Congress did not approve the Blaine Amendment, many states enacted the same or even broader restrictions in their own constitutions. Indeed, in the late nineteenth and early twentieth centuries, Congress required territories seeking admission to the Union to include such restrictions in their proposed constitutions.[19]

To many in the twenty-first century who look back at the fight over school aid, the vitriol is explicable only in terms of nativist Protestant bigotry against Roman Catholic immigrants. That source must remain an important part of any explanation. The historic hostility between Protestants and Ro-

---

17. Steven K. Green, *The Second Disestablishment: Church and State in Nineteenth-Century America* 259-261 (2010). See also Kurt T. Lash, *The Second Adoption of the Establishment Clause: The Rise of the Nonestablishment Principle*, 27 Ariz. St. L. Rev. 1085, 1118-1125 (1996).

18. The text of the amendment appears in McConnell, Garvey, and Berg, *supra* note 5, at 389.

19. See Kyle Duncan, *Secularism's Laws: State Blaine Amendments and Religious Persecution*, 72 Fordham L. Rev. 493, 513-514 (2003).

man Catholics was magnified by predominantly Anglo attitudes toward the Irish, who made up a large proportion of the antebellum Catholic migration to the United States.[20] But it is a mistake to see the debate only in terms of such bigotry. Opposition to support for public funding of religious schools predated significant Roman Catholic immigration, although opposition certainly intensified as immigration — and the attendant requests for public funding — increased.[21]

Most significantly, concerns about public funding of Catholic schools also related to particular features of mid-nineteenth-century Roman Catholic teaching. Vatican doctrine regarded core liberal democratic values, including religious liberty for all, as heretical.[22] According to such teaching, which was widely publicized in anti-Catholic publications, the faithful were expected to work toward a political order that officially and exclusively supported the Roman Catholic Church and suppressed other faiths. Given the common schools movement's core commitments to independent thought, emphasis on the authority of reason in secular matters, and consignment of doctrinal instruction to the private sphere, the conflict with Catholic teaching could not have been more stark. For the common schools movement, Catholic education — provided by members of religious orders subject to hierarchical control, with doctrine integrated throughout the curriculum — represented a threat to the fundamental mission of preparing children for republican citizenship.[23]

That hostility to funding "sectarian" schools was motivated by more than just anti-Catholic bigotry can best be seen in the patterns of funding for social welfare services provided by religious institutions. At the same time that states and localities uniformly rejected aid for parochial schools, many were willing to provide public funding for religious hospitals and orphanages, and courts regularly upheld such funding against legal challenges. A number

20. See generally Philip Hamburger, *Separation of Church and State* (2002).

21. See Green, *supra* note 17, at 251-259.

22. See Jeffries and Ryan, *supra* note 16, at 302-303; see also McConnell, Garvey, and Berg, *supra* note 5, at 391-392 (discussing the American reaction to Pope Pius IX's 1864 Syllabus of Errors, which emphatically condemned liberal democracy and rejected the idea of church-state separation). The text of the Syllabus of Errors is available at: http://www.ewtn.com/library/papaldoc/p9syll.htm.

23. See Green, *supra* note 17, at 259-271. Professor Gordon describes similar concerns about education raised by opponents of Mormonism. Sarah Barringer Gordon, *The Mormon Question: Polygamy and Constitutional Conflict in Nineteenth Century America* 198-200 (2002).

of distinctions can be drawn between funding for schools and these other institutions, including the fact that Protestant groups were also significant beneficiaries of public aid for hospitals and orphanages. Hospitals were easier to distinguish, because they were not primarily involved in the enterprise of religious indoctrination. In the Supreme Court's earliest encounter with an Establishment Clause challenge to public funding of a religiously affiliated entity, the Court in *Bradfield v. Roberts*[24] unanimously upheld a congressional appropriation to build a separate wing at a hospital owned and operated in the District of Columbia by a Catholic order. Under the enactment, the hospital was obliged to accept indigent patients, referred by officers of the District, for treatment of contagious diseases. In a brief and straightforward opinion, the Court characterized the corporation as neither "religious nor sectarian." As a hospital, it accepted and treated all patients. Accordingly, the appropriation aided the delivery of medical care rather than fostering an establishment of religion.

Religious orphanages, of course, inevitably engaged in religious formation of their charges, and courts did not question the permissibility of publicly funded institutions engaging in that activity. Most assumed that the orphanages taught the faith of the child's parent or parents, and thus substituted for that role. A number of jurisdictions refused to reimburse orphanages for educational expenses, but most approved a general subsidy for the care of children on terms equal to those of other providers.

So long as the First Amendment's nonestablishment principle applied to the federal government only, as was the conventional understanding in American law from the founding until the middle of the twentieth century, the occasions for Supreme Court engagement in issues of funding remained limited. During the republic's first century and a half, most public support for social welfare functions — most specifically, education of children — was provided by state and local government. The federal government, far smaller and narrower in focus than today, played a very limited role in such matters.

The Germination of Modern Law — *Everson v. Board of Education*

When, a half-century after *Bradfield,* the context changed from medical care to the education of the young, the scope of the Court's attention and the substance of its concerns altered dramatically. In the pathbreaking decision in

---

24. *Bradfield v. Roberts,* 175 U.S. 291 (1899).

Everson v. Board of Education,[25] rendered in 1947, all nine justices agreed that the nonestablishment principle now applied to state and local government as well as to the federal government. And, despite their disagreement on the outcome of the dispute, which involved reimbursement to parents for the costs of transporting children on public buses to Catholic schools, all nine justices likewise agreed on a historical narrative of the purposes of the Establishment Clause. *Everson* initiated a new regime, one that would thereafter control the financial relationship between government and religious entities in a vast array of social welfare contexts.

Everson constitutes a crucial step in what was at that time a quite fresh constitutional phenomenon — the federalizing of the law of religious liberty. This development was but a piece in the larger enterprise of reconstituting and federalizing the law of preferred liberties, broadly understood. At the time, the Court was composed almost entirely of justices appointed by President Franklin Roosevelt. This group had systematically repudiated the preexisting, strenuous protection of economic liberty under the federal Constitution. In place of that commitment, these justices had commenced the new constitutional project of explicitly applying the protections of the First Amendment to the actions of state and local government.

By 1947, this legal movement had already extended to freedom of speech, press, assembly, and, most notably, the free exercise of religion.[26] We will say more in later chapters about the connection between the exercise of religion and other constitutional rights of the people. At the time of *Everson,* however, it apparently seemed overwhelmingly logical and substantively appropriate to complete the jurisdictional expansion of First Amendment concerns by extending the Establishment Clause to state and local government.[27]

The simplicity of the facts of *Everson* masked its jurisprudential complexity. At the time the case arose, Ewing Township, a small community adjacent to Trenton, New Jersey, operated public elementary schools but not public high schools. Nor were Catholic schools, at any level, operating in the township. Acting under a state law, the township authorized reimbursement of bus fares to parents who sent their children to school in Trenton on existing public

25. *Everson v. Board of Education,* 330 U.S. 1 (1947).

26. *Cantwell v. Connecticut,* 310 U.S. 296 (1940).

27. This is exactly the way that Justice Black's majority opinion reasons out the incorporation question. The other opinions do not even mention it. See Ira C. Lupu and Robert W. Tuttle, *Federalism and Faith,* 55 Emory L. Rev. 19 (2006) (noting the absence of controversy on whether the Establishment Clause applies to states, at a moment when the Court had fierce internal conflict about application of other Bill of Rights provisions to the states).

buses. The state law required equal treatment of children in public and private schools, so long as the private schools were operated on a nonprofit basis. The Ewing Township Board of Education accordingly resolved to reimburse parents of children for bus fares necessary to attend Roman Catholic schools, as well as public high schools, outside the township.[28] A local taxpayer, arguing that support of transportation to religious schools violated both state and federal constitutions, filed the case originally in the New Jersey state courts.

In the years immediately preceding *Everson,* other state courts — acting under state constitutions alone — had been wrestling with this precise problem of financial support by government for transportation of children to Catholic as well as public schools.[29] The Supreme Court might just have left these issues to the law of the states, rather than jumping to a uniform and all-controlling federal approach, so there is reason to suppose that the Court perceived issues at stake larger than the allocation of the cost of getting children to school. After the highest court in New Jersey upheld reimbursement for these costs by Ewing Township, the Court likewise concluded that the scheme did not violate the First Amendment. Justice Black's opinion for the majority is justly famous, but not for its conclusion that the reimbursement scheme is constitutional. Rather, Black's opinion is oft-cited for its historical emphasis on the Framers' abhorrence of the persecutions that arose from enforcement of the coercive Anglican and Puritan establishments in England, and for its recitation of the colonial struggles over religious establishment, culminating in the battle (described earlier in this chapter) over the proposed Virginia assessment bill. The opinion is equally well-known for its invocation of the metaphorical "wall of separation," and its famous recitation of what the Establishment Clause signifies:

> The "establishment of religion" clause of the First Amendment means at least this: neither a state nor the Federal Government can set up a church.

28. 330 U.S. 62 at note 59: "The transportation committee recommended the transportation of pupils of Ewing to the Trenton and Pennington High Schools and *Catholic Schools* by way of public carrier as in recent years. On Motion of Mr. Ralph Ryan and Mr. M. French, the same was adopted" (opinion of Rutledge, J., dissenting).

29. The Supreme Court alludes to this pattern in *Everson.* 330 U.S. at 14, nn. 19-20. One earlier case about loans of textbooks to children in parochial schools had come before the Supreme Court on a challenge under the Due Process Clause of the Fourteenth Amendment, not the Establishment Clause. In *Cochran v. Louisiana Bd. of Educ.,* 281 U.S. 370 (1930), the Court concluded that such loans helped children and advanced state interests in good education, and rejected that challenge.

Neither can pass laws which aid one religion, aid all religions, or prefer one religion over another. Neither can force nor influence a person to go to or to remain away from church against his will or force him to profess a belief or disbelief in any religion. No person can be punished for entertaining or professing religious beliefs or disbeliefs, for church attendance or non-attendance. No tax in any amount, large or small, can be levied to support any religious activities or institutions, whatever they may be called, or whatever form they may adopt to teach or practice religion. Neither a state nor the Federal Government can, openly or secretly, participate in the affairs of any religious organizations or groups, and vice versa. In the words of Jefferson, the clause against establishment of religion by law was intended to erect "a wall of separation between church and State."[30]

This is a remarkable paragraph. It covers an amazingly large area of constitutional concern in a case about a seemingly narrow issue involving reimbursement for bus tokens. It ranges across issues of state coercion of religious experience ("No person can be punished for entertaining or professing religious beliefs or disbeliefs, for church attendance or non-attendance") in a case about nonestablishment, rather than free exercise, and in a context far removed from that kind of coercion. Alas, as the bottom line of this opinion comes into view, it becomes evident that this famous paragraph tells us nothing about how to resolve the problem of reimbursement for the cost of bus transportation to religiously affiliated schools.

Indeed, when the opinion turns to that problem, it strikes a very different and surprisingly conciliatory tone. Justice Black reminds his readers that the Constitution prohibits the exclusion of religiously affiliated schools from accreditation as satisfying compulsory education laws,[31] and likewise prohibits the exclusion of individual members of any community of believers or non-believers, "because of their faith or lack of it, from receiving the benefits of public welfare legislation."[32] With these propositions in mind, Black's opinion concludes that New Jersey's legislation, as applied in Ewing Township, "does not support [parochial] schools. Its legislation, as applied, does no more than provide a general program to help parents get their children, regardless of their religion, safely and expeditiously to and from accredited schools."

---

30. 330 U.S. at 15-16 (citation omitted).
31. *Pierce v. Society of Sisters,* 268 U.S. 510 (1925).
32. 330 U.S. at 16.

The dissenters in *Everson* found this inclusionary account deeply unsatisfactory. In a lengthy dissent for four justices,[33] Justice Rutledge reemphasized the story of post-Revolution disestablishment in Virginia. He argued that the reimbursement to parents for the costs of transportation aids the religious mission of parochial schools because it subsidizes the cost of getting children to school, a necessary element in the provision of education, even though it does not finance the teaching that takes place once the children arrive.

Was the particular religious character of the schools aided in New Jersey — and elsewhere at that time — relevant to the constitutional outcome? Neither Justice Black nor Justice Rutledge hinted at any such concern, which seems disturbingly hostile to a regime of religious pluralism and equality among faith groups. In a separate and far more revealing dissent, however, Justice Jackson (joined by Justice Frankfurter) focused on the precise question of the character of religious schools aided, and their ideological differences from the public schools. Jackson noted that the resolution of Ewing Township specified transportation only to public schools and Catholic schools as reimbursement-eligible. This was an act of discrimination, though probably only in theory; the record did not show any other private religious schools to which Ewing Township parents sent their children.

Jackson's concerns about the Catholic schools that benefited from the scheme extended far beyond any notion of formal evenhandedness among faiths. He explicitly highlights the character of Catholic education — longstanding in its insistence on education separate from that of other faiths, religiously mandatory on Catholic parents, designed to indoctrinate children in the faith, hostile to competing religious viewpoints, and hierarchically controlled. He explicitly contrasts the educational philosophy of such schools with that of the public schools: "Our public school, if not a product of Protestantism, at least is more consistent with it than with the Catholic culture and scheme of values. . . . It is organized on the premise that secular education can be isolated from all religious teaching, so that the school can inculcate all needed temporal knowledge and also maintain a strict and lofty neutrality as to religion. The assumption is that, after the individual has been instructed in worldly wisdom, he will be better fitted to choose his religion."[34] This appears to be the focal point of Jackson's opinion — that aid to the enterprise of Cath-

---

33. 330 U.S. at 28-74 (Rutledge, J., joined by Frankfurter, Jackson, and Burton, JJ., dissenting).

34. 330 U.S. at 23-24 (Jackson, J., dissenting).

olic education, as he understands its purpose, is in deep tension with a republican ethos of a free and independent citizenry, with each person trained to make personal decisions about politics, morality, and faith. This is not an abstraction about the general nonestablishment values of voluntarism and civil peace. Rather, it is a particularistic assessment of tension between a generically Protestant American ethos and the institutional arrangements, educational philosophy, universalizing ambition, and theological premises of the Church of Rome.[35] The other justices remained silent or euphemistic about these concerns, and emphasized a more sect-neutral historical narrative of the role of nonestablishment norms in minimizing sectarian competition for political power.

Everson remains a favorite of those with strong beliefs in minimizing state financial support of religious entities. Indeed, all the opinions are thick with rhetoric that supports such beliefs. Even the *Everson* majority, which upholds the reimbursement for bus tokens, characterizes that measure as going to "the verge of constitutional power" to aid religious schools. Thus, in the first Supreme Court decision ever to apply nonestablishment norms to state and local government, all nine justices strongly signaled that any substantial and direct program of government assistance to religious schools is unconstitutional.

Nevertheless, *Everson* has become over time a Rorschach test of constitutional impulses on the scope and meaning of the Establishment Clause, with images and traces of relevant themes for advocates on all sides of these questions. Indeed, the opinions contain the opening notes of virtually all the themes that would play through the Supreme Court in funding cases for the ensuing sixty-plus years. Should it matter if the aid goes to the beneficiaries of services, such as families with children traveling to school, rather than to the religious institutions themselves? Is it constitutionally significant that the aid — support for transportation — is prior, ancillary, or incidental to the educational process, rather than (like books, classrooms, libraries, or teachers) intrinsic to that process? Should the institutional and ideological character of beneficiary religious institutions make a constitutional difference?

These are questions of the form, substance, and consequences of the aid. All the opinions in *Everson* seem more intent on staking out the broad con-

---

35. At the time of *Everson,* the most prominent separationist group in the United States was called Protestant Americans United for Separation of Church and State. It now goes by the more denominationally neutral name of Americans United for Separation of Church and State.

stitutional ground that direct financial assistance to religious schools is prohibited than on dealing with the nuanced questions at the periphery of that ground. But neither the center nor the edges of the ground can be adequately understood without more rigorous theorizing of the prohibition on certain kinds of financial relationships between the state and religious entities.

At the core of the problem is a historically contingent story about tensions between Catholics and Protestants, suggested by the Jackson dissent in *Everson,* and a more abstract puzzle about the legal character of private activity that the state supports financially. In virtually all areas of constitutional law unrelated to religion, state financial support alone does not make the state accountable for the actions of its grantees and contracting partners. If the state helps to support a privately owned hospital, for example, with Medicare payments on behalf of residents, with subsidies for the purchase of experimental medical equipment, or (as in *Bradfield*) with construction grants, the state does not become constitutionally responsible for all that happens in that hospital. For example, the hospital need not honor the freedom of speech that the state must respect, nor provide due process of law in its treatment of patients.[36] Why, then, does the state ever bear constitutional responsibility for the inculcation of religious values by a private school, hospital, or other institution that happens to receive state financial assistance?

The anomaly here is more apparent than real. Unlike the rest of the First Amendment and many other constitutional commitments, with their focus on individual freedoms, the Establishment Clause operates uniquely as a limitation on the character of the state. The state may not act as a locus of worship, assert its own religious competence, nor commission private communities of worship to act as the state's instrument for the creation, maintenance, or transformation of religious identities. Once that limitation is recognized, various schemes of financial assistance can be appropriately categorized as either forbidden by that jurisdictional principle or outside of its scope. Of course, disputable line drawing is inevitable in such an enterprise, but the jurisdictional principle can provide both guidance and coherence to sketching the location of the boundaries.

The Court in *Everson* seemed divided into two camps on this principle,

36. See *Rendell-Baker v. Kohn,* 457 U.S. 830 (1982) (constitutional limits relating to free speech and procedural fairness do not attach to private schools receiving substantial public funding); *Blum v. Yaretsky,* 457 U.S. 991 (1982) (receipt of Medicaid payments for patients by nursing home does not make the Due Process Clause of the Fourteenth Amendment applicable to decisions by the nursing home to change the level of treatment for patients).

which at the time was, at best, dimly perceived. Those who sided with Justice Black may have believed that financing the transportation costs incurred by parents did not make the state responsible for the schools' mission of forming religious identity. The four dissenters may have seen the proximity of that agency differently — buses, after all, brought the children to the doorstep of those church schools. Alternatively, the dissenters may have been worried about drawing too fine a line on the question of proximity. Rather than, as Madison warned, dangerously entangling the question in precedents,[37] the dissenters may have opted for a posture of prophylaxis, in which any financial support of religious experience presented a risk of violation of the jurisdictional principle. Rutledge, in the principal dissent, worried about the difficulty of drawing lines between aid to families and aid to church schools, or between aid to ancillary functions and aid to the educational mission itself. Jackson and Frankfurter seem more explicitly concerned about the undemocratic character of the particular institutional beneficiaries of any such aid. All nine justices in *Everson,* however, were no doubt aware of Protestant American concern about the character of Catholic schools, and seemed committed to the message that broad programs of direct aid to those schools would be constitutionally unacceptable.

Because neither side in *Everson* identified with sufficient precision and clarity the deeper principle on which they may well have agreed, the causes of the ambivalence or division within the Court remained unarticulated for many years. And that division produced decades of decisions that, over time and in light of changes in the relevant religious institutions and ideas, increasingly confounded lawyers and policy makers who were trying to accomplish legitimate social ends with public resources while acting in fidelity to the Constitution.

In the quarter-century between *Everson* and the Court's iconic decision in *Lemon v. Kurtzman,*[38] very little happened on this front in the Supreme Court, while demographic and other changes began to alter dramatically the role of religious schools in the education of America's children. The largest systems of Roman Catholic schools in the United States had developed in response to the massive immigration from Europe between the mid–nineteenth century and the 1920s; those schools tended to be located in the great cities, especially in the East and Midwest. In addition, at mid–twentieth century, Roman Catholic schools far outnumbered the private religious schools

37. "Memorial and Remonstrance," par. 3.
38. *Lemon v. Kurtzman,* 403 U.S. 602 (1971).

of all other denominations combined, in part because of the Catholic emphasis on early and separate education.[39]

By the 1960s these patterns began to change. First, migration and immigration were changing the demography of the inner cities, making them
poorer, less white, and less Roman Catholic. Second, the decline in the number of men and women willing to enter Catholic teaching orders constricted
the supply of dedicated and inexpensive classroom teachers. In addition, religious schools sponsored by other religious traditions began to proliferate,
partly in response to the racial desegregation of the nation's public schools.

At the cusp of these changes, the Warren Court rendered its lone decision on the subject of government assistance to religious schools. In *Board of
Education v. Allen,*[40] a closely divided Court upheld New York State's program
in which local public school districts were obliged to loan, to parents of children in private schools, books that were used or had been approved for use
in the public schools. The program seemed to reflect a pragmatic legislative
judgment that New York's very many Catholic schools were in financial trouble, and that government subsidy of textbooks would decrease the chances
that some families would shift their children from religious schools to the
already-crowded public schools.

The majority emphasized that the books remained the property of the
public authorities, and that they were loaned to families for the benefit of children, not to the religious schools themselves. The dissenters, a group that included Justice Black, insisted that the New York scheme was not like *Everson*
at all, because (1) the relevant goods were intrinsic to the educational process;
(2) the religious schools stored the books over the summer and distributed
them each fall, thus making the structure of loans to families appear pretextual;
and (3) the decisions as to which books were properly approved for use in public schools would inevitably bring public and religious authorities into contact
and potential conflict over religious content or bias in the books.[41]

The Court's willingness to uphold a scheme that financed materials intrinsic to the educational process, and to do so in circumstances that suggested considerable benefit to the schools themselves as well as to the families, clouded yet further the constitutional question of state assistance to
religious entities. The jurisdictional principle for which we are contending

39. For discussion of the changing demography of religious schools over the course
of the twentieth century, see Ira C. Lupu, *The Increasingly Anachronistic Case against School
Vouchers,* 13 Notre Dame J. of Law, Ethics, & Public Policy 375, 386-388 (1999).

40. *Board of Education v. Allen,* 392 U.S. 236 (1968).

41. *Id.* at 251-254 (1968) (Black, J., dissenting).

seemed manifest in the *Allen* dissent but unacknowledged by the *Allen* majority. Perhaps in reaction to *Allen,* the Court's most strenuous interdiction of state assistance to religious schools soon appeared.

Strong Separation as Prophylaxis — the *Lemon* Era

Generations of lawyers and judges see the Supreme Court's decision in *Lemon v. Kurtzman* as iconic, because it purports to state the famous, frequently invoked (in the lower courts), and oft-ignored (in the Supreme Court) three-part "test" for satisfaction of the Establishment Clause — laws must have a secular purpose, reveal a primary effect of not advancing religion, and avoid "excessive entanglement" between the state and religious entities.[42] But *Lemon,* a case that arose in Pennsylvania, together with its companion case from Rhode Island, is central to the evolution of the jurisdictional principle that controls government funding of religious entities.

The Pennsylvania and Rhode Island cases had slight differences, but their essential features were highly similar. In both states, the overwhelming number of nonpublic elementary and secondary schools were operated under Roman Catholic auspices. Those schools faced financial troubles serious enough to threaten their viability; if they were forced to close, their former students would flood the public schools and cause considerable public expense. To avoid that catastrophe, the legislatures of the two states enacted schemes designed to aid the private schools (almost all religious, almost all Catholic) in their programs of secular instruction. Subject to certain limitations, the Rhode Island scheme authorized the state to supplement the salaries of teachers of secular subjects in private elementary schools. The teachers who received such supplements had to teach subjects offered in the public schools; could use only teaching materials used in the public schools; and had to agree not to teach a course in religion while receiving a salary supplement. The Pennsylvania scheme authorized state officials to pay for "secular educational services" provided in private schools. The payments would go directly to the private schools, and cover expenditures for teachers' salaries, textbooks, and instructional materials. The courses covered by such payments had to be in the secular subjects of mathematics, modern foreign languages, physical science, and physical education.

The common threads here are apparent. Both states were looking for

42. 403 U.S. 602, 612-613 (1971).

ways to subsidize private education, including in religious schools, without subsidizing the teaching of religion. Both states went a step beyond the New York program, upheld in *Allen*, which involved loan of secular textbooks only. By trying to restrict the aid to secular education, the states were invoking the long-standing and judicially approved practice of government support for the secular services provided by religious hospitals and orphanages.

In determining that both states' programs violated the Establishment Clause, the Court made a new, explicit, and powerful move. Chief Justice Burger's opinion characterized the system of Roman Catholic education as thickly imbued with a religious mission, a character that subsequent opinions would call "pervasively sectarian."[43] In light of that character, the Court reasoned, all teachers would be expected to carry the mission forward. The only way to prevent the state-subsidized teachers from advancing the religious mission, the Court assumed, would be for state inspectors to closely monitor the conduct of teachers. But neither statute required or even contemplated any system to ensure compliance with the limits on religious instruction by state-subsidized teachers.

More importantly, the Court held that no system of monitoring could keep the system within constitutional boundaries. Any effective system of monitoring, the Court reasoned, would involve "excessive entanglement" between the state and religious institutions. Through oversight of the curriculum and the conduct of teachers, inspectors would run a significant risk of either exercising undue state influence over the operation of religious schools or being drawn into the religious mission as a collaborator. This set of twin concerns strongly echoes Madison's assertion that establishments of religion risk the corruption of both state and church.

The focus on excessive entanglement shows that the logic of nonestablishment is concerned with something other than the conscience of taxpayers or the equality of sects. Instead, it is concerned about the character of civil government and the conduct of its agents. Specifically, civil servants should not exercise control over the curricula of religious schools, or censor the interactions between teachers and students in those schools. Such control — with its inevitable discretionary choices about forbidden and permitted content — effectively makes the state a coauthor of that content.

In light of those concerns, the Court was willing to impose a prophylactic rule on public support of primary and secondary religious schools. Any direct aid, in cash or kind, to the educational mission of such schools was

---

43. *Hunt v. McNair,* 413 U.S. 734, 743 (1973).

barred by the Establishment Clause, because such aid would inevitably involve the state as a subsidizer of religious indoctrination, or would produce "excessive entanglement" between public officials and representatives of the religious schools.

The foregoing account of *Lemon,* which emphasized the constitutional impossibility of separating religious formation and secular instruction within parochial schools, is reinforced by a decision, rendered the same day, involving public aid to higher education. In *Tilton v. Richardson,*[44] the Court upheld federal grants to private religiously affiliated colleges and universities for construction of new buildings. The legislation, which also provided aid to public and nonreligious private colleges, specifically barred the use of government-financed buildings "for sectarian instruction or as a place for religious worship."[45] In distinguishing this aid from that prohibited in *Lemon,* the Court emphasized that most institutions of higher learning do not have a primary mission of forming religious identity. College students are less impressionable than younger pupils, and even religious colleges typically segregate any religious instruction from secular classes, which constitute the vast majority of the course offerings. Accordingly, aid to the secular activities of such colleges does not require the sort of monitoring that the Court in *Lemon* viewed as constitutionally problematic in the context of parochial schools.

The Stresses of Prophylaxis

Following the Court's decision in *Lemon,* state legislators searched for alternative methods for aiding religious schools. With *Everson* (transportation) and *Allen* (secular textbooks loaned to families) as guideposts, legislators designed programs that offered various forms of educational assistance to children and families, rather than directly to religious schools. When these programs were challenged — as most were — courts faced the difficult task of deciding which forms of assistance impermissibly advanced the religious mission of the schools. As the post-*Lemon* decisions unfolded, borderline questions about the directness of the aid, its relationship to the educational program, and its potential diversion to religious use appeared with increasing frequency. The quarter-century that followed *Lemon*'s hard-to-satisfy ap-

44. *Tilton v. Richardson,* 403 U.S. 672 (1971).
45. *Id.* at 675.

proach produced a series of decisions that displayed highly splintered Courts and increasingly unpersuasive distinctions among various forms of aid.[46]

In several decisions in the mid-1970s, a Court unable to coalesce around any majority opinions struck down programs involving loans of educational materials to families and religious schools, and also struck down reimbursement for some testing expenses.[47] It also allowed states to provide diagnostic services in areas of speech and hearing while forbidding reimbursement for therapeutic services for the same conditions.[48] As reflected in Senator Daniel Patrick Moynihan's famous quip about atlases, it became impossible over time to distinguish persuasively the book loans upheld in *Allen* and the loans of maps, slide and film projectors, and other materials disallowed in these early post-*Lemon* decisions. At least some of the justices expressed concern that when the state loaned instructional materials either to families or directly to religiously affiliated schools, the materials might be diverted for use in religious instruction and would thereby have the primary effect of advancing religion. Although these loan programs typically included restrictions on such diversion, enforcement of the restrictions invited the same sort of entanglement problem as had the salary supplements struck down in *Lemon*. Of course, the textbook loan program upheld in *Allen* presented similar problems of entanglement, at the stage of both book approval and book use. But the substantive content of a book is fixed, and

46. In the first major post-*Lemon* decision, demography trumped other considerations. In *Committee for Public Education v. Nyquist*, the Court in 1973 struck down a variety of provisions in a scheme, enacted by the state of New York, designed to keep Catholic schools solvent. Several of the provisions involved indirect aid to families in the form of tuition tax credits, but this feature could not save the program from condemnation as an aid to the overall survival of Catholic elementary and secondary education, which the Court continued to perceive as "pervasively sectarian." Viewed through the lenses of that particular combination of demographics and institutional character, *Nyquist* may well have been consistent with the jurisdictional principle for which we contend.

47. See *Meek v. Pittenger*, 421 U.S. 349 (1975); *Wolman v. Walter*, 433 U.S. 229 (1977). The Court eventually overruled both *Meek* and *Wolman* in *Mitchell v. Helms*, 530 U.S. 793 (2000). Perhaps these cases turned on whether the state had made a credible claim that the materials really passed through the hands of families rather than going to the religious entities without mediation. But that was a slender reed, at best, to explain outcome differences, and led to persistent mockery and criticism of this line of decisions. See also *Levitt v. Committee for Public Education*, 413 U.S. 472 (1973) (invalidating reimbursement of schools for cost of administering state-mandated tests, in circumstances where teachers at the school prepared the tests).

48. *Wolman* approved state provision of diagnostic services, in areas like speech and hearing, to students; *Meek* had disapproved of state provision of therapeutic services for the same concerns.

the potential for its diversion for use in religious instruction is therefore somewhat easier to measure than materials with less determinate content, like a map, or instructional equipment, such as a film projector, which is devoid of substantive content.

In 1985, the uncertainty and social costs of the prophylactic theory in *Lemon* became starkly manifest in *Aguilar v. Felton*.[49] *Aguilar* involved a federal program that supported the use, in schools located in low-income neighborhoods, of public employees to teach remedial reading and mathematics in grades K-12. The program operated in both public and private schools. The teachers remained under control of public authorities, and, when in religious schools, taught classes in rooms from which the religious iconography had been removed. Because the program operated nationwide and included public schools on precisely the same terms as private schools (religious or otherwise), the demography of its beneficiaries was not materially skewed toward any particular faith, Roman Catholic or otherwise.

Nevertheless, a five-justice majority invalidated the program. Justice Brennan's opinion emphasized the new variable of "symbolic union" of church and state presented by the program; the risk of entanglement that accompanied the relationship between publicly employed teachers and the authorities in religious schools where the program's remedial teaching occurred; and the effective subsidy of religious instruction achieved by improving the learning skills of students. In light of all the circumstances, it was very difficult to see how the federal program rendered the government responsible for religious indoctrination or transformation. But the Court had never crisply identified that principle of responsibility as representing the core concern of restrictions on funding. So the decision in *Aguilar* — until its explicit overruling in *Agostini v. Felton* twelve years later[50] — stood for years as an outlier point of separationist reasoning. And it stood as well for the stark costs of this kind of reasoning, because the decision produced the consequence that children attending schools in economically poor neighborhoods, and in need of remedial education, could not receive that sort of help on school premises from dedicated public employees with no agenda of religious instruction in mind. At times, school districts set up off-school-site locations for this remedial instruction, but that only added to the financial costs or safety risks associated with the program. *Aguilar* was a sign that the funding cases had reached a point at which results had lost touch with any coherent, underlying narrative

49. *Aguilar v. Felton,* 473 U.S. 402 (1985).
50. *Agostini v. Felton,* 521 U.S. 203 (1997).

of the purposes of restricting government support for the secular instructional value being added by fully accredited, religiously affiliated schools.

The Rise of the Indirect Aid Paradigm

During the era of its most ardent insistence on a prophylactic denial of public support for religious schools, the Court kept alive a traditional and very different approach to that issue. Recall that in both *Everson* and *Allen* the Court upheld aid programs on the theory that the state provided bus tokens (in *Everson*) or textbooks (in *Allen*) to the schoolchildren, not directly to the religious schools. Moreover, the aid equally benefited children in private and public schools, and the aid itself had a fixed secular character. In other words, both *Everson* and *Allen* rested on an idea that secular aid provided to all children did not become constitutionally infirm simply because the aid enabled some children to attend religious schools. Those schools would certainly benefit indirectly by the eased burden on students and their families, but the government program did not directly provide such a benefit, and the state's assistance was peripheral to the enterprise of teaching religion. Or, as we put it earlier, the state is not responsible for the students' religious experience.

Although *Everson* and *Allen* thus foreshadowed contemporary developments, a series of decisions in the 1980s and 1990s, concerning what is now routinely called "indirect aid" — aid that flows initially through the intervening choices of individual beneficiaries, and flows to the benefit of religious entities only as a result of those intervening choices — crystallized this doctrinal line and, more importantly, its substantive underpinnings. If, as we have contended, the Establishment Clause is about state responsibility for the projects of religious formation and religious identity, the choice between state and private agency in channeling the flow of assistance to religious entities is appropriately of considerable constitutional significance.

The project of reenergizing the theory of intervening private choice began in *Mueller v. Allen* (1983),[51] a decision that upheld a Minnesota law that authorized deductions from income, for purposes of state income taxation, for various educational expenses, including "tuition, textbooks, and transportation." Deductible expenses included tuition paid at private, religiously affiliated schools. The deduction was capped at $500 per dependent in grades K-6, and $700 per dependent in grades 7-12.

51. *Mueller v. Allen*, 463 U.S. 388 (1983).

A narrow (5-4) majority of the Supreme Court upheld the program. Despite its superficial similarity to a program of tax credits for tuition paid at nonpublic schools, which the Court had invalidated (also 5-4) in *Committee for Public Education v. Nyquist* (1973),[52] the Minnesota program differed with respect to both demographics and program design.[53] The Minnesota scheme, unlike the New York scheme struck down in *Nyquist,* did not benefit only families of children in nonpublic schools. Nor were the religious schools in Minnesota overwhelmingly Roman Catholic in their religious character, as had been the situation in New York. Rather, like the exemption from taxation of real property that the Court had upheld in 1970 in *Walz v. Tax Commission,*[54] the Minnesota scheme benefited a broad class of beneficiaries, religious and otherwise.[55]

The opinion in *Mueller* revealed that the Court remained closely divided on the question of direct versus indirect aid, but it was also a significant step toward providing room to the states to create programs that combined beneficiary choice with aid to a broad class of institutions, secular and religious. Indeed, soon thereafter the Court made its most conspicuous move in favor of the beneficiary choice theory, in a case with highly sympathetic facts and — perhaps more important — considerable distance from the prototypical funding controversy involving thickly religious elementary and secondary schools.

In *Witters v. Washington Department of Services for the Blind,*[56] the Court ruled that the Establishment Clause did not preclude "the State of Washington from extending assistance under a . . . vocational rehabilitation assistance program to a blind person studying at a Christian college and seeking to become a pastor, missionary, or [religious] youth director." The assistance in question was a grant, from the state's Commission for the Blind, to be

52. See *supra,* note 46, discussing *Nyquist.*

53. The difference did not derive from the distinction between credits and deductions as tools of tax policy (as tax lawyers, not well versed in constitutional intricacies, sometimes assume).

54. *Walz v. Tax Commission,* 397 U.S. 664 (1970).

55. To the argument that the Court should analyze the precise distributional effects of the law with respect to religiously affiliated schools, then–associate justice Rehnquist famously declared, "We would be loath to adopt a rule grounding the constitutionality of a facially neutral law on annual reports reciting the extent to which various classes of private citizens claimed benefits under the law. Such an approach would scarcely provide the certainty that this field stands in need of, nor can we perceive principled standards by which such statistical evidence might be evaluated." 463 U.S. at 401.

56. *Witters v. Washington Department of Services for the Blind,* 474 U.S. 481 (1986).

used by Mr. Witters to help pay tuition at Inland Empire School of the Bible, a Christian college in Spokane.

To the surprise of those who had observed the Court's long string of closely divided rulings, Justice Marshall wrote for a unanimous Court in ruling that the Establishment Clause did not forbid the grant. Justice Marshall's opinion emphasized several crucial factors, including the actual transfer of the grant from the state to Witters, and then from Witters to the school. The opinion suggested that this movement of the funds through the hands of the individual beneficiary before going to the school made the grant analogous to a state employee using a portion of salary to contribute to a church, rather than analogous to a direct payment from state to school. He also emphasized the breadth of the class of institutions that might ultimately benefit from such grants, the likelihood that most of those institutions were secular, and the consequent unlikelihood that the scheme of aid to the blind was some sort of ruse to funnel state monies to sectarian schools. So described, and viewed as a whole, the system of vocational assistance grants thus could not be seen as having a "primary effect" of advancing religion.

The unanimity of the holding masked a crucial division among the justices. Justice Powell's separate concurrence for himself and two other justices (Justice Rehnquist and Chief Justice Burger) did not question Justice Marshall's reasoning, but argued for a broader understanding of the effect of intervening beneficiary choice.[57] Marshall saw intervening beneficiary choice as but one of many relevant factors, including the age and education level of the beneficiary, the total sum of state funds that wound up in the hands of religious entities, and the percentage of relevant state funds that ended up in such hands. To put it differently, Marshall seemed quite willing to analyze the religious demographics of the scheme's overall distributional outcome. For Powell, Burger, and Rehnquist, the question presented in both *Mueller* and *Witters* was much simpler. So long as the assistance program was formally neutral between secular and religious entities that provided the relevant service, and so long as the aid passed through the intervening choice of individuals, the state was not constitutionally responsible for any religious uses to which the aid was ultimately put. The demographics were constitutionally irrelevant.

The path defined by the approach to indirect financing championed by Powell, Rehnquist, and Burger in *Witters* foreshadowed the Supreme Court's validation, almost two decades later, of the school voucher scheme in *Zelman*

---

57. 474 U.S. at 490–492.

v. Simmons-Harris.[58] When that highly visible controversy involving the use of public vouchers, redeemable at participating secular or religious private schools in Cleveland, Ohio, arrived at the Court in 2002, the battle lines were obvious and well-set. The program, a state legislative response to the continued failure of the Cleveland public schools, included tuition vouchers worth $2,250 per year at private schools, secular or religious. Participating private schools had to agree to accept tuition of $2,500 per year for voucher students. Participation by schools was entirely voluntary, and no suburban public schools participated, even though they were offered considerably more on a per pupil basis to do so. If demand for vouchers exceeded supply, a lottery determined which students would receive vouchers, and a separate lottery then determined which school they would attend from a list of voucher schools their families had selected.

In the years of the program covered by the litigation, religious schools offered well over 90 percent of the seats available for voucher recipients. This occurred because most of the private schools in Cleveland had a religious character and the largest set of those — the Catholic schools — at the time charged tuition at or close to the permitted maximum of $2,500 per year. Religious schools that accepted voucher students were under no restrictions with respect to religious education or worship that might be required of such students.

In light of these facts, and the line of decisions over the preceding thirty-five years, the division on the Court was entirely predictable. One group of justices was inclined to follow Chief Justice Rehnquist's lead, and treat this program in precisely the same way the Court had treated the program in *Witters.* The schemes were formally neutral between secular and religious providers of the relevant services; they involved intervening private choices by beneficiaries; and they transferred public money through the hands of beneficiaries to religious schools. Moreover, like the textbook loan program upheld in *Board of Education v. Allen,* all these programs could plausibly be framed as designed to benefit families and students, rather than religious institutions that might gain from them incidentally. If the structure of intervening choice was all that the Establishment Clause required to break the connection between the state's material participation and the beneficiary's religious experience, the Cleveland program was on sound footing.

An opposing group on the Court was inclined to distinguish prior cases involving beneficiary choice. For these justices, the Cleveland voucher

---

58. *Zelman v. Simmons-Harris,* 536 U.S. 639 (2002).

scheme generated substantial financial assistance, most of which went to the ultimate benefit of the private religious schools (primarily Catholic) in Cleveland. As such, the program aided the project of religious inculcation at the elementary and secondary level, and thus — whatever the intentions of its designers — produced a "primary effect" of advancing religion.[59]

Various Establishment Clause decisions of the preceding twenty years suggested that Justice O'Connor's vote was the key to victory in *Zelman,* and that indeed appears to have been accurate. To gain that vote, Chief Justice Rehnquist's opinion for the Court emphasized that the Cleveland program involved not just the bare fact of private choice, but the quality of that choice. The chief justice described the program as one of "true private choice, in which government aid reaches religious schools only as a result of the genuine and independent choices of private individuals."[60]

This concept of "genuine and independent" choice played a crucial role in the *Zelman* opinion, and even more so in O'Connor's concurring opinion.[61] If Cleveland parents, especially among the poor, faced a stark choice between public schools that were both dangerous and educationally inadequate and private religious schools that were safe and educationally sound, they might well make a "nongenuine" choice of a school with religious attributes. That is, if the secular options were uniformly dreadful, parents might well opt for voucher schools despite deep reservations or disagreements concerning the religious training at those schools. The *Zelman* majority purported to solve that problem by emphasizing the improved choices among public schools in Cleveland, including newly created magnet schools and charter schools. O'Connor seized on this point, and elaborated it still further, emphasizing that it is the parents' actual experience of genuine choice, not simply the formal quality of that choice, that is constitutionally dispositive.

As we suggested in writings at the time of *Zelman,*[62] O'Connor was on the correct path, though she did not travel on it quite far enough. The proper constitutional concern in *Zelman* is not limited to the question of intentional favoring, preference, or support of religious schools by the state. The state is

59. 536 U.S. at 686-717 (Souter, J., joined by Breyer, Ginsburg, and Stevens, JJ., dissenting).

60. *Id.* at 649.

61. *Id.* at 663-676 (O'Connor, J., concurring).

62. Ira C. Lupu and Robert W. Tuttle, *Zelman's Future: Vouchers, Sectarian Providers, and the Next Round of Constitutional Battles,* 78 Notre Dame L. Rev. 917 (2003); Ira C. Lupu and Robert W. Tuttle, *Sites of Redemption: A Wide-Angle Look at Government Vouchers and Sectarian Service Providers,* 18 J. L. & Politics 537 (2002).

constitutionally responsible for religious experience when it creates financial incentives that will steer its citizens into such experience even if they would choose to avoid it but are willing to tolerate it to attain some other valuable good. The arrangements in Cleveland included some steps to avoid such steering — in particular, the provision of new, amply funded secular public school options. It was those options that apparently convinced O'Conner that, from the perspective of parents making such choices, the selection of a religious school was both sincere (that is, "genuine") and uncoerced by the state (that is, "independent").

These policy arrangements, however, which had been made at the state legislative level, could have provided sturdier protection against coerced choice of, or state steering toward, religious schools. Most significantly, Ohio could have required, as the city of Milwaukee did in similar circumstances,[63] that religious schools permit voucher students to opt out of religious instruction, worship services, or both. In addition, the state could have demanded the participation in the voucher scheme of high-quality suburban public schools. Moreover, if the state had offered an amount per student closer to what it would have spent per student in the public schools, it might have induced additional secular private schools into accepting voucher students. We do not claim that any of those options were, in and of themselves, constitutionally required, though the case for that seems strongest with respect to the opt-out possibility. We do suggest, however, that policies of this sort, each of which expands the universe of choices and reduces the likelihood that the state was steering children into religious experience, would have made considerably more persuasive the case for the constitutionality of the Cleveland voucher scheme.

To put the point more broadly, indirect financing — the reliance on individual beneficiaries to choose between, and then direct the use of state resources toward, secular or religious providers — is an important mechanism for accomplishing the requisite disconnection of the state from responsibility for the people's religious experience. *Zelman* is too thinly reasoned and invites comparisons to illicit "money laundering" as a way of evading constitutional norms. A thicker version of the underlying prohibition on state responsibility for religious experience might have led to a different result in *Zelman,* and a reconstruction of the Cleveland program (or similar programs in other places or different service contexts) that better fits those norms.

63. *Jackson v. Benson*, 578 N.W. 2d 602 (Wis. 1998).

Rethinking the Problem of Direct Aid

Shortly before the full crystallization of the indirect aid theory in *Zelman v. Simmons-Harris,* a splintered Court had already begun to rethink its approach to indirect aid. Recall that the decisions from *Lemon v. Kurtzman* (1971) to *Aguilar v. Felton* (1985) had relied quite explicitly on the overall institutional character of the entities being assisted — that is, the Court had viewed religiously affiliated elementary and secondary schools as "pervasively sectarian." Accordingly, these decisions had invalidated a number of programs that offered assistance directly to the educational program in such schools — whether in the form of additional teaching personnel, salary supplements for private school teachers, instructional materials, or otherwise.

How these schools were characterized was an important factor in those decisions. If the schools truly were "pervasively sectarian," aid to their educational mission inevitably set up that perfect double bind, of inevitable religious advancement or excessive entanglement, that had been fatal in *Lemon* and its progeny. This conceptual apparatus had been pressed to the breaking point in *Aguilar v. Felton,* in which the Court had ruled unconstitutional the provision of public employees to teach remedial reading and mathematics in schools, including religious schools, in poor areas. The risk of diversion of these efforts to religious instruction seemed vanishingly small, and the likelihood of constitutionally troubled relationships between these public employees and religious school personnel also seemed most unlikely. Neither had been proven in the litigation in *Aguilar.* Moreover, *Aguilar* involved a federal program, applicable to public and private schools nationwide, rather than a state program that appeared targeted at the schools of a particular religious faith.

Aguilar, which had been decided by a 5-4 vote, thus seemed ripe for overruling once the balance on the Court shifted ever so slightly. In response to that sense of ripeness and change, the Board of Education of the City of New York initiated an attempt to get relief from the prevailing court order against operating the federal program in religious schools in the city. In 1997, in *Agostini v. Felton,*[64] a new 5-4 majority indeed overruled *Aguilar* and terminated the injunction. As Justice O'Connor explained, three changes in the law — two of which had emerged in decisions concerning indirect aid — pushed toward overruling *Aguilar.* First, an earlier decision,[65] which allowed

---

64. *Agostini v. Felton,* 521 U.S. 203 (1997).
65. *Zobrest v. Catalina Foothills School District* (1992). Larry Zobrest was a profoundly deaf high school student entitled under the federal Individuals with Disabilities Act to a

the use of a publicly employed interpreter for a hearing-impaired student in religious school, had established a presumption that public employees could be trusted to aid students in a religious school without contributing to the enterprise of religious indoctrination. If trust was appropriate when an interpreter was translating religious instruction and worship services, it was all the more so in *Agostini,* where the public employees were teaching entirely secular subjects. Second, *Witters* had established that not all aid that supports the educational mission of a religious school is constitutionally impermissible. Third, the breadth of the class of beneficiaries of the remedial instruction program, which operated nationwide in both public and private schools, helped guarantee that its overall effects were secular and not religious.

Agostini, which merged considerations that had long been thought to belong to separate categories of indirect versus direct aid, thus set the stage for the most recent and dramatic reconfiguration of the law of government financial assistance to religious entities. In *Mitchell v. Helms,*[66] a splintered Court in 2000 upheld the application to religious elementary and secondary schools of a federal program that loaned books, instructional materials, and computers to state and local educational authorities, for use in schools in poor areas. The program restricted all the materials loaned to "secular and non-ideological use"; that is, the borrowing schools were prohibited from using these materials in religious instruction.

This scheme was in a number of ways similar to the remedial instruction program upheld in *Agostini* — in particular, it was national in scope, was aimed at the same set of schools and schoolchildren, and included restrictions on religious use. In one vitally important way, however, the program challenged in *Mitchell* was different from that in *Agostini* — the materials loaned to schools in *Mitchell* were in the hands of religious school employees

---

government-provided hearing interpreter at school. He attended a Catholic high school, and state authorities had denied him the statutory benefit of a hearing interpreter because the aid would (the state asserted) unconstitutionally facilitate his religious education. In a 5-4 opinion by Chief Justice Rehnquist, the Supreme Court ruled that the aid at issue in *Zobrest* met the dual criteria of (1) beneficiary choice and (2) formal neutrality between the secular and religious entities that might attain some material benefit from the scheme. To the majority, the fact that the hearing interpreter would be a state-provided human interface between Mr. Zobrest and his religious experience at the school was of no constitutional import. The interpreter was equivalent to a hearing aid, and the majority saw no reason why the families of students with such remediable needs should be forced to choose secular over religious schools. Here, as in *Witters,* the aid recipient and not the state was responsible for the choice to employ the aid in ways that produced religious experience and materially benefited religious entities.

66. *Mitchell v. Helms,* 530 U.S. 793 (2000).

rather than public employees. Under the presumptions that had operated in the *Lemon* era, to the effect that teachers in parochial school systems would inevitably engage in religious indoctrination of their students, this quality of the program in *Mitchell* would undoubtedly have been fatal. Indeed, in *Meek v. Pittenger*[67] and *Wolman v. Walter,*[68] both decided in the 1970s, the Court had invalidated state programs almost exactly like the one challenged in *Mitchell,* on the very ground that parochial school teachers would use such aids to the educational program to assist in religious instruction, or that excessive entanglement would be the inevitable result of any effort to be sure that the teachers did not do so.

The Court's very different and splintered response in *Mitchell* stands at the cusp of a new era, its precise contours yet to be determined, in cases of direct aid. No single opinion gained a majority of the justices' votes. A plurality of four justices — Thomas (the opinion's author), Kennedy, Scalia, and Chief Justice Rehnquist — joined an opinion that seemed to overthrow all restrictions on aid to religious entities, so long as secular entities were treated similarly.[69] That is, the *Mitchell* plurality asserted that the only constitutionally mandatory criteria for such a funding program were those of (1) secular purpose and (2) no favoring of religious institutions over their nonreligious counterparts. In a significant divergence from prior decisions, Justice Thomas's opinion insisted that the risk of diversion of aid to religious instruction was constitutionally irrelevant. And, in its most dramatic sections, the opinion attacked and repudiated the doctrine that barred all direct aid from going to "pervasively sectarian" schools. It asserted an anti-Catholic provenance of that doctrine, and insisted that it be buried.[70]

The most important opinion in *Mitchell,* at least for now, was that of Justice O'Connor, joined by Justice Breyer.[71] They agreed with the plurality's outcome — that the federal program under which computers, books, and other instructional materials were loaned to state and local authorities for distribution to schools in poor areas did not violate the Establishment Clause. Although the concurring opinion ignored the plurality opinion's attack on the bar to aiding "pervasively sectarian" schools, O'Connor agreed that the

67. *Meek v. Pittenger,* 421 U.S. 349 (1975), *overruled, Mitchell v. Helms,* 530 U.S. 793 (2000).

68. *Wolman v. Walter,* 433 U.S. 229 (1977), *overruled, Mitchell v. Helms,* 530 U.S. 793 (2000).

69. 530 U.S. at 802-829 (plurality opinion).

70. *Id.* at 826-829 (plurality opinion).

71. *Id.* at 836-864 (O'Connor, J., joined by Breyer, J., concurring).

crucial constitutional question involved the character of the aid, rather than the character of the aided institution.

With respect to the character of the aid, O'Connor took a great leap forward from her opinion in *Agostini,* in which she had asserted the constitutional trustworthiness of public employees. Here, in *Mitchell,* she argued that teachers and others employed by religious schools could likewise be trusted to comply with restrictions on use of the loaned materials — that is, to not divert them to religious use. Moreover, she concluded that a system of affidavits of compliance and very occasional inspection by public officials was sufficient to prevent such diversion without risking "excessive entanglement."

Because the *Mitchell* concurrence is the narrowest opinion in support of the outcome in the case, it represents the controlling law.[72] And it marks a significant departure of emphasis and method — not of substance — from what had gone before in cases involving direct aid. No longer is the character of an institution dispositive of its eligibility for government financial support. Rather, even houses of worship themselves can be eligible for some forms of support. The crucial constitutional variables emerge from an inquiry into the content and context of the aid, and the safeguards against diversion of that aid to the inculcation of religious values.

As has been the case since *Everson,* government may not act in ways that render it responsible for the formation and reinforcement of the religious character of individuals. What has changed over time are the Court's doctrines for enforcing that Establishment Clause norm. Gone are the presumptions that certain kinds of entities engage in pervasive and continuous religious indoctrination. Accordingly, the prophylactic bar (flowing from those presumptions) on aid to thickly sectarian entities has likewise disappeared. In their place is a more narrowly focused prohibition against the use of material government support in any program of religious worship or inculcation. Government must have in place safeguards against such use to accompany that support, and the safeguards must be enforceable in ways that minimize constitutionally dangerous interactions. On this new and more refined narrative, those enforceable safeguards keep the state at a constitutionally safe distance from the enterprise of religious indoctrination.

To pull this chronological account together — by the middle of 2002 the Establishment Clause law controlling government aid to religious institutions had crystallized around two discrete themes. First, as established in the crucial *Mitchell* concurrence, direct aid by government to such institutions is permissi-

72. See *Marks v. United States,* 430 U.S. 188 (1977).

ble if that aid is used only in activities with exclusively secular content, and the governmental entity providing such assistance creates constitutionally adequate safeguards against diversion from secular to religious experience. In addition, programs of direct aid may not favor religious entities over secular ones. Second, following *Zelman v. Simmons-Harris*, programs that distribute aid to religious entities through intervening, genuine private choices are consistent with the Constitution even if the aid is ultimately used for religious activities. The intervening choices absolve the government of responsibility for the religious experience. With respect to indirect aid, like direct aid, government may not favor religious entities over their secular counterparts, and the choice between religious and secular providers must be genuine and independent.

Faith-Based Social Services

Constitutional limits on public aid for religious education were rarely applied to public funding of religiously affiliated hospitals and orphanages. At the height of the Court's prophylactic application of the Establishment Clause, the federally financed Medicare and Medicaid programs funneled substantial sums to religiously affiliated hospitals. These voucher-like programs, which financed the secular health-care choices of patients, no doubt satisfied the relevant constitutional concerns, but they were not the subject of litigation. With the exception of the Court's 1988 decision in *Bowen v. Kendrick*,[73] involving federal grants for social services to religious entities under the Adolescent Family Life Act, virtually all the Supreme Court's decisions in the past sixty years about government aid to religious entities have involved aid to education. In its most important contribution to constitutional doctrine, *Bowen* clarified that the issues raised by the Court's funding decisions are not limited to educational services. At least in principle, constitutional concerns about government support for religious experience should attach to any financial relationships between the government and religiously affiliated institutions.

By the middle 1990s, questions of participation by religious entities in government-financed social services of many different types had bubbled up for increased attention. The primary cause of this expanded focus was the

---

73. *Bowen v. Kendrick*, 487 U.S. 589 (1988). Bowen broke no new ground at the time of decision; the Court's opinion continued to insist that direct aid to faith-based social services not fund specifically religious activities, nor be directed to "pervasively sectarian" organizations.

Charitable Choice provisions of the welfare reform laws enacted by Congress in 1996.[74] These provisions required that, as a condition of federal assistance for social services to welfare beneficiaries, state and local governments not discriminate against service providers with a religious character.

During the remaining years of the Clinton administration, the full import of these provisions was not tested. The set of constitutional norms that had been in place since *Lemon v. Kurtzman* appeared to constrain substantially any attempt to fully comply with the Charitable Choice provisions. In particular, the doctrine that barred government aid to pervasively sectarian entities suggested that houses of worship could never be recipients of direct government grants, and executive branch officials at the federal level were not inclined to test the continued vitality of that doctrine.

That reluctance to push for and test the possibility of constitutional reform changed dramatically during the administration of George W. Bush. Operating under the rubric of the Faith-Based and Community Initiative (FBCI), the federal government began to press state and local governments to comply with the Charitable Choice provisions. Indeed, by executive orders[75] and a series of regulations emerging from the major federal agencies engaged in social service financing, the theme of nondiscrimination against religious providers soon became a dominant administrative concern. Of course, the relevant services went far beyond those of education. A wide range of services were financed under the initiative, including emergency shelter, affordable housing, adoption and foster care services, literacy, and treatment for substance abuse, among others. Some of these services — substance abuse treatment, in particular — invited the strong possibility of religious content.

After a period of federal-state regulatory adjustment and lower court litigation,[76] the constitutional contours of the FBCI eventually fell into place. This process was aided immeasurably by the Supreme Court's decisions in *Mitchell v. Helms,* which clarified the permissible scope of direct financing,

74. See Personal Responsibility and Work Opportunity Act of 1996, Pub. L. No. 104-193, 110 Stat. 2105 (codified as amended in various sections of 42 U.S.C., including 42 U.S.C. sec. 604a *et seq.* [1996]).

75. Exec. Order 13198 (creating seven agency centers on Faith-Based and Community Initiative) (Jan. 29, 2001); Exec. Order 13199 (declaring the policy in favor of inclusion of faith organizations in social service efforts, and creating White House Office on Faith-Based and Community Initiative to develop, lead, and coordinate efforts to implement that policy) (Jan. 29, 2001).

76. For a full discussion, see Ira C. Lupu and Robert W. Tuttle, *The Faith-Based Initiative and the Constitution,* 55 DePaul L. Rev. 1 (2005).

and *Zelman,* which reinforced the relevant criteria for indirect, beneficiary choice financing. Those Supreme Court decisions, the congressional enactments on Charitable Choice, and the FBCI represented all three branches of the federal government moving toward relaxing the limitations on government financial assistance, for secular purposes, to religious institutions.[77]

Even with two major (and recent) Court decisions as lodestars, the Bush administration's efforts fell somewhat short of full constitutional clarity and adequacy. In particular, its formula for the limitations on direct government aid was framed ambiguously as a prohibition on using government funds for "inherently religious activities, such as worship, religious instruction, or proselytization." This formulation suggested the possibility that government might permissibly finance social services that include a religious component, because social services are not "inherently religious." Litigation in the lower courts, including one very prominent decision about the provision of faith-based rehabilitation services to persons incarcerated for crime,[78] repeatedly rejected that line of thinking.

The Obama administration has retained but renamed the initiative, which is now known as Faith-Based and Neighborhood Partnerships. Moreover, the administration has ordered all federal agencies to amend the regulations to bar the use of direct government aid in all "explicitly religious activities." This is a considerable improvement over the ambiguous formulation of "inherently religious activities," and to the best of our knowledge the

77. This is not to say that the now-prevailing distinction between direct and indirect assistance, and the battery of rules within each category, neatly solves all questions for religion-state partnerships in the delivery of social services. The model of indirect financing, which permits religious content in the delivered service, works well with preexisting and well-established deliverers of service, such as health-care providers or private schools, with respect to which vouchers or certificates as a form of payment will blend smoothly into existing operations. For religious entities considering bringing a new service online, in need of start-up capital, and uncertain of the rate of usage by government beneficiaries, indirect financing may be considerably suboptimal. Moreover, the choice of direct financing by the government brings with it strict constitutional limitations on religious content, and that will inhibit some religious entities from participating. In addition, direct financing involves an increased hazard of religious discrimination (or perceptions of such discrimination) by government officials when they are choosing just a few religious providers (out of a larger number of applicants) for direct grants or contracts, as compared with the diffused judgment of private beneficiaries with respect to which provider among many to patronize. Even this cursory glance at the choice between financing methods reveals its complexities and administrative shortcomings, however constitutionally sound this structure may be.

78. *Americans United for Separation of Church and State v. Prison Fellowship Ministries,* 509 F. 3d 406 (8th Cir. 2007).

litigation front has been quiet with respect to these partnerships since Obama took office. Whether this is the product of increased constitutional certainty, improved administrative compliance, more restrictive rules on taxpayer standing to bring these actions in the federal courts, or reduced willingness on the part of separationist groups to litigate this set of issues is difficult to say, though we suspect all these considerations are in the mix.

The Future of Limits on Public Funding

This chapter has taken the reader through the long and winding story of the Supreme Court's handling of cases involving material government assistance to religious entities. Whatever might be said, not all kind, about the periods of internal contradiction and messy detail in the period from *Everson* (1947) to *Zelman* (2002), we think the Court has now arrived at a set of workable rules for both indirect and direct assistance.

The replacement of justices over time could of course destabilize these rules. In particular, the rules about direct financing now rest on a two-justice (O'Connor and Breyer) concurring opinion in *Mitchell v. Helms*. The replacement of Justice O'Connor by Justice Alito, who has given strong hints that he is less oriented to a strenuous version of the Establishment Clause than his predecessor, suggests that the *Mitchell* plurality — with its strong overtones of no restrictions on the religious content of government-aided services, so long as the overall program has a secular purpose and does not favor religion — may soon become the governing law. Were that to happen, the distinctiveness of religious institutions as targets of government assistance might soon fade away.

But the combination of restrictive taxpayer standing rules[79] and reduced litigation about such matters suggests that the Supreme Court may have little engagement with this subject for a lengthy period, and that the current doctrines — in part because they seem quite workable for all concerned — may be in place for a considerable time. On that assumption, it remains to ask the normative questions about whether the prevailing approach is constitutionally sound.

As we have suggested from the very beginning of this chapter, we perceive the underlying constitutional norm as a limitation on government re-

---

79. Although *Flast v. Cohen,* 392 U.S. 83 (1968), had opened the door for taxpayer suits that challenged, under the Establishment Clause, government funding of religious entities, several recent decisions in the Supreme Court have made it considerably more difficult for taxpayers to mount such lawsuits. *Arizona Christian School Tuition Organization v. Winn,* 131 S. Ct. 1436 (2011); *Hein v. Freedom from Religion Foundation,* 551 U.S. 587 (2007).

sponsibility for religious indoctrination. That norm informs *Everson,* and it continues to inform *Zelman* and the *Mitchell* concurrence. To be sure, modes of enforcement of that norm have varied. *Lemon* may have overenforced it by excluding all material assistance to thickly religious schools, and perhaps the *Mitchell* concurrence underenforces it by allowing the government to rely heavily on nondiversion affidavits from officials at religious entities. Modes of enforcement aside, the deeper question remains — why should the Constitution block the government from assuming responsibility for religious worship or indoctrination, through instruction or otherwise?

At the first and most obvious level, it seems plain to us that government should be barred from pursuing religious ends. The salvation of souls is not the government's business, and any attempt to make it so would compromise completely the government's secular identity, and would undermine the peace treaty among all religious sects to refrain from struggle to control the machinery of government. All this is commonplace and incontrovertible in the contemporary constitutional world. Over and over, all the justices agree on the singular proposition that material aid by government to religious entities must be aimed at secular purposes, and not religious ones. The provision of goods such as education, health care, and adequate shelter will always qualify as secular goals; ensuring the people's spiritual welfare and the correctness of their religious beliefs will never so qualify.

The more complex question for contemporary constitutionalists is why the government operates under restrictions with respect to the use of religious means to achieve secular ends. If religious schools educate children well, and substance abuse programs with thick religious content are especially efficient at weaning their clients permanently from drugs or alcohol, why should government not be free to include them in programs of direct assistance? And, if their efficiency meets or exceeds that of their secular counterparts, isn't it invidious discrimination to exclude them from streams of assistance for which those counterparts are eligible?

One quick and incomplete answer is that religious providers are not completely excluded from all such streams. The voucher mechanism makes their participation constitutionally possible, so long as beneficiaries are making a genuine, independent choice among a range of religious and secular providers. But voucher funding may not be a practical business model for providers of some types of service.[80]

---

80. Consider, for example, a teen abstinence program. Young people are not likely to want to identify themselves to the government as consumers of such services. Nor is a tuition-

This set of concerns forces us to confront the question of why direct government support of religious means to secular ends — in minimizing the hazards of active teen sexuality, for example, including disease or pregnancy — should be off-limits to the state. One plausible answer is that means and ends are not always so neatly separated, nor is the difference between them always accurately perceived. The government's decision makers may be utterly indifferent to religious transformation as an end, and be genuinely concerned only with a good social policy result. But decision makers might well be concerned with both, and hide their religious ends behind the concern for equal or fair treatment of religious means. Even worse in some cases, the government's decision maker may be predominantly concerned with religious ends, and be interested in aiding religious social services primarily to achieve such ends. Broad discretion in decision makers — for example, in the awarding of grants or contracts for direct assistance — will make it very difficult for outside parties to be confident that the government is using religion entirely as a means, because of its efficacy, rather than an end, because of its theological truth.

Moreover, even if decision makers are exclusively focused on the efficacy of religion as a means to secular ends, constitutional concerns remain. As chapter 2 emphasized, purely ecclesiastical questions are outside the scope of governmental competence. This proposition has the identical force when the government purports to resolve internal religious disputes over such questions. In addition, religious people are rightly concerned when the state uses religion as an instrument of social responsibility. Madison described this as an "unhallowed perversion of the means of salvation"[81] — strong words, but to the point of this discussion. The state lacks competence to choose and control religious experience, and it threatens both its own secular identity and the jurisdictional realm of faith when it coordinates with religious authority in an attempt to maximize social outcomes. Suppose, for example, the state's social scientists learn that one form of Protestant Christianity is far

---

based system for allocating the costs of providing the service efficient. Providers will be unable to predict how many will show up for each session; the numbers may vary considerably from session to session; the basic costs of providing the service, including rent of space and counselor salaries, will not vary in direct proportion to the number of users; and the program might never get off the ground without an initial capital infusion that only direct financing can provide. So the absence of a direct assistance option may mean that the religion-based abstinence program will not come into being or survive, while a comparable secular program may find direct government financial assistance that will get it started and keep it going.

81. "Memorial and Remonstrance," par. 5.

better than all other faith traditions for making inroads on the problem of substance abuse, or that some faiths are far worse than others in responding to problems of domestic violence. Should decision makers rely on these findings in allocating grants and contracts? Should grant officers press religious leaders who have such grants or contracts to revise their teachings in the direction revealed by the more efficacious faith traditions?

We recognize that the particular rules and doctrines by which these concerns are made manifest may vary by time and circumstance. We are certainly not committed to the precise details of *Zelman,* which underemphasizes the dangers of the state incentivizing religious experience, and we see the instability and imprecision of the particulars that emerge from the *Mitchell* concurrence. Indeed, even a version of the *Mitchell* plurality view — equal opportunity for religious and nonreligious providers, and readily demonstrable secular purpose — might be defensible, but only so long as the government provides a strenuous guarantee of adequate alternatives, religious and secular. Where the market does not readily generate a full measure of such alternatives, the hazards of steering beneficiaries to religious experience and thus being responsible for indoctrination are considerable. Similarly, the state cannot directly support private actors who exclude from services eligible beneficiaries based on religious identity or cooperation, because such support makes the state responsible for the religious qualities on which the provider insists.

From *Everson* to *Zelman* and beyond, the core constitutional concern has been the state's responsibility for religious experience. When the state chooses religion as an end, or itself selects religion as a means, it is fairly held responsible for the indoctrination that may ensue. And the secular state is barred by the Establishment Clause from undertaking any such responsibility. For this reason, the standard model of state action, under which actions of private parties that the state assists are ordinarily not attributed to the state,[82] cannot be squared with the constitutional distinctiveness of religion. When the state materially aids religious institutions, constitutional limitations on the character of the state must play a part in the form and content of such aid.

---

82. See the decisions cited *supra,* note 29.

PART II

Religion Inside Government

The view of the Establishment Clause that we have advanced thus far is focused on the character of government. At times, that character may be revealed by the relationship between government and religious institutions, discussed in Part I, or by the interactions between a sometimes responsive government and religiously motivated people, discussed in Part III. The character of government is revealed most sharply, however, in the messages and pronouncements of government itself. Some of these messages, such as the national motto or the Pledge of Allegiance, come from the government speaking as the government. Other messages may represent the view of agents of the government, ranging from public school teachers all the way to the president of the United States. At times, it is difficult to determine whether these agents are speaking for the government or only for themselves. Or, to put it in terms of our jurisdictional approach, it is sometimes difficult but always necessary to determine whether these agents are expressing their own religious character rather than attributing a religious identity to the state.

Our oldest and most persistent legal conflicts over government-sponsored religious messages emerge from the operation of public schools, and chapter 4 addresses that set of problems. Because children are legally compelled to attend school, and schools frequently engage in the enterprise of character formation, a public school's messages present an intriguing amalgam of rights-based and jurisdictional considerations. The paste only thickens when we recognize that students and others within the schools have their own rights to speak and exercise religion, and sometimes do so in ways that collide with the interests of others.

When government-sponsored religious messages appear elsewhere, the mix of rights claims and jurisdictional impediments that appears is usually quite different. Chapter 5 thus broadens the inquiry into more recent controversies provoked by government-sponsored religious messages in a wide variety of contexts other than the public schools. This is the stuff of front-page controversies over government-supported displays, including seasonal presentation of the symbols of religious holidays; permanent displays of the Ten Commandments, and of Latin crosses as war memorials; and government-sponsored prayer at gatherings of lawmakers and citizens. These kinds of disputes, where rights claims are weakest, have generated intensely divisive and difficult contexts in which to work out the relevant legal boundaries. Chapter 5 offers suggestions — substantive, remedial, and otherwise — for doing just that.

CHAPTER 4

Religious Expression in Public Schools

Historical as well as conceptual concerns motivate the choice to focus on religious expression in public schools before turning to other contexts in which government expresses its character. The rise of government-supported common schools in the nineteenth century produced the first pointed clashes over the religious content of public education (and, hence, over government-sponsored religious speech).[1] Moreover, the characteristics of religious exercises in public schools make this context an unusually rich one in which to observe the interaction of structurally based and rights-based conceptions of nonestablishment.

The rights-based narrative is easy — we are tempted to say too easy — to develop. For children up to the midteen years, attendance at school is compulsory. School-sponsored worship puts the state in competition with parents and guardians, who have their own rights to control the religious upbringing of their wards.[2] Even if children (or their parents, speaking for them) have the right to opt out of participation in religious exercises, the social pressure to conform is considerable, and schools have strong disincentives to make

1. For worthwhile accounts of the nineteenth-century conflicts, see Joan DelFattore, *The Fourth R: Conflicts over Religion in America's Public Schools* 12-60 (Yale University Press, 2004); Rosemary Salamone, *Visions of Schooling: Conscience, Community, and Common Education* 10-41 (Yale University Press, 2000). See also Ian Bartrum, *The Political Origins of Secular Public Education: The New York School Controversy, 1840-1842*, 3 NYU J. L. & Liberty 267 (2008).

2. *Pierce v. Society of Sisters*, 268 U.S. 510 (1925); *Meyer v. Nebraska*, 262 U.S. 390 (1923). See also *Wisconsin v. Yoder*, 406 U.S. 205 (1972) (Free Exercise Clause supports exemption from affirmative duty of parents to send children to accredited school until they reach age sixteen).

students aware of their rights.[3] In addition, school-sponsored religious exercises are frequently intended to have character-forming consequences, rather than a merely ritualistic effect. Complicating the picture further are the rights of students — and sometimes of teachers and other school personnel — to express their own religious convictions, rather than those of the government. All these rights-based considerations swirl about the subject of religious expression in public schools.

Since the middle of the nineteenth century, however, considerations of the government's character have played a role in the way such disputes have been understood. As close analysis will reveal, such considerations are at the core of these issues, and even more deeply at the center of such disputes in contexts (discussed in the ensuing chapter) other than public schools.

Historical Clashes over School-Sponsored Religious Exercises

Contemporary constitutional consciousness of the problem presented by school-sponsored religious exercises typically goes back no further than the school prayer cases of the early 1960s.[4] Those decisions were indeed a watershed, for reasons we will elaborate below. Political and legal conflicts in the United States over such exercises, however, date from more than a century earlier. And the political and religious origins of such disputes reveal their potential to implicate the deepest themes of nonestablishment.

As is so often true in the United States and elsewhere, and most especially in the relationship between religion and the state, diversity produces struggles for cultural dominance. The curriculum in the earliest common ("public") schools in the nineteenth century frequently emphasized themes of divine providence and individual morality typical of Protestantism,[5] and the reading materials in such schools frequently included the King James Bible rather than the Douay Bible used in Catholic churches.[6] Immigration

---

3. Students have such opt-out rights with respect to recitations of the Pledge of Allegiance; see *West Va. Bd. of Educ. v. Barnette,* 319 U.S. 624 (1943). But we suspect that teachers and other school officials rarely call attention to this, either out of ignorance, concern that disclosure of rights will be seen as encouragement for their exercise, or desire to avoid open divisiveness among students.

4. *Abington Sch. Dist. v. Schempp,* 374 U.S. 203 (1963); *Engel v. Vitale,* 370 U.S. 421 (1962).

5. Salamone, *supra* note 1, at 14-18; DelFattore, *supra* note 1, at 14-31 (describing conflicts in New York City).

6. DelFattore, *supra* note 1, at 21.

from Ireland and elsewhere had swelled the Catholic population of a number of urban centers, but Protestant majorities and their political leaders ignored complaints about the religious favoritism of these schools and rejected demands by Catholic leaders for public funds for a separate system of schools.[7]

Despite the eruption of open conflict, sometimes to the point of physical violence, in New York City, Philadelphia, and Boston in the mid–nineteenth century, authorities were unwilling to change these pro-Protestant practices.[8] Indeed, these practices were typically defended as nonsectarian, because virtually all Protestants could comfortably participate in them. It was Catholics who were perceived as "sectarian," a label that would stick in both law and culture for another century or more.[9]

Long before the Supreme Court explicitly ruled in the 1940s that the religion clauses of the First Amendment applied to states and localities,[10] the linked issues of public funding of religious education and government sponsorship of religious exercises in public schools rose to prominence on the national agenda. In the mid-1870s, the proposed Blaine Amendment, which would have explicitly applied the First Amendment's religion clauses to the states, had as its central focus a prohibition on public funding of "sectarian" (read "Catholic") schools.[11] But the debate over the Blaine Amendment also included a focus on religious exercises in public schools.[12] Although the amendment failed at the federal level, the political forces driving it remained a part of the nation's constitutional consciousness long thereafter.

Moreover, by the late nineteenth and early twentieth centuries, state courts had begun to adjudicate cases about compulsory religious exercises

7. For a more elaborate exposition of the "de facto Protestant establishment" in the early republic, see Mark DeWolfe Howe, *The Garden and the Wilderness: Religion and Government in American Constitutional History* (1965).

8. Salamone, *supra* note 1, at 18-23; DelFattore, *supra* note 1, at 14-51.

9. See chapter 2, on school funding disputes, for additional discussion of the label "sectarian" as a euphemism for Roman Catholic.

10. *Cantwell v. Connecticut*, 310 U.S. 296 (1940) (Free Exercise Clause applies to the states). Seven years later, in *Everson v. Bd. of Educ.*, 330 U.S. 1 (1947), the Court similarly held that the Establishment Clause applied to the states.

11. For a thorough account of the history of the Blaine Amendment, see Steven K. Green, *The Blaine Amendment Reconsidered,* 36 Amer. J. L. Hist. 38 (1992); Philip Hamburger, *Separation of Church and State* 287-334 (Harvard University Press, 2002).

12. Michael W. McConnell, John H. Garvey, and Thomas C. Berg, *Religion and the Constitution* 389 (Wolters Kluwer, 3rd ed., 2011) (noting that some versions of the Blaine Amendment affirmed that "this article shall not be construed to prohibit the reading of the Bible in any school or institution").

in the public schools. The supreme courts of Wisconsin and Illinois ruled that school-sponsored prayer and Bible reading violated their respective state constitutions;[13] the supreme court of Colorado ruled that the King James Bible was "nonsectarian" but that Catholic children could opt out of Bible reading exercises;[14] and the Ohio Supreme Court famously upheld the Cincinnati school board's decision to stop religious exercises in the public schools.[15]

As early as the 1920s, the Supreme Court began to impose significant constitutional limits on compulsory education. In *Pierce v. Society of Sisters*,[16] the Court invalidated an attempt by Oregon to require all children to attend the state's public schools. The opinion denied that the state had power to "standardize its children" and asserted that "the child is not the mere creature of the state."[17] Instead, those who "nurture him and direct his destiny" have the right and duty to "prepare him for additional obligations."[18] Here we see the early invocation of a jurisdictional theory of the sort advanced in chapter 1. The Court recognized that the family, and not the state, is the primary source of authority in the religious formation of children.

And in *West Virginia Board of Education v. Barnette*,[19] which in 1943 eliminated compulsory saluting of the American flag by children in the public schools, the Court took yet another dramatic step toward limiting any totalitarian pretensions of the state, even in a time of world war. Justice Jackson's most famous pronouncement in *Barnette* would echo twenty years later when the first school prayer case came before the Supreme Court: "If there is any fixed star in our constitutional constellation, it is that no official, high or petty, can prescribe what shall be orthodox in politics, nationalism, religion, or other matters of opinion or force citizens to confess by word or act their faith therein."[20] The language of *Barnette*'s operative prohibition — "no official . . . can . . . force citizens to confess by word or act their faith [in state-imposed orthodoxy]" — resonates powerfully with our thesis that the state lacks political authority over the subject of belief in a deity or other ultimate concern.

13. *State ex rel. Weiss v. Dist Bd., Sch. Dist. No. 8, City of Edgerton,* 76 Wis. 177 (1890); *Ring v. Board of Education,* 245 Ill. 334 (1910).

14. *Vollmar v. Stanley,* 255 P. 610 (Colo. 1927).

15. *Board of Education of Cincinnati v. Minor,* 23 Ohio St. 211 (1872).

16. *Pierce v. Society of Sisters,* 268 U.S. 510 (1925).

17. *Id.* at 535.

18. *Id.* at 535.

19. *West Virginia Board of Education v. Barnette,* 319 U.S. 624 (1943).

20. *Id.* at 642.

The School Prayer Cases

Engel v. Vitale (1962)[21] and *Abington School District v. Schempp* (1963)[22] are the two most famous Establishment Clause decisions in Supreme Court history. High school students studying American government or history are likely to learn of these decisions, and to appreciate that they represent a watershed in the American constitutional ethos.[23]

The long-simmering tensions between Protestants and Catholics over the financing and content of public education provide the oft-overlooked backdrop for the decisions.[24] Justice Black, who wrote for the Court in *Engel*, had also written the opinion fifteen years earlier in *Everson*, which had held that the Establishment Clause applies to the states and suggested firm limits on state power to provide financial assistance to religious schools. The combination of compulsory education, a ban on state funding of Catholic schools, and state-sponsored "nonsectarian" religious exercises in public schools represented a deeply unfair and divisive favoring of some faiths over others. If the state was not going to pay for Catholic schools, many of the justices realized, officially sanctioned Protestant prayer and devotional Bible reading in public schools had to go.

But *Engel* and *Abington* are about more than just favoritism for Protestants. On the surface, the two decisions are very different. *Engel* involved a simple monotheistic prayer, composed by the New York Board of Regents. The board intended the prayer to embrace as wide a range of beliefs as possible. Here is the prayer in its entirety: "Almighty God, we acknowledge our dependence upon Thee, and we beg Thy blessings upon us, our parents, our teachers and our Country."[25] The prayer was made available to school boards in New York State for exercises at the beginning of school, though many school boards did not use it. Parents who objected to having their children recite the prayer could have them excused, and the New York State courts upheld the exercise on the basis of that opt-out provision.[26] The New York

---

21. *Engel v. Vitale*, 370 U.S. 421 (1962).

22. *Abington School District v. Schempp*, 374 U.S. 203 (1963).

23. For a highly critical view of that watershed, see Steven D. Smith, *Constitutional Divide: The Transformative Significance of the School Prayer Decisions*, 38 Pepperdine L. Rev. 945 (2011).

24. See generally John C. Jeffries and James Ryan, *A Political History of the Establishment Clause*, 100 Mich. L. Rev. 279 (2001).

25. 370 U.S. at 422.

26. *Engel v. Vitale*, 176 N.E. 2d 579 (N.Y., 1961).

courts reasoned that the state was not coercing anyone to pray, and therefore respected religious liberty and voluntarism.

Justice Black refused to see the case in terms of the rights of students and their families. Instead, he focused on the role of state officials in writing the prayer, and saw that authorship as the core constitutional wrong. Drawing on the painful English history of struggles over the content of the *Book of Common Prayer*,[27] Black concluded that opt-out rights could not cure the constitutional flaws of the Regents' Prayer. The opinion is deceptively simple. It includes no overarching standard for judging Establishment Clause claims about state-sponsored speech or anything else. Instead, it asserts that state-sponsored prayer inevitably leads to "hatred [and] disrespect" from those who hold contrary beliefs, and that the Regents' Prayer cannot be saved by its intended denominational neutrality.[28]

The Court's opinion in *Abington,* on its facts and in the analytical approach taken by Justice Clark for the majority, has a very different feel. The Commonwealth of Pennsylvania had not authored any official prayers. Instead, state law required the reading of at least ten verses from the Bible each day. At Abington Senior High School, students chose and read these verses over the public address system, followed in turn by the Lord's Prayer and the Pledge of Allegiance.[29] Unlike *Engel,* the Court's opinion has a decidedly doctrinal character. It emphasizes the state's obligation to remain "neutral" on religious questions, in the sense of the state not putting its official support "behind the tenets of one or of all orthodoxies."[30] And it frames, for the first time, an Establishment Clause test: "[W]hat are the purpose and the primary effect of the enactment? If either is the advancement or inhibition of religion then the enactment [violates the constitution]."[31]

In hindsight, this proclamation of an Establishment Clause test for all seasons represented the Supreme Court losing its way. The test appears to condemn — without anything resembling adequate explanation — Thanksgiving Day proclamations, the national motto, and virtually all government-sponsored religious messages and symbols. Neither the country nor the Court was prepared for the full implications of such a test, and it has never been judicially applied with its full rigor. We will have much more to say about this in chapter 5.

Despite these differences in tone and approach, *Engel* and *Abington*

27. 370 U.S. at 425 *et seq.*
28. *Id.* at 431 *et seq.*
29. 374 U.S. at 205-208.
30. *Id.* at 222.
31. *Id.*

have far more in common than the setting of public schools and the question of the validity of a school-sponsored religious exercise. Both acknowledge the social pressure on students to participate, but both explicitly disclaim the necessity of coercion as an element of an Establishment Clause violation. These are not decisions about free exercise rights — rather, they are emphatically decisions about Establishment Clause duties.

Moreover, though the facts seem different, the undercurrents are identical — both cases involve conspicuous attempts by government to exploit a union of patriotism and religiosity. The Regents' Prayer does this by combining those themes in a single sentence — "we beg [God's] blessings upon us, our parents, our teachers and our Country." The Abington arrangement used the longer form — Bible reading, the Lord's Prayer, and the Pledge of Allegiance, which by 1963 had been amended to include the words "under God." Were students not instructed by this sequence to make connections among the God of the Pledge, the Lord of the Bible, and the Father whose name is hallowed in the Lord's Prayer? Of course, the principle in *Engel* and *Abington* does not require plaintiffs to show that the challenged religious exercise mixes religiosity and patriotism. All school-sponsored prayers are forbidden. But the facts of the two leading cases reinforce our central theme that the jurisdictional focus of nonestablishment norms is designed to limit the state's tendency to affiliate itself with divine authority.

A thought experiment may help illuminate the significance of the jurisdictional theory in the context of school prayer. Imagine a very small public school — an old-fashioned one-room schoolhouse, where all the children in a single, religiously homogeneous community receive their formal education. The school's principal desires to institute a daily prayer but wants to avoid any legal challenge. The principal develops a policy under which every family with a child in the school receives a card to return each morning to the school. The card reveals the proposed prayer, discloses fully the parents' right to object to the prayer, and allows parents to check a box for "prayer" or "no prayer." The children return the cards anonymously, and the policy offers iron-clad guarantees that no one in authority can or will know how any particular family responds. (Nor will the children know, unless their parents choose to disclose this information.) The teacher will lead the class in prayer only if, on a given day, every family whose child is in attendance checks "prayer." If only one family checks "no prayer," or returns a blank card or no card at all, the teacher will not recite the prayer. Under this scenario, the school will sponsor a prayer only if the family of each child has made a knowing and completely voluntary waiver of the right to object. Is that practice consistent with the Establishment Clause?

On a rights-based theory, it is hard to see why the school should not be free to proceed with this arrangement. Each family has the right to object, fully protected by a daily, risk-free opportunity to exercise the right. If all families knowingly and voluntarily waive that right, and affirmatively approve the prayer, the rights-based objection to the prayer vanishes altogether.

On a view of nonestablishment that emphasizes the government's character, however, the waiver process is completely ineffective and wholly irrelevant as a legal matter. The restrictions of the Establishment Clause bind the structures of government and those acting as its agents. Government may not align itself with divine authority. That proposition can be changed through the processes of constitutional amendment, but it may not be set aside by individual waivers.[32]

This understanding of the school prayer cases, though explicit in *Engel* and *Abington,* has tended to bleach out under the harsh light of developments — including an escalating and misplaced emphasis on coercion and individual rights — of the past forty-plus years. As the next few sections will show, restoring this understanding will clarify the appropriate resolution of many of the subsequent controversies over religious speech in schools. On the jurisdictional view, not all these cases have been correctly decided, and some are much easier than the 5-4 splits in the Supreme Court make them appear.

In the Wake of the School Prayer Cases

Three distinct categories of disputes arose in the wake of the school prayer cases of the early 1960s. The first involves the relationship between curricular decisions in public schools and issues of religious doctrine. Most of these disputes have been triggered by the question of teaching Darwinian evolution in

32. As we know from other constitutional contexts, structural restrictions in the Constitution may not be waived. Here, the most apt analogy may be the rule that parties cannot by silence or explicit waiver confer jurisdiction on the federal courts. See *Sosna v. Iowa,* 419 U.S. 393, 398 (1975); *Mitchell v. Maurer,* 293 U.S. 237, 244 (1934). The analysis would be conceptually identical, however, if both houses of Congress unanimously enacted and the president signed a bill making the Speaker of the House the commander in chief of the armed forces. The assignment of that power to the president is a matter of structure, and the assent of both the president and Congress cannot alter or reassign the authority that attaches to the relevant office. Similarly, Congress and the president cannot by mutual consent alter the Constitution's requirements of bicameralism and presentment. See *INS v. Chadha,* 462 U.S. 919 (1983) (overturning statutory grant of veto to one house of Congress); *Clinton v. New York,* 524 U.S. 417 (1998) (Congress may not authorize the president to change a law by exercising a line-item veto).

the public schools, but courses that purport to address the Bible as literature or the role of religion in history also may fall under this category. The second category of cases, which arose in the 1980s, involves state support for displays or activities that touch on religion but do not require students to recite or even listen to a state-prescribed form of worship. The third involves claims that the state must treat student-sponsored religious expression in public schools as well as it treats comparable secular communications. For important reasons, which we explore in Part III, this last set of claims is driven by concerns of freedom of speech and equality rather than religious liberty.

Religion and the Public School Curriculum

Ever since the Court's opinion in *Abington,* lawyers and scholars have echoed the standard mantra that public schools may teach about religion or the Bible "objectively as part of a secular program of education."[33] In *Abington,* Justice Clark's opinion explicitly distinguished such teaching, in history or literature, for example, from state-sponsored devotional religious exercises. *Abington,* however, prohibits far more than just those exercises. On *Abington's* juris- dictional account of the Establishment Clause, the public school curriculum may not advance, defend, or expressly challenge propositions that rest solely on religious doctrine.

That account helps make the best sense out of *Epperson v. Arkansas* (1968),[34] which struck down an Arkansas statute that made it unlawful "to teach the theory or doctrine that mankind ascended or descended from a lower order of animals."[35] The Arkansas law did not merely exclude a deli- cate or controversial subject, like sex education, from the curriculum.[36] The state did not prohibit teaching about the subject of human origins. Instead, it barred schools from teaching a specific, scientifically grounded theory of human origins.

Nor did the law merely accommodate the beliefs of parents who wanted their children to learn only the account of human origins embodied in a fun- damentalist Protestant interpretation of the book of Genesis, which we refer

33. 374 U.S. at 225.

34. *Epperson v. Arkansas,* 393 U.S. 97 (1968).

35. 393 U.S. at 98-99. For good discussions of *Epperson,* see Edward J. Larson, *Trial and Error* (Oxford University Press, 1985); Jay Wexler, *The Scopes Trope,* 93 Georgetown L. J. 1693 (2005).

36. 393 U.S. at 112-113 (Black, J., concurring).

to as "creationism."[37] The state could have made human biology a voluntary course, or allowed students to opt out of portions of the course that covered human origins. Instead, the state effectively barred schools from teaching evolution to all students, including those willing to learn it. As an accommodation, the law thus swept far too broadly, and burdened third parties whose religious interests were in no way threatened by an opportunity to study the science of animal biology, including the theory of evolution.[38]

Seen in this light, the law served no purpose other than to protect a particular account of religious truth against possible contradiction from science. Under a jurisdictional version of the Establishment Clause, that purpose is impermissible. If the state is limited to the realm of the material and temporal, it may not promote or defend a divinely revealed narrative of human origins. Such a narrative is, of course, best promoted affirmatively — by teaching creationism as scientific truth — but a religious truth claim can also be promoted by the second-best approach of protecting it against competing claims of scientific truth, including that arising from Darwinism.

This view of *Epperson* renders unquestionably correct the outcome in *Edwards v. Aguillard* (1987),[39] in which the Court struck down a Louisiana act requiring "balanced treatment for creation-science and evolution-science in public school instruction." The Louisiana law was designed to create a choice for the biology teachers in the state's public schools. These teachers could either stop teaching theories of evolution or give equal time to the evidence that animal species, including humans, had come into being at a time and within ways suggested by creationism.

As the Court in *Edwards* realized, professional teachers of science would find both options unpalatable. Very few teachers trained in the natural sciences would bring into their biology classes the "evidence" that many species of life had appeared on Earth only within the last five to six thousand years. These teachers would know that this "evidence" was not a product of scientific methods, which invite falsifiability by counterevidence, but was designed to promote a particular version of religious truth. Accordingly, teach-

---

37. We recognize that not all fundamentalists subscribe to the idea that the book of Genesis is a literally accurate account of human origins. See generally Peter J. Smith and Robert W. Tuttle, *Biblical Literalism and Constitutional Originalism*, 86 Notre Dame L. Rev. 693 (2011).

38. As we will discuss in chapter 7, religious accommodations that significantly burden third parties are a kind of forced subsidy, akin to compulsory tax support, payable by some to facilitate the religious experience of others.

39. *Edwards v. Aguillard*, 482 U.S. 578 (1987).

ers would tend to present no theory of human origins — precisely the result condemned by *Epperson* as driven by an effort to protect religious truths. Whether the law functioned to protect creationism against competition from theories of evolution, or to advance creationism by dressing it up in the normatively appealing garb of science, this regime put the state's curricular machinery behind a comprehensive religious doctrine about God's role in the origin of species.[40]

Other subjects for instruction in public schools may present problems more subtle than that associated with the stark struggle between evolution and creationism. One would hope and expect that a course in the history of Western civilization would address the role of Christianity in the rise of the nation-state system; religion as a potent source of inspiration, conflict, and persecution over many centuries; and the historical evolution of Islam, among other themes. Here, too, however, teachers should not be presenting or protecting religious truths, or taking a position on the religious merits of particular faith communities, in the guise of teaching the subject of history.

The Ten Commandments and Moments of Silence

To most casual observers of the Supreme Court's struggles with government support of religious symbols and messages, issues of state-sponsored displays of the Ten Commandments did not appear on the constitutional radar screen until 2005. In fact, the first case at the Court involving the Ten Commandments was *Stone v. Graham* (1981),[41] which invalidated a Kentucky statute that required a posting of "a durable, permanent copy of the Ten Commandments" on the wall of "each public elementary and secondary school classroom in the Commonwealth."[42] In a brief unsigned opinion, six justices concluded that the posting requirement lacked a secular purpose and therefore violated the Establishment Clause.

The Court's explanation was cursory, but the outcome seems correct.

---

40. The sweeping rejection by a federal district court in Pennsylvania of any support in the science curriculum of public schools for the theory of "intelligent design" as an account of human origins rests on similar conclusions about the religious premises of that theory. *Kitzmiller v. Dover Area School District*, 400 F. Supp. 2d 707 (M.D. Pa. 2005). See generally Frank S. Ravitch, *Marketing Creation: The Law and Intelligent Design* (2012).

41. *Stone v. Graham*, 449 U.S. 39 (1980).

42. *Id.* at 39, n. 1 (citing 1978 Ky. Acts, ch. 436, §1 [effective June 17, 1978], Ky. Rev. Stat. §158.178 [1980]).

The state attempted to distinguish the school prayer cases by pointing to two features of the statute. The law did not require — or even invite — students to recite the Commandments. Moreover, the law required each display to expressly assert that the Commandments have a legitimate secular status, because they have been adopted "as the fundamental legal code of Western civilization and the Common Law of the United States."[43] Of course, the Commandments include injunctions against murder, larceny, perjury, and other misdeeds that secular legal codes quite universally condemn. But they attribute these injunctions to God's revealed word and also include other precepts that cannot be justified or explained in secular terms (most obviously, the commandments to observe monotheism, refrain from taking the Lord's name in vain, abstain from the creation of graven images, and honor the Sabbath).[44]

If the appropriate Establishment Clause standard required official coercion of students, Kentucky's posting requirement would be unproblematic. The state forced no student to read, respect, recite, acknowledge, or believe any of the contents of the Ten Commandments. Through our jurisdictional lens, however, the case looks quite different. The claim that the Commandments had been adopted as the legal code of Western civilization and the common law of the United States lacks any historical justification or warrant.[45] Once we dismiss that claim of the historical relevance of the Commandments to the development of American law, what remain are (1) an unadorned claim by the state that the authority of some of its own civil law derives from divine command, not from the people of Kentucky; and (2) additional assertions by the state about the power of the God of the Bible as a source of governing norms for religious life. Under *Engel* and *Abington,* the state may not communicate these ideas to its schoolchildren.

By contrast, *Wallace v. Jaffree* (1985)[46] presented the much more difficult problem of the constitutionality of an Alabama statute authorizing public school teachers to set aside a period of silence "for meditation or voluntary prayer" at the beginning of the school day. The five-justice majority of the

43. *Id.*

44. The Commandments appear in Exodus 20:1-17 and Deuteronomy 5:4-21.

45. See generally Steven K. Green, *The Fount of Everything Just and Right? The Ten Commandments as a Source of American Law,* 13 Journal of Law and Religion 101 (2000).

46. *Wallace v. Jaffree,* 472 U.S. 38 (1985). We discuss the Supreme Court's leading decisions concerning displays of the Ten Commandments disconnected from the context of public schools, and the assertions that such displays are justified by an account of the historical development of American law, in chapter 5.

Supreme Court rested its judgment against the state on the narrow point that the relevant enactment in the case had explicitly authorized silent "prayer" as well as meditation, and accordingly had endorsed the idea of voluntary prayer in schools. Because a prior statute had authorized a moment of silence in the public schools, the Court concluded that this subsequent enactment lacked a secular purpose of its own.

Wallace seems to us to be wrongly decided. So long as the state does not sponsor any particular religious expression, the nonestablishment principle does not condemn an acknowledgment that some students will choose to pray silently during a moment of meditation. Such an acknowledgment is not an impermissible act of reverence by the state. Moreover, because the school prayer cases had thrown into doubt the legality of silent prayer in schools, the Alabama statute could sensibly have been viewed as an attempt to clarify that students were free to pray during the moment of silence. Perhaps some members of the Court saw the Alabama statute as a hostile response to the school prayer cases, and perhaps it was just that as a political matter within the Alabama state legislature. But seeking political credit for acknowledging religious practice and belief is not an unconstitutional motivation for action. Most importantly, the state's action did not put the authority of the state behind a deity, or otherwise claim religious authority for the state.

Wallace seems of a piece with *Aguilar v. Felton,*[47] a case from the same term, discussed in the previous chapter. Both represent an approach to church-state separation that has lost touch with any inner logic. When the state promotes a religious belief, or the superiority of a religious life over an irreligious one, it has crossed the Constitution's jurisdictional boundary. By contrast, when the state acknowledges that some of its citizens (for themselves or their children) value a religious life, the government may be appropriately responding to the religious impulses and practices of its people.

Decisions like *Wallace* had predictable social consequences. The decision could easily be perceived, by both its supporters and its critics, as hostile to religious impulses in American public life. What began to emerge from that clash of sensibilities, which ripened in the years of the Reagan presidency, was a deliberate framing by conservative social forces of a counterstory, in which American religiosity was portrayed — sometimes accurately — as a victim of official discrimination.

---

47. *Aguilar v. Felton,* 473 U.S. 402 (1985), *overruled,* Agostini v. Felton, 521 U.S. 203 (1997).

Claims of Equal Access

As we described in chapter 1, the jurisdictional account of the nonestablishment principle did not take firm hold of American constitutional consciousness. Because the school prayer cases seemed so driven by the special context
of compulsory education of minors, those decisions were easily and readily understood in the popular culture as being about parents' and children's
rights to be free from unwanted religious experience in the public schools.
This sensibility was quietly but firmly reinforced by decisions like *Marsh v.
Chambers* (1983),[48] upholding a practice of prayer by a state legislative chaplain, and *Lynch v. Donnelly* (1984),[49] which rejected a constitutional attack
on the inclusion of a nativity scene in a city-sponsored Christmas display. If
government is free to sponsor religious messages outside the context of public schools, it would seem perfectly logical to conclude that the prohibition on
school-sponsored prayer is entirely about coercion of children.

A thoroughly rights-focused view of the school prayer cases can both
expand the decisions' ambit in schools and shrink their scope elsewhere.
Some school administrators demonstrated the expansionist tendency
through efforts to make the public schools a religion-free zone. At its extreme,
this meant excluding various forms of student-initiated, private religious expression from various public school contexts. Those determined to protect
the rights of students seized on particularly vivid examples of this kind of
exclusion, such as that involving the middle school student whose teacher
refused to accept her essay about the life of Jesus as an exercise in biographi-
cal writing.[50] And, at times, administrators' efforts to bar religious expression
from public schools took the stronger form of official policy, including the
exclusion of student religious groups from the roster of organizations eligible
for school sponsorship.

Eventually, advocates for student religious organizations challenged
school officials who excluded such groups. The first case of this variety to
reach the Supreme Court was *Widmar v. Vincent*,[51] which involved a decision
by the University of Missouri (Kansas City) to exclude Cornerstone, an organization of evangelical Christians, from meeting on campus. Unsurprisingly,

---

48. *Marsh v. Chambers,* 463 U.S. 783 (1983).

49. *Lynch v. Donnelly,* 465 U.S. 668 (1984).

50. *Settle v. Dickson,* 53 F. 3d 152 (6th Cir. 1995) (upholding decision by teacher and
school to exclude the essay on grounds of its inconsistency with prescribed guidelines for
research and writing).

51. *Widmar v. Vincent,* 454 U.S. 263 (1981).

the Court ruled (8-1) that because the university had opened its facilities to a very wide range of student organizations, it had created a "public forum" for speech and association. Accordingly, the university's exclusion of Cornerstone represented impermissible discrimination against the group based on the content of its speech. Any religious expression was attributable to Cornerstone and its members, not to the state. Because the state is not responsible for the content of the speech, the Establishment Clause does not apply. The question of state responsibility for the content of speech is very important and sometimes quite difficult, but that issue was simple and straightforward on the facts of *Widmar.*

Despite the Court's decision in *Widmar,* a significant number of school administrators continued to believe that the school prayer cases represented a sweeping constitutional prohibition on "prayer in public schools," whether or not the government was responsible for the religious expression. On a rights-oriented view of the school prayer cases, that belief was not implausible. Unlike university students, elementary and most secondary school students are minors, and compelled to attend school. In that respect, students represent a "captive audience" for religious expression, whether the messages are delivered by teachers or by classmates. Accordingly, some administrators refused to permit student religious clubs, akin to Cornerstone, to meet during school activity periods when other student organizations were free to meet. Ultimately, in *Bender v. Williamsport School District,*[52] the U.S. Court of Appeals for the Third Circuit upheld such an administrative decision.

The U.S. Congress responded to court decisions like *Bender* by passing the Equal Access Act,[53] which forbids all public secondary schools that receive federal funds and permit noncurricular student groups to meet on school property from excluding any such group based on its religious or political character. In *Westside Board of Education v. Mergens,*[54] the Supreme Court upheld the act against the board's assertion that it violated the Establishment Clause to permit a Christian club, whose student members would read the Bible and worship together, to meet on school premises.

Although the Court voted 8-1 to reject the Establishment Clause defense offered by the Westside Board, justices were significantly divided on how to approach the question. Justice O'Connor's opinion asserted, in an oft-

52. *Bender v. Williamsport School District,* 741 F. 2d 538 (3rd Cir. 1984), *appeal dismissed for lack of appellant's standing,* 475 U.S. 534 (1986).
53. 20 U.S.C. sec. 4071.
54. *Westside Board of Education v. Mergens,* 496 U.S. 226 (1990).

quoted phrase, "[T]here is a crucial difference between *government* speech endorsing religion, which the Establishment Clause forbids, and *private* speech endorsing religion, which the Free Speech and Free Exercise Clauses protect."[55] But the portion of the opinion in which this idea appears received only four votes. Justices Kennedy and Scalia did not join it, not because they rejected the government-private speech distinction, but because they rejected the endorsement test as applied to government speech.[56] And Justices Brennan and Marshall did not join this part of the opinion, because they saw the milieu of high school as profoundly different from that of college. Brennan and Marshall believed that the school must take special steps to distance itself from a student religious group and thereby avoid any misperception that the school endorsed its religious message.[57]

Thus, the fact that eight justices agreed in the result in *Mergens* masked profound internal disagreement on the Court about religious speech in public schools. One faction, which Justice Thomas would ultimately join when he took a seat on the Court a year later, took the narrowest, rights-oriented view of the school prayer cases, and understood them as being entirely about coercion of students. A middle group, led by O'Connor, focused on state endorsement as the central question, and presumed that responsibility for the content of the speech, not just its setting, was the key to decision. Yet a third faction urged special sensitivity to the potential that students would mistakenly believe that the state endorsed religious beliefs, and thus feel official or peer pressure to participate.

Lee v. Weisman — Graduation Prayer and the Move of Coercion to Center Stage

The mixture of the school prayer cases, uncertain signals from the Supreme Court about state-sponsored religious messages, and legal pressure to give equal treatment to private religious expression in public schools eventually produced the perfect storm. In *Lee v. Weisman*,[58] the Court considered a challenge to prayer at a public school commencement exercise in Providence, Rhode Island.

55. *Id.* at 250.
56. *Id.* at 261 (Kennedy, J., joined by Scalia, J., concurring in part and concurring in the judgment).
57. *Id.* at 262-270 (Marshall., J., joined by Brennan, J., concurring in the judgment).
58. *Lee v. Weisman*, 505 U.S. 577 (1992).

Lee represents a crossover point, not widely noticed, in school prayer litigation. The decisions from the 1960s involved daily religious exercises, with attendant repetition of religious themes, pressure to participate, and persistent burden on the religious autonomy and privacy of those who chose not to participate. In contrast, prayer at commencement is a highly infrequent experience, in a social context in which ceremonial prayer is quite common. After the Providence School Board lost in the U.S. Court of Appeals, the litigation quickly took on the trappings of a "movement" case for conservatives, who were focused on limiting or rolling back the strictures of the school prayer cases. The city of Providence hired Charles Cooper, a former political appointee in the Reagan Justice Department, to represent it in the Supreme Court. Cooper's advocacy stressed a narrow, rights-oriented view of nonestablishment. Religious coercion, he argued, was a necessary element of an Establishment Clause violation, and no such coercion infected the enterprise of ceremonial prayer at commencement.[59]

Cooper's argument nearly succeeded. As we discussed in chapter 1, Justice Kennedy's opinion for a five-justice majority appeared to accept the argument that coercion was indeed a necessary component of such a violation.[60] But his opinion also accepted the idea, hotly contested, that middle school or public school commencements represented coercive settings. Objecting students would be unwilling to skip graduation in order to avoid a prayer, or to remain seated while others stood in respectful silence while the prayer was being uttered.[61] *Lee* thus establishes, at least for minors, a very low threshold of what constitutes coercion. Although Kennedy focused primarily on coercion, he also emphasized factors relevant only in a jurisdictional theory — for example, the official invitation to a clergyman to lead the prayer, and the instructions given by the school to the clergyman who agreed to do so.[62] These elements had nothing to do with the prayer's coercive quality, but nevertheless played an important role in the judicial narrative and disposition of the case.

Justice Scalia's dissent in *Lee* was biting and powerful.[63] He emphasized all the themes that would narrow the ambit of the Establishment Clause —

59. See transcript of oral argument in *Lee v. Weisman,* available at http://www.oyez .org/cases/1990-1999/1991/1991_90_1014/argument.
60. 505 U.S. at 593-596.
61. 505 U.S. at 593-596.
62. 505 U.S. at 586-592.
63. 505 U.S. at 631-646 (Scalia, J., joined by Rehnquist, CJ., and White and Thomas, JJ., dissenting).

foremost, that those who claim a violation of the clause must show overt state coercion, such as official punishment for refusal to stand for the prayer. Recall that *Engel* and *Abington* had said precisely the opposite — that a showing of coercion, however weak or strong, was *not* necessary to demonstrate a breach of the Establishment Clause. Beyond that, Scalia emphasized the majority's countervailing right to celebrate graduation with a ceremonial invocation, if that is the choice of the community.

Because its premises were both unsteady and in tension with the school prayer cases, *Lee v. Weisman* generated litigation in ways that the school prayer cases never had. The latter were very clean-cut in their constitutional imperative. Public schools could sponsor no daily religious exercises. No doubt, some school systems — defiantly or quietly — continued to do so after 1963, but litigation on the subject was relatively rare. By contrast, *Lee v. Weisman* ushered in a period of turmoil, as school administrators and lawyers struggled to determine the parameters of the relevant constitutional norm.

Lee is a Rorschach test. On one view, it may ultimately represent a significantly narrowed view of the Establishment Clause. If coerced participation in religious exercises is indeed a necessary element of a constitutional violation, many otherwise questionable practices in public schools should raise no problem. For example, suppose a public school offers an elective course in Bible studies, taught from a particular religious perspective. Participation would be entirely voluntary, hence noncoercive and in no conflict with the Constitution.

Alternatively, one might read *Lee* to broaden considerably the ambit of the school prayer cases. If the relevant concept of coercion extends to any source of social pressure on a captive audience of children within the school, then all forms of student-initiated religious proselytizing and organizing raise Establishment Clause questions, even if the school takes an entirely passive role in the conduct.

Yet a third, middle way of reading *Lee* is also possible. If school sponsorship of the religious exercise is a necessary element of any constitutional violation, then privately initiated religious speech by students — at commencement exercises or otherwise — might not present a constitutional problem, regardless of the social or psychological pressures it may generate.[64]

64. On any of these interpretations of *Lee,* one is left with questions about the coercion variable. For example, is state-sponsored ceremonial prayer unconstitutional at state university commencements (see *Tanford v. Brand,* 104 F. 3d 982 [7th Cir. 1997], which upheld school-sponsored prayer at university commencement), gatherings of members of the armed forces (see Ira C. Lupu and Robert W. Tuttle, *Instruments of Accommodation: The Military*

In the wake of *Lee v. Weisman,* which substantially muddied the waters of Establishment Clause theory, conflict and litigation became widespread. A wide range of organizations produced guidelines and advice for school administrators caught in the middle of this particular culture war cross fire.[65] Civil liberties groups on both sides of that war mobilized resources to help embattled parties. Groups on the left supported those who challenged religious expression in schools and the administrators who opposed such expression;[66] groups on the right supported those who sought to engage in religious expression in schools and the administrators who promoted or defended that expression.[67] With lawyers coming at them from both left and right, it was small wonder that administrators sought guidance, and even less wonder that they felt trapped no matter what decision they made.

Public Duties versus Private Rights — Attributing Responsibility for the Message

As the law developed, it increasingly focused on the "crucial difference between *government* speech endorsing religion, which the Establishment Clause forbids, and *private* speech endorsing religion, which the Free Speech and Free Exercise Clauses protect."[68] This approach framed the relevant question in terms of competing private rights — the right to be free of government-sponsored religious messages versus the right to engage in private worship, proselytizing, or religious association. The next major case in the Supreme

---

Chaplaincy and the Constitution, 110 W. Va. L. Rev. 89 [2007]), or other public settings in which such religious expression is commonplace? We discuss in chapter 5 the more general question of the validity of state-sponsored ceremonial prayer in settings outside of elementary and secondary public schools.

65. See, e.g., Charles C. Haynes and Oliver Thomas, *Finding Common Ground* (Freedom Forum First Amendment Center, 1994). The U.S. Department of Education has promulgated regulations on aspects of this subject for all federally funded elementary and secondary schools. See "Guidance on Constitutionally Protected Prayer in Public Elementary and Secondary Schools," Feb. 7, 2003, available at http://www2.ed.gov/policy/gen/guid/religionandschools/prayer_guidance.html.

66. The principal players on this side are the ACLU Program on Religious Freedom and Belief, Americans United for Separation of Church and State, and the Freedom from Religion Foundation.

67. The principal players on this side of the disputes are the American Center for Law and Justice, the Alliance Defense Fund, and the Becket Fund.

68. *Westside Board of Education v. Mergens,* 496 U.S. at 250.

Court about "prayer in school," a challenge to the practice of pregame prayer by students at public high school football games, perfectly illuminated this frame. Was this school-sponsored prayer, from which students had the right to be free, or student-initiated prayer, in which students had the right to engage? That was the question put to the Court in *Santa Fe Independent School District v. Doe* (2000).[69]

At the threshold, this is the correct constitutional inquiry. If the Establishment Clause is a jurisdictional limit on the state's power to affiliate itself with religious authority, attributing the fully private speech of some students to the state is misplaced. That some students want to worship or spread God's word at school does not present the dangers at which the clause is aimed. Instead, those activities represent the students' constitutionally protected conduct.

Of course, aggressive religious proselytizing in a school can develop into a form of harassment.[70] Children should have the right to be free of unwanted religious entreaties, in precisely the same way they have the right to be free of unwanted sexual attention. Where an audience is captive, its members have a right to resist and reject unwanted speech. But antiharassment rules should be religion-neutral, and their scope and enforcement are primarily a matter of administrative discretion, bounded by the speech rights of those doing the proselytizing.[71] The Free Exercise Clause adds nothing to those private rights of free speech,[72] and the Establishment Clause subtracts nothing from those rights.[73]

School-sponsored religious activities, however, trigger nonestablishment norms, which are religion-specific. So the opening question in many school-based Establishment Clause cases is whether the government or a private party is responsible for the challenged expression. The Establishment Clause applies only if the challenged speech is properly attributable to the government.[74]

69. *Santa Fe Independent School District v. Doe,* 530 U.S. 290 (2000).

70. In *The Good News Club: The Christian Right's Stealth Assault on America's Children* (PublicAffairs, 2012), Katherine Stewart argues that the rise of evangelical Christian clubs at the elementary school level has made such harassment commonplace.

71. For the Supreme Court's most recent exposition of those rights, see *Morse v. Frederick,* 551 U.S. 393 (2007).

72. See chapter 6 for a discussion of the significant overlap in rights between the Free Speech Clause and the Free Exercise Clause.

73. See *Capitol Square Review and Advisory Board v. Pinette,* 515 U.S. 753 (1995) (private speech in a public forum on government property is not limited by the Establishment Clause).

74. See *Pleasant Grove City v. Summum,* 555 U.S. 460 (2009). The most comprehensive

The facts of *Santa Fe Independent School District v. Doe* easily placed the challenged speech on the government side of that line. The background atmosphere in the school was hostile to virtually anyone who was not a member of the evangelical Christian community.[75] Teachers as well as students had been disrespectful of Mormons and Roman Catholics. Out of fear of reprisal, the plaintiffs successfully asked to litigate anonymously (hence the "Doe" designation). School officials had persistently and aggressively tried to maintain their preexisting practices of prayer, at commencement and at high school football games, in the face of court orders to the contrary. The policy ultimately struck down by the courts, including the Supreme Court, involved a school-sponsored student election on the question of whether football games should be preceded by an "invocation" over the public address system, followed by a student election of the student spokesperson to deliver the invocation. Neither the written policy nor its background left any doubt that the "invocation" would be in the form of a prayer. Indeed, the school district had enacted a "fallback policy" that the invocation must be "nonsectarian and nonproselytizing" only if the courts enjoined the district's preferred policy, which would have imposed no such limitation, and hence would have permitted prayer in the name of Jesus.[76]

The six-justice majority in *Santa Fe* found the district responsible for the content of the pregame invocations, and determined that the invocation policy violated the Establishment Clause. But the themes that had pushed *Lee v. Weisman* toward a rights-based analytical model surfaced in *Santa Fe* as well. Justice Stevens's opinion emphasized the coercion associated with pregame prayer. Football players, cheerleaders, band members, and students who just wanted to join their classmates under the Friday night lights were forced to listen to the prayer as a condition of participation.[77]

However sociologically and psychologically real these coercive pres-

---

academic work on the problem of attributing Establishment Clause responsibility for speech includes Claudia Haupt, *Mixed Public-Private Speech and the Establishment Clause,* 85 Tulane L. Rev. 571 (2011); Mary Jean Dolan, *Government Identity Speech and Religion: Establishment Clause Limits after Summum,* 19 William & Mary Bill of Rights L. J. 1 (2010); Caroline Maia Corbin, *Mixed Speech: When Speech Is Both Private and Governmental,* 83 NYU L. Rev. 605 (2008).

75. The facts in the paragraph are recited in the opinion of the 5th Circuit Court of Appeals in *Santa Fe Ind. Sch. Dist. v. Doe,* 168 F. 3d 806, 809-811 (5th Cir. 1999). See also 530 U.S. at 294, n. 1 (quoting the district court's order to all in the community to stop trying to ferret out the plaintiffs' identity in order to harass and intimidate them).

76. *Santa Fe Independent School District v. Doe,* 530 U.S. at 297-298.

77. 530 U.S. at 311-313.

sures may have been, a jurisdictional theory makes them irrelevant. For reasons we have developed in this work, unanimous community consent to the pregame prayers would not be sufficient to validate them. In contrast, pregame prayer led by the football team's captain, voluntarily accompanied by teammates who chose to engage in that practice, would be a protected exercise of religious freedom, even if it left some teammates feeling uncomfortable and excluded. And the football coach, obviously an agent of the school in that pregame moment, is constitutionally obliged to remain officially indifferent to the prayer — neither joining in it nor demonstrating hostility toward those who do or don't participate.[78]

Our approach to the issue of religious expression in the public schools illuminates the perennial controversy about religious content in speeches by students, valedictorians or otherwise, at public school commencements.[79] As applied to this issue, the rhetoric of rights tends to get trapped between the rights of students to speak and the rights of others not to be forced to hear religious messages at public ceremonies. The jurisdictional view focuses not on the competing rights, but rather on the question of official responsibility for the content of student remarks.

At the extremes, these cases are easy. If school officials provide student speakers with no substantive limits on content, the state is not responsible for that content. And if school officials require students to include a prayer, or affirmatively collude with students to include a prayer, the Establishment Clause constraints of *Lee* and *Santa Fe* are triggered. Cases between these extremes, however, are more difficult. For example, what if school administrators instruct students that commencement speeches must be "appropriate to the occasion"? What if administrators review the text of student speeches in advance to be sure that they are "appropriate to the occasion"? Do such practices render the school responsible for any religious content that appears in the speech?

In these ambiguous circumstances, we are inclined to recognize a significant degree of official discretion. Administrators fearful of litigation and community upset should be free to discourage or forbid religious content in

78. See *Borden v. Sch. Dist., Township of East Brunswick*, 523 F. 3d 1353 (3rd Cir. 2008) (in order to prevent a likely violation of the Establishment Clause, school district may bar public high school football coach from any form of participation in pregame prayer by members of the school's football team).

79. See, e.g., *Jones v. Clear Creek Ind. Sch. Dist.*, 977 F. 2d 963 (5th Cir. 1992); *Adler v. Duval County Sch. Bd.*, 112 F. 3d 1475 (11th Cir. 1997); *ACLU v. Black Horse Pike Regional Bd. of Education*, 84 F. 3d 1471 (3rd Cir. 1996) (en banc).

student speeches, just as they may forbid vulgar remarks, insults to teachers and fellow students, and politically controversial assertions. A commencement is not a "public forum" for speech, so student speakers do not have a right to express a religious viewpoint. But student speech should not be reflexively attributed to the state, even when the state imposes general criteria such as occasion-specific appropriateness. Accordingly, the provision of such criteria in advance, or even the application of such criteria to the speech prior to its delivery, does not make the state responsible for its content.

Thus, an administrator's failure to remove a prayer or religious reference from a speech by a student at commencement does not make the state constitutionally responsible for the content of the speech. Establishment Clause principles do not protect an audience from hearing a prayer, or from a misperception (however reasonable) of the authorship of a message. Instead, the Establishment Clause protects against efforts by the government to associate itself with, or claim for itself, religious authority. When a student speaker, independently and voluntarily, invokes claims about the role and authority of God, the student is not making those assertions on the state's behalf, even if they are being made at a state-sponsored event.

Similar concerns about rights, responsibilities, and discretion are raised by questions about the freedom of public school teachers to express their own religiosity to their students. At the poles, these cases too are simple. On their own time and away from their place of employment, teachers have full rights under the Free Exercise Clause and the free speech clause to live, practice, and communicate their faith. In contrast, when acting as agents for their public employers, teachers must scrupulously respect Establishment Clause limitations on the state's authority to indoctrinate students in religious faith, because the official actions of teachers are fully and appropriately attributed to the state.[80]

80. The current controversy in many European countries about veiled Muslim women represents an echo of similar conflicts in the United States over the identifiable dress of Catholic priests and members of Catholic religious orders. For a trenchant essay on the problem, see Martha Nussbaum, *Veiled Threats,* New York Times Opinionator (online), July 11, 2010, available at http://opinionator.blogs.nytimes.com/2010/07/11/veiled-threats/. In the past, several American states prohibited public school teachers from wearing any full-dress religious garb. In 1923, for example, Oregon enacted a statute forbidding public school teachers from wearing religious garb in a public school classroom. The state courts upheld this law against constitutional challenge. (See *Cooper v. Eugene Sch. Dist. No. 41,* 301 Ore. 358 [1981]. In the spring of 2010, the Oregon legislature finally repealed the law. Press Release, Northwest Religious Liberty Association, April 2, 2010, available at http://www.nrla.com/article.php?id=86. For discussion of decisions from the European Court of Human Rights on similar issues,

Between these poles, however, lie a number of situations in which questions of attribution are more difficult. Because teachers, while on the job, are agents of the school system, public school administrators need discretionary space in which to manage the tensions between accommodating the religious freedom of teachers and avoiding situations that present risks of Establishment Clause litigation and liability. For example, in *Roberts v. Madigan* (1990),[81] the Tenth Circuit correctly rejected a lawsuit by Roberts, a fifth-grade teacher in Denver, Colorado, who had been instructed by his principal Madigan to keep his Bible (from which he read during silent reading time in the school day) out of sight during classroom hours; to take down a classroom wall poster that read "You have only to open your eyes to see the hand of God"; and to remove two books on Christianity from his personal library collection, available for student borrowing, in the classroom. No one had accused the teacher of improper proselytizing, but, in these cumulative circumstances — including some expressions of concern by parents — the principal did not need to await a court order to take steps that would avoid the risk of violating the Establishment Clause. Roberts's rights to pursue his faith outside the classroom remained fully respected.

The case of *Wigg v. Sioux Falls School District 49-5*,[82] decided by the Eighth Circuit in 2004, presented a closer question. The school district permitted the Good News Club, an evangelical Christian organization that provides after-school programs for young children, to offer classes in the district's elementary schools. But it barred teachers employed by the district from leading the club's programs in any of the district's public schools. Barbara Wigg, a public elementary school teacher who wished to teach in Good News Club programs that began just as the school day ended, challenged the prohibition on First Amendment grounds. A federal district court upheld the policy as applied to the school where a teacher was employed during school hours, but

see Claudia Haupt, *Transnational Establishment*, 80 Geo. Wash. L. Rev. 991 (2012].) Although the statutory language of the bans on teachers' religious apparel appeared to treat all faiths equally, there was little doubt that these enactments were aimed at keeping Catholic religious personnel from teaching in the public schools. Like those American enactments, the European proposals are not neutral among faiths — indeed, the European efforts make little or no effort to be seen as religion-neutral. In the context of public schools, these kinds of dress codes are fairly characterized as religious discrimination, barred by religious liberty and equality norms, rather than as an attempt to further nonestablishment concerns. Religious garb may invite questions, but wearing it cannot be seen in and of itself as an act of proselytizing.

81. *Roberts v. Madigan*, 921 F. 2d 1047 (10th Cir. 1990), *cert. denied*, 505 U.S. 1218 (1992).
82. *Wigg v. Sioux Falls School District 49-5*, 382 F. 3d 807 (8th Cir. 2004).

struck it down as applied to all schools at which a particular teacher was not employed during the school day.[83] The Eighth Circuit more sweepingly invalidated the entire policy, on the ground that the Good News Club programs took place after hours, and that the district therefore had no Establishment Clause–related interest in restricting Ms. Wigg's participation, regardless of where she taught during the school day.[84]

On the facts and circumstances in *Wigg,* we are inclined to say that the district court got this one right. The staff hours at the school where Barbara Wigg taught ran from 7:30 A.M. to 3:30 P.M. Students were dismissed at 3:00, and the Good News Club program ran from 3:00 until 4:00. Several students from Ms. Wigg's combined second- and third-grade class attended the Good News Club sessions at the same school. We are no fans of the Supreme Court's endorsement test, and its emphasis on what reasonable observers may perceive, but in this case it seems inevitable that eight- and nine-year-old children would be unable to distinguish their religious instruction at the Good News Club from the rest of their learning experience in the public schools. If Ms. Wigg led Good News Club sessions anywhere but the school at which she taught, this association would not be nearly so strong.

We recognize that the close overlap between regular school hours and Good News Club hours may have made it impossible for any teacher to get to another school in time to do both kinds of teaching. Public school teachers certainly have a general right to engage in religious teaching on their own time and in private space, but in this situation Ms. Wigg was not entirely on her own time or in private space. More generally, teachers have no right to advance their own religious convictions in circumstances that significantly compromise the state's Establishment Clause responsibilities.

Conclusion

As we reflect on the material relevant to school-sponsored religious exercise, it is not difficult to see why the questions are tumultuous. The school prayer cases provided a necessary companion to a constitutional policy of no-aid to religious schools. And the milieu in which they developed suggested a perfect mesh between jurisdictional concerns about the state's authority and rights-based concerns about religious coercion of impressionable minors. But the

83. *Wigg v. Sioux Falls School District 49-5,* 274 F. Supp. 2d 1084 (D.S.D. 2003).
84. 382 F. 3d at 812-816.

connection between school prayer and public aid to religious schools has receded in the face of demographic and doctrinal change, and the jurisdictional focus on the scope of state authority has been the subject of harsh and persistent cultural attack. The far narrower theme of anticoercion is what remains most vibrant and readily comprehensible among the American people.

A focus on voluntary participation in religious activities, rather than official authority to sponsor them, has profound implications. Outside the context of schools, state-sponsored religious messages are far less vulnerable to an anticoercion focus. Questions concerning the validity of such messages thus present a harder and cleaner test of our thesis about the constitutional mandate of a government with a secular character for a religious people. Accordingly, the next chapter faces up to those questions. Does the Constitution demand that the United States government refrain from official proclamation of trust in God, no matter the extent to which our people continue to do so?

CHAPTER 5

Religious Expression in the Public Square

Once we turn our attention away from public schools, a purely jurisdictional theory of the Establishment Clause faces more difficult questions. In the school setting, the jurisdictional theory is frequently reinforced by a rights-based approach. The targets of any government-sponsored religious expression there are impressionable minors, present by compulsion, subject to peer pressure, objects of state-directed character formation, and under the primary religious influence of their parents or guardians. Every one of those characteristics helps buttress a rights-based objection to state-sponsored religious exercise in public schools.

Away from that setting, most or all of these conditions shrink or disappear. Government-sponsored religious expression typically addresses adults, who are voluntarily present, religiously autonomous, and typically not the direct objects of state-directed character formation. Adults who encounter unwanted religious messages, state-sponsored or otherwise, can usually just avert their eyes and ears. What is the constitutional problem presented by such messages, when sponsored by the state?

If the Establishment Clause protects no more than the right to be free from religious coercion, the answer may well be that these messages present no constitutional problem at all. By contrast, a jurisdictional theory, designed to limit the character of the state, must grapple more broadly with the question of forbidden expression. The list of official messages that appear problematic under a jurisdictional theory is very long, and includes some very familiar items. The Pledge of Allegiance, the national motto (In God We Trust), the prayers spoken by legislative chaplains,[1] the naming of American cities after saints or other reli-

---

1. See *Marsh v. Chambers*, 463 U.S. 783 (1983).

gious icons, presidential Thanksgiving proclamations, a congressionally declared National Day of Prayer, the Supreme Court crier's call of "God save the United States and this Honorable Court" — all these and more are drawn into presumptive constitutional doubt by our jurisdictional theory of nonestablishment.

This long and familiar list reflects the historical role of religion in American public life. At the time of the framing of the Constitution and Bill of Rights, government-sponsored messages containing religious themes were abundant and noncontroversial. Indeed, the political rhetoric of that generation was replete with references to a divine Providence who superintends us all. For example, Thomas Jefferson's Bill to Establish Religious Freedom in Virginia,[2] which forbids the state from coercing anyone to attend or materially support any enterprise of religious worship, begins with an explicit reference to an "almighty God" who has "created the mind free," and invokes the "plan of the holy author of our religion" to act through the faculty of human reason rather than through coercion of the body or mind.[3]

The founding generation was highly aware of the horrendous history of religious coercion, so it's hardly a surprise that the Founders were primarily concerned with eliminating that coercion. And constitutional controversy and litigation in the nineteenth century, as well as in the first three-fourths of the twentieth century, focused on state financial support for religious schools and coercive religious exercises in the public schools.

The Supreme Court did not confront the Establishment Clause problems presented by government-sponsored religious messages in noncoercive environments until the early 1980s. Since that time, the Court has decided a handful of these cases, but each decision has been marked by deep uncertainty about the appropriate legal principles. Without the anchoring base of a concern for coercion, and in the face of an elaborate history of governmental acknowledgments of God, the courts have found it very difficult to conceptualize the grounds from which to reason about Establishment Clause limitations. As this chapter will highlight, this line of decisions has been characterized by (1) uncertainty about the relevant constitutional injury; (2) concern about the hazard of unsettling long-standing practices; (3) uneasiness about potentially arbitrary line-drawing; and (4) worry about the appearance of judicial hostility to religion. We hope to offer paths out of this crippling anxiety.

2. Merrill D. Peterson, ed., *Thomas Jefferson: Writings* 347 (Library of America, 1984).
3. For discussion of the significance of this oft-overlooked feature of the Virginia bill, see Steven D. Smith, *The Rise and Fall of Religious Freedom in Constitutional Discourse*, 140 U. Pa. L. Rev. 149, 161-166 (1991).

The Supreme Court and Religious Displays — the Legacy of a Bad Start

One might have expected from the fiery separationist rhetoric in *Everson* (1947)[4] that federal courts would have immediately confronted lawsuits over religious displays. The school prayer cases of the early 1960s certainly seemed to invite such litigation. But it was not until the challenge to state legislative prayer in 1983 in *Marsh v. Chambers*[5] and to a city-sponsored nativity scene in 1984 in *Lynch v. Donnelly*[6] — almost two centuries after ratification of the Bill of Rights, more than thirty years after *Everson,* and more than two decades after the school prayer cases[7] — that the Supreme Court encountered the constitutional problem presented by government-sponsored religious messages away from the setting of public schools.

Taken alone, *Marsh* seemed to suggest a narrow, history-based exception to the sweeping principles, announced in the school prayer cases and later expanded upon in *Lemon. Marsh* involved a challenge by a Nebraska state legislator to the state's practice of employing a chaplain, paid with public funds, who opened each legislative session with a prayer. At the time of the litigation, the chaplain was a Presbyterian minister, Robert Palmer, who had been in the position for eighteen years. In upholding the practice, the six-justice majority in *Marsh* relied explicitly on the fact that, in 1789, the first Congress approved the hiring of a congressional chaplain only three days before sending the Establishment Clause (together with the rest of the Bill of Rights) to the states for ratification.[8] Thus, the Court reasoned, the first Congress did not believe that the Establishment Clause barred them from hiring and paying a chaplain, who opened legislative sessions with prayer. More generally, the *Marsh* opinion gave weight to the fact that "the opening of sessions of . . . deliberative bodies with prayer is deeply embedded in the history and tradition of this country."[9]

At the time, *Marsh v. Chambers* seemed fully explicable on these sorts of historical grounds. Perhaps *Marsh* stood for the narrow proposition that practices that would otherwise violate nonestablishment norms are constitutionally acceptable if they are both long-standing and widespread. On that

---

4. *Everson v. Bd. of Educ.,* 330 U.S. 1 (1947).

5. 463 U.S. 783 (1983).

6. *Lynch v. Donnelly,* 465 U.S. 668 (1984).

7. *Abington Sch. Dist. v. Schempp,* 374 U.S. 203 (1963); *Engel v. Vitale,* 370 U.S. 421 (1962).

8. 463 U.S. 783, 786-787 (1983).

9. *Id.* at 786.

reading, *Marsh* did not narrow the controlling constitutional norms; it carved out a historical exception to them. If that were the case, other state-sponsored religious practices that came into being well after 1791, and were less widespread, would not get the benefit of the exception, and might well be condemned by the Establishment Clause.

That reading of *Marsh* was short-lived. Just one year later, in *Lynch v. Donnelly,* a five-justice majority rejected a challenge to the inclusion of a nativity scene in a city-sponsored Christmas display. The various opinions in *Lynch* foreshadow almost perfectly the next three decades of constitutional strife over these issues. The themes that appear, nearly full-blown, in *Lynch* include the following:

The Relaxation of Governing Norms

The Court refused to be confined to any overarching Establishment Clause principles.[10] Although government-sponsored Christmas displays lacked the historical pedigree of legislative prayers, Chief Justice Burger's opinion explained that the challenged display was nevertheless analogous to other religiously themed messages sponsored by the government, including the national motto and annual Thanksgiving proclamations of the presidents.[11] The opinion concluded that the secular purposes of promoting commerce and seasonal goodwill justified the inclusion of a nativity scene in a broader Christmas display. The *Lynch* opinion refused to be bound by the guideposts in *Lemon,* but offered little in the way of alternative norms for judging such displays.[12]

---

10. 465 U.S. at 679 ("In the line-drawing process we have often found it useful to inquire whether the challenged law or conduct has a secular purpose, whether its principal or primary effect is to advance or inhibit religion, and whether it creates an excessive entanglement of government with religion. . . . But, we have repeatedly emphasized our unwillingness to be confined to any single test or criterion in this sensitive area") (citation omitted).

11. 465 U.S. at 675-676.

12. *Id.* at 685. The Court dismissed the district court's detailed findings about the primary effects of the display upon people within the Pawtucket community, *Donnelly v. Lynch,* 525 F. Supp. 1150, 1174-1178 (D.R.I. 1981), by emphasizing that the effects of the display were no different than the effects of other, constitutionally permissible displays. 465 U.S. at 681-683.

The Role of Government Acknowledgment of the People's Religious Belief

The Court opinion in *Lynch* emphasizes the broad range of situations in which government acknowledges the religious beliefs of its people.[13] But not all acknowledgments of religion have the same character; indeed, the idea of acknowledgment is deeply ambiguous. Sometimes an acknowledgment simply recognizes that another holds particular beliefs. At other times, an acknowledgment affirms the truth of those beliefs. For Establishment Clause purposes, official recognition is fundamentally different from official affirmation.

Imagine, for example, that a city puts cartoonish images of ghosts and witches on the lawn of city hall in the days leading up to Halloween. It would seem foolish indeed to treat that display as an affirmation of the city's official position that such creatures exist. Now imagine that the city puts a crucifix on that same lawn during Easter week. Unless accompanied by an appropriate disclaimer, that display could plausibly be viewed as an affirmation of the truth of particular Christian beliefs represented by the crucifix. Nothing in *Lynch,* however, gives any hint about how or whether courts are to distinguish between recognition of the people's holiday spirit and affirmation of religious truth. Indeed, the Court's reference to the nativity scene on display — populated, in the Court's words, with "angels, shepherds, kings, and animals,"[14] present to bear witness to the birth of God's Son — as an acknowledgment of the "historical origins" of the Christmas holiday appeared to give the government wide latitude to engage in affirmation of religious truth.

The Lynch Concurrence — the Birth of the No-Endorsement Test

Concurring in *Lynch,* Justice O'Connor expressed concern that the majority opinion failed to articulate a standard by which to judge the constitutional validity of government-sponsored religious messages.[15] In her separate opinion, which has profoundly shaped the law on this subject for the past quarter-century, O'Connor first introduced the endorsement test. She offered this test as a method for distinguishing permissible acknowledgments of religion from impermissible government affirmations of religious truth.[16] The theory underlying this test,

13. 465 U.S. at 677-678.
14. *Id.* at 671.
15. *Id.* at 687 (O'Connor, J., concurring).
16. *Id.* at 688 (O'Connor, J., concurring).

which O'Connor fleshed out in far more detail in *County of Allegheny v. ACLU,*[17] focuses on an observer's potential experience of alienation and exclusion. As O'Connor wrote in *Lynch,* "Endorsement sends a message to non-adherents that they are outsiders, not full members of the political community, and an accompanying message to adherents that they are insiders, favored members of the political community. Disapproval sends the opposite message."[18]

The endorsement test appealed to widely held intuitions that the Establishment Clause bars the government from affirming particular religious truths. The test quickly gained wide support. Among other qualities, the test resonated with contemporary, rights-based notions of equal protection and nondiscrimination. Scholars applauded the endorsement test as reflecting a sensible view of the values protected by the Establishment Clause, and as charting a reasonable pathway between the Scylla of relentless extirpation of all public acknowledgments of religion and the Charybdis of limitless government power to promote religious faith.[19] Lower courts seized on it as a useful norm to apply in post-*Lynch* cases.[20]

Eventually, in *County of Allegheny v. ACLU*, a case involving a nativity scene and a Hanukkah menorah, a Supreme Court majority adopted the endorsement test for measuring the constitutionality of government-sponsored religious displays. But the test was a failure from the start. Even those members of the Court who accepted the test in *Allegheny County* could not agree on how to apply it.[21] The opinions in *Allegheny County* exposed the core reason for that disagreement — the test relies on the perceptions of a hypothetical "objective observer" whose identity and characteristics are deeply contested. That observer is supposed to be reasonable and fully informed about all relevant customs and practices of the community. The standard assumes

---

17. *County of Allegheny v. ACLU,* 492 U.S. 573 (1989).

18. 465 U.S. at 688.

19. Donald L. Beschle, *The Conservative as Liberal: The Religion Clauses, Liberal Neutrality, and the Approach of Justice O'Connor,* 62 Notre Dame L. Rev. 151 (1987); Note, *Developments in the Law — Religion and the State,* 100 Harv. L. Rev. 1606, 1647 (1987); William P. Marshall, *"We Know It When We See It": The Supreme Court and Establishment,* 59 S. Cal. L. Rev. 495 (1986).

20. See, e.g., *Barnes-Wallace v. City of San Diego,* 607 F. 3d 1167 (9th Cir. 2010); *Newdow v. Roberts,* 603 F. 3d 1002 (D.C. Cir. 2010); *ACLU v. Grayson County,* 591 F. 3d 837 (6th Cir. 2010); *Stratechuk v. Bd. of Educ.,* 587 F. 3d 597 (3rd Cir. 2009); *Weinbaum v. City of Las Cruces,* 541 F. 3d 1017 (10th Cir. 2008).

21. Compare *County of Allegheny,* 492 U.S. 573, 598-602 (Blackmun, J.), with *id.* at 637-645 (Brennan, J., concurring in part, dissenting in part), with *id.* at 632-637 (O'Connor, J., concurring).

that there is a neutral place — occupied by someone without any religious self-identity — from which to observe, but virtually no one thinks that such a neutral place exists. In *Lynch,* Justice O'Connor believed that the inclusion of a nativity scene in a broader Christmas display did not affirm the religious meaning of Christmas. Unsurprisingly, many equally reasonable observers thought otherwise, typically because they viewed the nativity scene from the perspective of those who do not celebrate Christmas.[22]

From the perspective of a jurisdictional theory of nonestablishment, the endorsement approach suffers from flaws far deeper than uncertainty or bias in its application. More to the heart of the problem, the test asks the wrong question. State endorsement of sentiments that make some people feel like political outsiders is not a constitutional wrong. Every time the state takes a strenuous moral position — war over peace, social welfare over pure individualism, rights of sexual freedom over condemnation of certain forms of adult consensual intimacy — some citizens may feel excluded from the polity, while others are reaffirmed in their beliefs. Religion is not distinctive in this regard. No consistent constitutional account can rest on a universal right to be free from state disparagement of deeply held beliefs.[23]

The endorsement test grew out of the *Lynch* concurrence, and it gathered strength because it offered a bridge over a middle ground full of quicksand. But if the nonestablishment principle is jurisdictional, intended to limit the claims the state may make about its own character, a test that focuses on the experience of observers looks in the wrong direction. That principle is not implicated when the state, through its rhetoric, recognizes the secular manifestations of the people's religion. The state is free to express wishes for the people's joy, including the joy of religious celebrations. The state may wish Christians a merry Christmas or acknowledge the experience of Muslims at Ramadan. In doing so, the state does not join in worship or affirm the truth of what believers worship in these events, but simply acknowledges holidays celebrated by some and wishes believers well.

22. Laurence Tribe, *American Constitutional Law* 1292-1294 (Foundation Press, 2nd ed., 1988) (criticizing application of endorsement from adherent's perspective). See generally, Steven D. Smith, *Symbols, Perceptions, and Doctrinal Illusions: Establishment Neutrality and the "No Endorsement" Test,* 86 Mich. L. Rev. 266 (1987).

23. For a defense of such an antidisparagement view, see Christopher L. Eisgruber and Lawrence G. Sager, *Religious Freedom and the Constitution* (Harvard University Press, 2007). We critique this view in a review of Sager and Eisgruber's work; see Ira C. Lupu and Robert W. Tuttle, *The Limits of Equal Liberty as a Theory of Religious Freedom,* 85 Texas L. Rev. 1247 (2007).

Likewise, the state may lament or condemn the people's misdeeds, including those committed in God's name. The state may speak out against discrimination against racial, ethnic, or sexual minorities, whether or not such discrimination is defended by religious doctrine,[24] or condemn the terrorism associated with the radical version of Islam that motivated the 9/11 attackers. In such cases, the state does not reject the theological basis for the claims, but only condemns the temporal consequences of those beliefs. What the state may not do is assert its own theological basis for approval or condemnation of religiously motivated practices. To do so would be to cloak itself in divine authority, or claim comprehensive jurisdiction over the people's spiritual welfare.

The Lynch Dissent — Religious Meaning Lost, and the Concept of Ceremonial Deism

Dissenting in *Lynch,* Justice Brennan argued that *Lemon's* general principles should apply, and that the city's sponsorship of the nativity scene ran afoul of those principles.[25] He conceded, however, that the *Lemon* test's mandate of secular purpose and primary secular effect was not easily reconciled with the long history and widespread acceptance of a variety of religious practices and references in public life. Some of these, he argued, accommodated private religious commitment — that is, they involved removal by government of obstacles to privately chosen religious practice. Making Christmas Day a public holiday, and thereby giving most public employees and public school children the entire day to be with their families, constitutes such an accommodation. Less persuasively, Brennan argued that some government practices, such as Thanksgiving proclamations, originated in state-reinforced religious commitment but now could be justified by wholly secular purposes.[26]

Least persuasively of all, Brennan argued that some government practices could be understood and defended as "ceremonial Deism" — practices that had "lost through rote repetition any significant religious content" and were appropriately used in "solemnizing public occasions" or "inspiring commitment to meet some national challenge in a manner that simply could not

24. *Catholic League for Religious & Civ. Rights v. City & County of San Francisco,* 567 F. 3d 595 (9th Cir. 2009).

25. *Lynch v. Donnelly,* 465 U.S. 668, 687 (1984) (Brennan, J., dissenting).

26. *Id.* at 692.

be fully served in our culture if the government were limited to purely nonreligious phrases."[27] Brennan put the national motto and the reference to God in the Pledge of Allegiance in this category.

This argument for reconciling the nonestablishment principle with official claims of a relationship between God and the American nation just cannot work on its own terms.[28] Perhaps the names of cities and places, like St. Paul, Las Cruces, or Corpus Christi, can be defended on grounds of religious meaning lost, particularly where the reference is not in English.[29] San Francisco is a vibrant city, and no one thinks of it as a shrine or tribute to St. Francis. But the national motto and the words "under God" in the Pledge are not surrogates for secular places or ideas. They are intended to invoke a connection between God and the American polity.

Moreover, calling a religious practice "ceremonial" can only damage the constitutional defense of it. The very notion of using such invocations to solemnize an occasion or to inspire a national commitment completely belies the underlying premise that such phrases have lost their religious meaning. If that were so, how would such phrases serve to inspire or solemnize? And why should we believe that secular phrases could not equally solemnize or inspire?[30] Before the Congress added the words "under God," the Pledge was no less a commitment to fidelity to the republic.

Justice Brennan's argument in the *Lynch* dissent for ceremonial Deism served the practical purpose of making his view seem less threatening to long-standing public expressions, but as a conceptual matter the argument defeats itself. If the national motto and the current version of the Pledge are constitutionally defensible — and we have our doubts, expressed later in this chapter — the defense will have to be on other terms.

The Bad Start Compounded

A majority of the Court came together in the *Allegheny County* decision to adopt the endorsement test, and despite its deep flaws, it remains the only systematic approach that has garnered five votes in the Supreme Court. Lower

---

27. *Id.* at 717.

28. See Steven B. Epstein, *Rethinking the Constitutionality of Ceremonial Deism,* 96 Colum. L. Rev. 2083 (1996).

29. See B. Jessie Hill, *Of Christmas Trees and Corpus Christi: Ceremonial Deism and Change in Meaning over Time,* 59 Duke L. J. 705 (2010).

30. *Abington Sch. Dist. v. Schempp,* 374 U.S. 203, 281 (1963) (Brennan, J., concurring).

courts have fastened tightly upon the endorsement test as the metric for adjudication, though their typical method involves close reasoning by analogy to the facts involved in various Supreme Court decisions.[31]

But that process of analogical reasoning is itself made problematic because the justices who accepted the test disagree about its application. In *Allegheny County,* that majority agreed only on the impermissibility of a county-sponsored, stand-alone nativity scene, prominently displayed on the landing of the main staircase in the county courthouse. That same majority divided on whether the test barred a county-sponsored Hanukkah menorah next to a Christmas tree. Similar strains appeared in the Ten Commandments cases,[32] discussed below.

Justice Kennedy's dissent for four justices in *Allegheny County* represents the other side of the deep chasm on the Supreme Court in cases involving government-sponsored religious messages. Kennedy attacked the subjectivity and unpredictability of the endorsement test,[33] and argued more generally that the Establishment Clause did not constrain the government from broadly acknowledging the people's religious beliefs and practices, whether or not anyone was made to feel like an insider or outsider on religious grounds.[34] An Establishment Clause violation required either coercion or some sort of government-sponsored proselytizing, wrote Kennedy. Accordingly, he and those who joined him would have permitted the county to display the nativity scene on the courthouse stair landing as well as the Hanukkah menorah near the Christmas tree. Both represented noncoercive, nonproselytizing acknowledgments of the respective holidays.

But these justices, too, have recognized that the Establishment Clause imposes some limit on government sponsorship of religious messages, even if noncoercive. Justice Kennedy's opinion asserted: "I doubt not, for example, that the Clause forbids a city to permit the permanent erection of a large Latin cross on the roof of city hall. This is not because government speech about religion is per se suspect, as the majority would have it, but because such an obtrusive year-round religious display would place the

---

31. See, e.g., *Am. Atheists, Inc. v. Duncan,* 2010 U.S. App. LEXIS 17249 (10th Cir. 2010), *cert. denied,* 132 S. Ct. 12 (2011); *Sonnier v. Crain,* 2010 U.S. App. LEXIS 16237 (5th Cir. 2010); *Newdow v. Rio Linda Union Sch. Dist.,* 597 F. 3d 1007 (9th Cir. 2010); *Am. Atheists, Inc. v. City of Detroit Downtown Dev. Auth.,* 567 F. 3d 278 (6th Cir. 2009).

32. *McCreary County v. ACLU of Kentucky,* 545 U.S. 844 (2005); *Van Orden v. Perry,* 545 U.S. 677 (2005).

33. *County of Allegheny v. ACLU,* 492 U.S. 573, 669 (1989) (Kennedy, J., dissenting).

34. *Id.* at 668 (Kennedy, J., dissenting).

government's weight behind an obvious effort to proselytize on behalf of a particular religion."[35]

Kennedy never explains the extent to which this conclusion is driven by the size of the cross (large), the type of cross (Latin), the place of the cross (roof of city hall), the duration of the display (year-round), the particularity of the display (Christian), or the presumed intent of the display ("obvious effort to proselytize on behalf of a particular religion"). Nor does he explain why proselytizing by government is constitutionally inappropriate, or why such a display should be seen as proselytizing rather than merely an affirmation of beliefs among those who already share them.

In light of its rejection of the endorsement test, Kennedy's opinion cannot be interpreted as a judgment that the display of the cross would make some citizens feel like political outsiders. The rhetorical purpose of this example seems only to show that Kennedy's approach to the Establishment Clause imposes some limit on state-sponsored religious communications outside of schools. Without further explanation, however, nothing in his example would give any more guidance to public officials and lower courts than the endorsement test that he so severely criticizes.

With the Supreme Court so divided, and the underlying standards so poorly conceived, few legal observers were surprised when, on the same day in 2005, the Court struck down a Ten Commandments display in a Kentucky courthouse *(McCreary County v. ACLU of Kentucky)*[36] and upheld a monument, inscribed with the Commandments, on the grounds of the Texas State House *(Van Orden v. Perry)*.[37] In *McCreary County*, the county officials had recently posted the display, and their comments at the ceremony unveiling the display demonstrated an unmistakable religious intent.[38] Among other things, county officials approved a resolution that celebrated the Commandments as the source of Kentucky's legal code. During the course of the litigation, the officials had also surrounded the Commandments with documents, from Anglo-American legal history, that explicitly referred to God. Justice Souter, in an opinion for five justices, applied the endorsement test, and emphasized the expressly religious purpose of the county officials.[39] In its focus on religious intent, the Court's decision in *McCreary County* differs markedly from its holding in *Allegheny County*, which enjoined the court-

35. *Id.* at 661 (1989) (Kennedy, J., dissenting).
36. *McCreary County v. ACLU of Kentucky*, 545 U.S. 844 (2005).
37. *Van Orden v. Perry*, 545 U.S. 677 (2005).
38. *McCreary County v. ACLU of Kentucky*, 545 U.S. at 856.
39. *Id.* at 861-862.

house nativity scene on the basis of the display's likely effect on reasonable observers.[40]

Simultaneously, the Court handed down its opinions in *Van Orden v. Perry,* which upheld a larger and more permanent stone display of the Commandments on the Texas State House grounds. The different outcome of the two cases bewildered most nonlawyers but surprised very few well-informed lawyers. The former quite reasonably assumed that a state-sponsored display of the text of the Ten Commandments either always violated the Constitution or never did. In sharp contrast, the latter had perceived from the time the Court had originally granted review that one or more justices would find some Solomonic way of splitting the cases.

Solomonic or not, Justice Breyer did just that.[41] In *Van Orden,* his vote and the four votes of the *McCreary County* dissenters trumped the votes of the four justices he had joined in the *McCreary County* majority. To put the matter slightly differently, our reasonable nonlawyers were right that most citizens would treat the two cases identically. And indeed, eight justices did exactly that. Those eight justices, however, divided 4-4; four thought both displays violated the Constitution, and four thought neither did so. This left room for a single justice to split his votes and produce different outcomes in the two cases.

Chief Justice Rehnquist's *Van Orden* plurality, like Chief Justice Burger's opinion in *Lynch* and Justice Kennedy's *Allegheny County* dissent, framed the issue in a way that resonates, but only in part, with the theory we espouse: "Our cases, Januslike, point in two directions in applying the Establishment Clause. One face looks toward the strong role played by religion and religious traditions throughout our Nation's history. . . . It can be truly said, therefore, that today, as in the beginning, our national life reflects a religious people. . . . The other face looks toward the principle that governmental intervention in religious matters can itself endanger religious freedom."[42]

The *Van Orden* plurality's first face, in which "our national life reflects a religious people," is quite in line with the notion that the Constitution permits government acknowledgment of the religious character of its people. The "other face," however, does not focus, as we would, on the character of the government. Rather, similar to Kennedy's dissent in *Allegheny County,* the other face is rights-focused, and looks to the question of coercion. If no one

---

40. *Id.* at 869.

41. Justice Breyer joined in *McCreary County,* and wrote a separate concurrence in *Van Orden. Van Orden v. Perry,* 545 U.S. 677, 698 (2005) (Breyer, J., concurring).

42. *Van Orden v. Perry,* 545 U.S. 677, 683 (2005).

is coerced, the plurality implies, then the threat to "religious freedom" may be nonexistent.

At least some of Justice Breyer's decisive concurrence maps reasonably well onto the plurality opinion. Both emphasized that the Texas display had been a gift to the state from the Fraternal Order of Eagles, whose actions and words apparently manifested a secular purpose of helping to fight juvenile delinquency. But Breyer, who realized the apparent inconsistency of his votes in the two cases, conceded that *Van Orden* was a "borderline case."[43] What for Breyer resolved the case in the state's favor was the age of the display. Reasoning from the premise that the central purpose of the Establishment Clause is to avoid political divisiveness on religious grounds, he asserted that the Texas display had stood for over forty years and had caused little divisiveness, while a court order to remove the display — and similar court orders for other displays — would cause significant social conflict.[44] This he contrasted with the more recent *McCreary County* display, which had generated conflict and litigation from its very inception.[45]

For a variety of reasons, we think Justice Breyer's focus on divisiveness is misplaced.[46] First, all sorts of government policies, whether they touch on religion or not, may cause intense divisiveness — issues of war and peace quickly come to mind. No one ever asserts that government is constitutionally forbidden from initiating or ending armed conflict because of deep divisions in the country over the wisdom of either action. Second, a number of social issues, like abortion, contraception, and same-sex intimacy, inevitably stir disagreement on religious lines, among others. Government cannot be constitutionally disabled from legislating on a subject just because the subject may provoke religious factionalism. Third, judges have an extremely limited capacity for measuring religious divisiveness. The Ten Commandments monument had not triggered a lawsuit during its forty-year existence, but that does not necessarily reflect widespread acceptance of the display. Instead, those who opposed the display might reasonably have feared social animosity

43. *Id.* at 700 (Breyer, J., concurring).

44. *Id.* at 699 (Breyer, J., concurring).

45. Justice Breyer's opinion met with considerable scorn in the legal academy. See, e.g., Douglas Laycock, *Government-Sponsored Religious Displays: Transparent Rationalizations and Expedient Post-Modernism,* 61 Case West. Res. L. Rev. 1211 (2011); Steven K. Green, *Religion Clause Federalism: State Flexibility over Religious Matters and the "One-Way Ratchet,"* 56 Emory L. J. 107 (2006).

46. For an extended argument to this effect, see Richard W. Garnett, *Religion, Division, and the Constitution,* 15 Wm. & Mary Bill of Rts. J. 1 (2006).

or reprisal if they challenged it.[47] Fourth, Breyer's notion of divisiveness runs in two directions. It provoked him to vote to invalidate the Cleveland school voucher scheme,[48] which he thought would ultimately produce divisiveness, but to preserve the Texas monument, the removal of which he predicted would be divisive. If a concern about potential divisiveness authorizes both invalidation and validation of controversial policies, the concept is nothing more than gazing into the future and attempting to exercise seat-of-the-pants social prudence, stamped with a religion clause label.

Breyer's underlying theory of divisiveness founders on the shoals of categorical underinclusion (why just religious divisiveness?), subject matter overbreadth (on which issues is potential for religious divisiveness constitutionally fatal?), unresolvable empirical uncertainty, and substantial manipulability. These defects, however, do not necessarily mean that his emphasis on the age of the monument is completely misplaced. To be sure, protecting long-standing religious displays tends to privilege those faiths that first and most aggressively claimed the government square — an odd kind of constitutional "squatters' rights." On the other hand, Breyer's emphasis on the historical origins of the Texas display highlights important concerns about the kinds of injuries at issue in challenges to religious displays, as well as the discretion of judges to remedy such injuries. We return to those concerns at the end of this chapter.

Since the decision in 2005 in the Ten Commandments cases, four new justices (Roberts, Alito, Sotomayor, and Kagan) have been appointed to the Supreme Court. Thus far, we have only preliminary indications about where they stand on religion clause issues, although Roberts and Alito have signaled tolerance for government-backed religious displays.[49] As of this writing, the Court has agreed to hear, in its 2013-2014 term, the case of *Town of Greece v. Galloway,*[50] a challenge to the practice of town-sponsored prayer at the opening of each month's meeting of the town board.

Cases about legislative prayer have been roiling the lower courts for many years. The attention of the Court, with new personnel, to just such a

47. *Santa Fe Independent School District v. Doe,* 530 U.S. 290 (2000) (describing threats of reprisal against parties who complained about school-sponsored prayer at public high school football games).

48. *Zelman v. Simmons-Harris,* 536 U.S. 639, 717 (2002) (Breyer, J., dissenting).

49. See *Salazar v. Buono,* 559 U.S. 700, 130 S. Ct. 1803 (2010) (Kennedy, J., joined by Alito, J., and Roberts, CJ.); see also 130 S. Ct. at 1821-1824 (Alito, J., concurring).

50. The case is an appeal from the decision in *Galloway v. Town of Greece,* 681 F. 3d 20 (2nd Cir. 2012) (Calabresi, J.).

case makes this an unusually opportune moment to reconsider the basic questions raised by challenges to government sponsorship of messages with religious content.

A Theory of Permissible and Impermissible Acknowledgments

The nonendorsement test looks in the wrong direction. The test presumes an individual right to be free from state promotion of a religious message that, to a "reasonable observer," makes some people feel like religious outsiders. In close cases — and many of them are indeed close — this approach has continually foundered in both the Supreme Court and the lower courts.

In contrast to the individualistic premises that underlay the endorsement test, we believe that the concerns of nonestablishment are far better served by an approach that focuses on the relationship between the challenged message and the state's claims of its own character. The government's message triggers Establishment Clause concerns when the message asserts a connection between God's authority and the state's. So, to use Justice Kennedy's example, a cross placed on top of city hall would violate the clause, but not because it is a "proselytizing" symbol, nor because it may alienate some non-Christians as well as some Christians. Rather, whatever its effect on the populace, such a placement of the symbol at the core of Christianity aligns the city with a distinct set of religious beliefs, and with a comprehensive theological view of human flourishing.[51] It is that sort of effort to combine religious with government authority that the clause puts off-limits.

A theory of acknowledgment does not distinguish, as many commentators and judges intuitively do, between symbols of Christianity and more generic symbols of monotheism,[52] or any kind of theism. The wellspring for

---

51. Lower courts have recently and prominently ruled against government-sponsored displays of crosses as generic memorials for the dead. *Trunk v. City of San Diego,* 629 F. 3d 1099 (9th Cir. 2011), *cert. denied,* 2012 U.S. LEXIS 4665 (June 25, 2012); *American Atheists, Inc. v. Duncan,* 616 F. 3d 1145 (10th Cir. 2010), *cert. denied sub nom. Utah Highway Patrol Ass'n v. Am. Atheists, Inc.,* 132 S. Ct. 12 (2011). The use of a cross, or any other symbol of a particular faith, on the gravesite of a particular person in a government-owned cemetery — for example, at Arlington Memorial Cemetery — is permissible as an accommodation of the wishes of the decedent and/or his family. Such a display, chosen by the family, does not align the government with the religious meaning of the chosen symbol.

52. This has been a popular distinction, usually framed in the language of sectarian versus nonsectarian cases about legislative prayer in the wake of *Marsh.* See, e.g., *Wynne v. Town of*

that intuition seems to be some unarticulated notion that government may adopt and express the religious identity of its people, so long as it does so inclusively. Monotheism may be more inclusive than Christianity, but no religious position can possibly include everyone. Our society includes atheists and polytheists, all of whom are excluded by affirmations of monotheism. Indeed, we suspect that the rise in the number of those who openly avow atheism, and the intensity with which some of them assert their equal status, has something to do with the fever pitch of this debate. While sectarian discrimination in the distribution of material burdens and benefits is of course a matter of constitutional concern, the existence or scope of such discrimination is not the central focus of the Establishment Clause. When a government-sponsored prayer offends the clause, the prayer's relative degree of inclusiveness cannot save it. And when a government-sponsored prayer — say, by a military chaplain at a soldier's funeral — does not offend the clause, its constitutionality is not compromised by the choice of god or gods to whom the prayer is addressed.

The principle and approach for which we contend do not put off-limits all state recognition of religious experience and belief. The secular government created by the Constitution must be able to govern the people, many of whom are religious. Government should remain free to acknowledge the religiosity of its people without claiming religious authority for itself. The foundations of this proposition are evident in the pre–Bill of Rights Constitution. The Preamble seeks only liberty's blessings, not God's.[53] Other provisions in the Constitution give government officers the choice of religious oath or nonreligious affirmation of fidelity to the Constitution, and explicitly bar religious tests for federal office.[54] A government with its own religious character would have insisted that officeholders affirm that character. By contrast, our government, with no religious character, is officially indifferent to the religious choices of all.

Beginning with the Court's opinions in *Marsh v. Chambers* and *Lynch v. Donnelly* — its very first decisions on religious displays that don't concern schools — the concept of acknowledgment has played a crucial role.[55] The Supreme Court has never systematically addressed the idea of acknowledgment, however, and the concept is subject to both misunderstanding and ma-

---

Great Falls, 376 F. 3d 292 (4th Cir. 2004) (town council may not open its meetings with prayers that make frequent and specific Christian references).

53. U.S. Const., Preamble.

54. U.S. Const., Art. I, §3; Art. II, §1; Art. VI, para. 3.

55. *Lynch v. Donnelly,* 465 U.S. 668 (1984); *Marsh v. Chambers,* 463 U.S. 783 (1983).

nipulation. In an earlier work, we suggested three categories of acknowledgment: historical, reverential, and cultural.[56]

A historical acknowledgment of religion states an accepted fact about the past — for example, the Pilgrims who emigrated to Plymouth believed that the Church of England did not hold or practice the true Christian faith. A cultural acknowledgment of religion makes a similarly descriptive claim about the present — for example, many Christians celebrate Christmas because they believe that is the day Jesus Christ, the Son of God, was born. Finally, a reverential acknowledgment involves an overt commitment by the speaker — for example, "we believe that God gave Moses the Ten Commandments, to serve as divine law for our lives."

As we explain, acknowledgments of the historical role of religion in America, including among its founders, are the least problematic under the Constitution. In sharp contrast, reverential acknowledgments present the most severe constitutional issues, because they tend to involve the state in acts of worship and thus are thoroughly inconsistent with the idea of government as having a secular character. The most difficult cases are those of cultural acknowledgment, because they tend to echo current beliefs and practices, and therefore invite the possibility of being intended as, or being misunderstood to be, reverential as well as cultural.

The Permissibility of Historical Acknowledgment

The first understanding of acknowledgment is the most defensible, restrictive, and uncontroversial of the three. The government may officially recognize the significance of religious groups, movements, and ideas as a part of our cultural and national history. For example, the National Park Service, which maintains the Mormon Pioneer National Historic Trail, may explain why the pioneers were emigrating. Such acknowledgments of religion are rooted in facts, not theology, and involve entirely descriptive rather than normative claims about religion.

The sharpest illustration of this distinction arises in public schools, which are permitted by the Constitution to teach about religion but forbidden to engage in religious indoctrination. That distinction, however, some-

---

56. Ira C. Lupu and Robert W. Tuttle, *The Cross at College: Accommodation and Acknowledgment of Religion at Public Universities*, 16 Wm. & Mary Bill of Rts. J. 939 (2008) (hereafter Lupu and Tuttle, *The Cross at College*).

times proves elusive or difficult to administer. For example, when some school systems have attempted to implement programs of instruction about religious topics, the classes have been challenged because teachers redirected the courses to serve devotional purposes.[57] Thus, even if it is uncontroversial as a matter of principle that government may acknowledge the historical significance of religion, implementation of the principle — especially in public primary and secondary schools — is likely to present problems of administration because of the difficulty of controlling those who provide the lessons about religion's significance.

Even if government actors focus on a factual account of past religious movements or ideas, those descriptions may nonetheless present questions of accuracy, and thus invite questions about the descriptions' legitimacy as historical acknowledgments. Debates over display of the Ten Commandments offer a useful illustration. Proponents of such displays often argue that the displays acknowledge the Commandments' role as the historical foundation of the common law.[58] Many medieval and early modern legal writers made the same assertion, although very few contemporary legal historians would agree. Modern scholarship generally locates the roots of the common law tradition in pre-Christian Anglo-Saxon sources.[59] The persistence of proponents' historical claims in the face of significant evidence to the contrary suggests that the argument from history may be a pretext for normative claims about the divine authority of the Commandments. As we discuss below, officials (and reviewing courts) often interweave descriptive acknowledgments of religion with normative religious claims. In those cases, unpersuasive descriptive assertions should be evaluated with a deeply skeptical eye.

The controversy over the display of the cross in Wren Chapel at the College of William and Mary provides an excellent example of the use and misuse of claims of historical acknowledgment. For many years the cross occupied a space on the altar of the chapel, and was removed only during non-Christian worship. When, in the fall of 2006, President Gene Nichol decided to remove the cross from its default position on the altar and allow it to be placed there only during Christian worship, a bitter controversy erupted. Those who

57. *Gibson v. Lee County Sch. Bd.*, 1 F. Supp. 2d 1426 (M.D. Fla. 1998); *Crockett v. Sorenson*, 568 F. Supp. 1422 (W.D. Va. 1983); *Wiley v. Franklin*, 497 F. Supp. 390 (E.D. Tenn. 1980).

58. Steven K. Green, *"Bad History": The Lure of History in Establishment Clause Adjudication*, 81 Notre Dame L. Rev. 1717 (2006).

59. Brief of Baptist Joint Committee, American Jewish Committee, American Jewish Congress, and the Interfaith Alliance Foundation, as Amici Curiae in Support of Respondents, 2003 U.S. Briefs 1500, at *20-*23.

opposed the decision to remove the cross from its default place frequently argued that permanent display of the cross represented an acknowledgment of religion's historical role at the college.[60] And it is quite true that the college was largely founded for religious purposes and maintained its identity as a church institution until at least the Civil War.[61]

But a closer examination of the history of the chapel and cross reveals significant weaknesses with the argument that the permanent display of the chapel cross represents a historical acknowledgment of the role of religion at the college. In the 1931 restoration of the Wren Building, the chapel's Victorian-era configuration was removed and replaced with the present reproduction of mid-eighteenth-century design of worship space.[62] The decision to replicate eighteenth-century design was an explicit attempt to link the identities of the College of William and Mary and Colonial Williamsburg.[63] Those identities find their distinctiveness, and help attract students and tourists, by emphasizing the links among the town, the college, and the nation's founding generation.

In a representation of an eighteenth-century chapel, however, the altar cross is glaringly anachronistic. Anglican churches of that era did not place crosses on the altar because Anglicans of that time viewed such adornments as remnants of Roman Catholicism.[64] That belief continued well into the nineteenth century, until the Oxford Movement led many Anglican congregations to adopt a more ornamented style of worship.[65] Instead of a cross, the altar of an eighteenth-century Anglican church would have been adorned with a communion plate and cup, often made of silver or gold.[66]

---

60. See, e.g., Linda Arey Skladany, *Editorial — Cross Controversy Is Less about Religion Than History and Heritage*, Richmond Times-Dispatch, Mar. 7, 2007, at A-15; J. Edward Grimsley, *Editorial — What Would the Founders Think Today?* Richmond Times-Dispatch, Feb. 8, 2007, at A-13.

61. Lupu and Tuttle, *The Cross at College*, at 944-953.

62. James D. Kornwolf, *"So Good a Design": The Colonial Campus of the College of William and Mary; Its History, Background, and Legacy* 64 (College of William and Mary, 1989).

63. Parke Rouse Jr., *A House for a President: 250 Years on the Campus of the College of William and Mary* 180-85 (Dietz Press, 1983).

64. Lupu and Tuttle, *The Cross at College*, at 985.

65. John Edward Joyner III, *The Architecture of Orthodox Anglicanism in the Antebellum South*, diss., Ga. Inst. of Tech, College of Architecture (Dec. 1998), at 1-6, 25. On the Oxford Movement, see generally Larry Crockett, *The Oxford Movement and the 19th-Century Episcopal Church: Anglo-Catholic Ecclesiology and the American Experience*, 1 Quodlibet J. (Aug. 1999), *available at* http://www.quodlibet.net/crockett-oxford.shtml.

66. Lupu and Tuttle, *The Cross at College*, at 985.

The anachronistic placement of the cross thus undermined rather than corroborated the purported intent to acknowledge the school's religious origins. Because the cross display is not an accurate representation of eighteenth-century worship space, the display communicates a different message — that the chapel is *now* a place set apart for Christian worship; it was not originally constructed for that purpose. Other religiously distinctive symbols could have been justified as historical acknowledgments. For example, churches of the colonial era often had an altarpiece inscribed with the Ten Commandments or displayed a communion plate and cup on the altar. But the altar cross lacks any plausible connection to eighteenth-century worship practice. Permanent display of the cross thus lacks the accuracy necessary to qualify as a historical acknowledgment.

The Impermissibility of Reverential Acknowledgment

The second category of religious acknowledgment represents a core violation of the nonestablishment principle. The historical version of acknowledgment is descriptive, but acknowledgment as an expression of reverence is not only normative but also performative. It represents an act of worship by the political community. As such, it aligns the state with divine authority, and reinforces a totalitarian conception of government's role.

Explicit judicial defense of the state's reverential acknowledgment has surfaced only recently in contemporary Establishment Clause jurisprudence, and has not yet commanded a majority of the Court. Concurring in *Van Orden v. Perry,* Justice Scalia wrote, "There is nothing unconstitutional in a State's favoring religion generally, honoring God through public prayer and acknowledgment, or, in a nonproselytizing manner, venerating the Ten Commandments."[67] For Scalia, the people collectively — acting through their agent, the government — may properly engage in worship of God.

Scalia's idea of acknowledgment as reverence would permit official expressions of support for religion, public religious displays, and prayer before civic events. Scalia derived his understanding of permissible religious acknowledgment from a reading of Establishment Clause history, and that history also provides the two limiting principles of his account of acknowledgment. Such acknowledgments, he asserted, violate the Establishment Clause only if individuals are compelled to participate in the communal religious

67. *Van Orden v. Perry,* 545 U.S. at 692 (2005) (Scalia, J., concurring).

activity, or if the activity involves religious claims that are narrower and more specific than the inclusive monotheism embraced by the Founders.[68] Government must not promote or denigrate any specific faith, but is otherwise free to support or engage in generically monotheist worship and religious expression.

Justice Scalia's approach is utterly inconsistent with our understanding of nonestablishment. He would permit government to exhibit a religious character — sponsoring and writing prayers, hosting worship — so long as the state remains within this generically monotheist framework. Moreover, Scalia's purported limiting principle of generic monotheism permits the government to manifest a religious character strongly associated with its past, but forbids that character to evolve in keeping with the changing beliefs of the people. Scalia would allow the government to manifest a religious character, even in its authority over what could become a secular people. Moreover, Scalia's stance invites judges and other government officials to empty religious symbols of their distinctive meaning for particular faith traditions in order to fit those symbols, perhaps disingenuously, within the framework of generic monotheism.[69]

The prohibition on reverential religious acknowledgment is easy to state but in some cases far more difficult to apply. It is bounded by the concept of historical acknowledgment, described above, and that of cultural acknowledgment, analyzed below. For reasons we discuss in later sections of this chapter, courts may be inclined to significantly underenforce the prohibition on reverential acknowledgment. But we should at least take our best shot at stating the norm before explaining the difficulties of full judicial enforcement.

As we outlined in chapter 1, the core concern of nonestablishment relates to the claimed character of government. Nonestablishment helps preserve liberty and forestall totalitarianism by separating and constraining power. The principle demands that the government remain secular in its claims of authority, and leave assertions of divine and comprehensive author-

68. *Id.* at 692 (2005) (Scalia, J., concurring); *McCreary County v. ACLU of Kentucky,* 545 U.S. at 893-895 (Scalia, J., dissenting).

69. See *Salazar v. Buono,* 130 S. Ct. 1803, 1820 (2010) (Kennedy, J., joined by Alito, J., and Roberts, CJ.): "[A] Latin cross is not merely a reaffirmation of Christian beliefs. It is a symbol often used to honor and respect those whose heroic acts, noble contributions, and patient striving help secure an honored place in history for this Nation and its people. Here, one Latin cross in the desert evokes far more than religion. It evokes thousands of small crosses in foreign fields marking the graves of Americans who fell in battles, battles whose tragedies are compounded if the fallen are forgotten."

ity over human souls to private institutions and individual beliefs. Accordingly, the most constitutionally troublesome messages sponsored by government express the idea that the nation (or the state, or its subdivisions) acts with authority from God. Any and all assertions by government of a Christian identity (or a Jewish, Islamic, Hindu, or atheistic identity) fall squarely within the prohibition. They do so not because of their exclusivity, however obnoxious that may be to the idea of equal citizenship, but because such claims purport to align the state with some account of divine authority.

The decision by Congress to include the words "under God" in the Pledge of Allegiance raises a profound question, which the Supreme Court has dodged, of compliance with this prohibition.[70] Recitation of the Pledge in public schools injures some students in a particularized way. As Professor Laycock has argued, pressuring students to affirm God as a condition of showing their patriotism subjects some of them to a thoroughly unreasonable choice.[71]

Even outside the context of public schools, however, the Pledge's claim that the United States stands in a relationship with God appears to represent a core violation of the Establishment Clause. And here, we concede, the crucial question may be one of interpretation. Does the Pledge signify that the United States is blessed by God? That it has a special relationship with or mission from God? That it obeys God's will? Or is the Pledge perhaps more benign, as a representation of the thought that the government is "under" — beneath, lower than, inferior to — some transcendent ordering? This latter meaning might be seen as a disclaimer that the United States has God on its side, though it still seems to affirm the existence of God.

Whatever the meaning, this part of the Pledge is no longer about patriotism alone. We can imagine a court, acting out of a sense of institutional restraint, choosing what we describe as the more benign interpretation of the Pledge. More likely, we can imagine a court choosing the even more benign but less plausible explanation that "under God" qualifies as a historical acknowledgment, because it implicitly refers to religious beliefs held by America's Founders

---

70. *Elk Grove Unified Sch. Dist. v. Newdow*, 542 U.S. 1 (2004) (challenge to Pledge dismissed on grounds that noncustodial father could not assert his daughter's rights to challenge recitation of the Pledge at her school). A number of lower courts have decided the question, and have resolved it in favor of the state. See, e.g., *Freedom from Religion Found. v. Hanover Sch. Dist.*, 626 F. 3d 1 (1st Cir. 2010), *cert. denied*, 2011 U.S. LEXIS 4435 (U.S., 6/13/11), and cases cited therein.

71. Douglas Laycock, *Theology Scholarships, the Pledge of Allegiance, and Religious Liberty: Avoiding the Extremes but Missing the Liberty*, 118 Harv. L. Rev. 155 (2004).

and great leaders.[72] Choosing the latter helps save the constitutionality of the Pledge by purporting to weaken the reverential linkage between government and higher authority. In any event, we think that schools in which the Pledge is recited are civically obliged to explain the historical provenance of all the words in the Pledge, including the fact that "one nation under God" comes directly from the Gettysburg Address. From a rights-based perspective, fully appropriate in this setting, schools should also undertake the affirmative obligation to remind students of their opt-out rights.[73]

The national motto, In God We Trust, also has a slightly ambiguous character because of the unstated antecedent to the pronoun "we." Perhaps the "we" refers to the people[74] rather than to the government that "we" have established. On that view, the motto might just be presumptuous, not unconstitutional. The ambiguity is removed, however, when the motto appears on the coins and currency of the United States. The government, and only the government, can coin money.[75] If, as we contend, the United States is constitutionally disabled from officially entering into any relationship of trust, or mistrust, with divine authority, then the motto's claim stands on fragile ground.

Does the ban on reverential acknowledgment extend to irreverential acknowledgment? A fellow scholar has asked us whether the Establishment Clause should bar a town-sponsored sign like "Good without God" or "In God We Do Not Trust."[76] For those who subscribe to a theory of nonendorsement or nondisparagement, this case seems easy, because the sign seems to make atheists into political insiders and religious believers into outsiders. We reject that theory, and the case may seem to fall outside the nonestablishment norm, because it appears to disclaim divine authority and therefore to leave any such claims in private hands. So long as the town respects private religious freedom, does such an assertion engender constitutional harm? We think there are good arguments that it does. A secular state doesn't disclaim God. Instead, it disclaims competence over all religious questions, including the existence or nonexistence of God.[77]

72. See, e.g., *Freedom from Religion Found. v. Hanover Sch. Dist.*, 665 F. Supp 2d 58 (D.N.H. 2009), *aff'd*, 626 F. 3d 1 (1st Cir. 2010), *cert. denied*, 2011 U.S. LEXIS 4435 (U.S., 6/13/11).

73. *West Va. Bd. of Educ. v. Barnette*, 319 U.S. 624 (1943).

74. U.S. Const., Preamble.

75. U.S. Const., Art. I, §8, cl. 5.

76. For the question, we thank Professor Nelson Tebbe of Brooklyn Law School.

77. *Lee v. Weisman*, 505 U.S. 577, 591 (1992) ("In religious debate or expression the government is not a prime participant, for the Framers deemed religious establishment antithetical to the freedom of all").

The Uneasy Case for Cultural Acknowledgment

Courts frequently use a third conception of acknowledgment, linked to contemporary culture. This approach is probably the most frequently invoked, but is also the most constitutionally perilous, largely because of its inherent ambiguity. In a cultural acknowledgment, the state may recognize the important role of religion within the social and political community. By contrast to the historical version, cultural acknowledgment focuses on the current significance of religion among the people. But the two versions are alike — and distinguishable from the reverential account — in that they are both descriptive. The government acknowledges religion but does not engage in worship or proclaim its own religious character. The ambiguities of cultural recognition arise from the frequent difficulties of separating the descriptive act of acknowledgment from the government's normative and reverential promotion of religious experience.

Chief Justice Burger's opinion for the Court in *Lynch v. Donnelly*[78] still represents the most prominent example of cultural acknowledgment. In rejecting a challenge to the inclusion of a nativity scene in a city-sponsored Christmas display, the Court pointed to the history of public recognition of religion and focused particularly on long-standing practices related to religious holidays. For example, presidents and Congress issue proclamations that commemorate religious holidays; government closes its offices and gives its workers paid vacations; and cities across the country erect displays to publicly celebrate the holiday season.

Cultural acknowledgments respond to the religious experiences and preferences of the populace, but response to popular demand alone cannot justify the acknowledgment. If demand were sufficient, the government would have virtually unlimited discretion to highlight, celebrate, and affirm the religious beliefs of the majority or politically influential. One method, however weak, for preserving cultural acknowledgments while impeding reverential ones is judicial insistence that official recognition of religion must manifest a secular purpose, determined by each specific factual context.[79] In *Lynch,* the Court found such a purpose in the celebration of the Christmas holiday, which has taken on independent secular significance as a widely shared time of vacation and exchange of gifts, and thus become part of the broader culture. Within the broad context of a display celebrating this cul-

78. *Lynch v. Donnelly,* 465 U.S. 668 (1984).
79. 465 U.S. at 679.

tural holiday, the Court reasoned, the city should be able to include a reference to the religious roots of the holiday.[80]

Not all acts of alleged cultural recognition pass this test. In *County of Allegheny v. ACLU,*[81] a splintered Supreme Court invalidated a display of a stand-alone nativity scene on the landing of a prominent staircase in the county courthouse but upheld the display of a Christmas tree alongside a Hanukkah menorah and peace sign outside the county municipal building. The display of the nativity scene alone, the Court ruled, celebrated the religious meaning of the holiday and lacked connection to the day's secular significance. In our terms, this quality of the nativity scene's display appropriately led to an inference that its sponsors, both public and private, acted out of reverence. In contrast, as seven justices concluded, the combination of multiple holiday symbols with a peace sign in the outdoor display supported the argument that this arrangement recognized the cultural significance of the holiday season for many in the Pittsburgh area.[82]

Similarly, the Court's disposition of the Ten Commandments cases, decided in 2005, manifested precisely the same distinction between displays designed to recognize secular aspects of culture and displays designed to promote religious ideals. In *McCreary County* the majority parsed the history of the display of the Decalogue in the county courthouse and concluded that public officials had posted the document for the purpose of celebrating its religious content.[83] By contrast, all five justices who voted to uphold the Ten Commandments monument in *Van Orden* reasoned that the state accepted and displayed the monument to advance the secular purpose of fighting juvenile delinquency through moral education.[84]

The Ten Commandments cases sharply reinforce the constitutional requirement that cultural acknowledgments of religious symbols or sentiments must credibly resonate with secular meaning and purpose. Sometimes the argument for cultural acknowledgment is just not credible, and

---

80. 465 U.S. at 675. The Court suggested that the nativity scene might be viewed more literally as a historical acknowledgment. *Id.* at 680. Despite the Court's suggestion, the inclusion in the display of "the Infant Jesus, Mary and Joseph, angels, shepherds, kings, and animals," *id.* at 671, precludes recognition of the display as an attempt to re-create historical fact.

81. *County of Allegheny v. ACLU,* 492 U.S. 573 (1989).

82. 492 U.S. 613-621 (Blackmun, J., for plurality); *id.* at 623 (O'Connor, J., concurring in part and concurring in the judgment); *id.* at 637 (Brennan, J., concurring in part and dissenting in part).

83. *McCreary County v. ACLU of Kentucky,* 545 U.S. 844, 864 (2005).

84. *Van Orden v. Perry,* 545 U.S. 677 (2005), *id.* at 698 (Breyer, J., concurring).

falls away as a pretext. For example, during the controversy over the Wren Chapel cross at the College of William and Mary, the idea of cultural acknowledgment surfaced through an argument offered to defend permanent display of the cross. Some opponents of the college president's decision claimed that the preexisting display of the cross commemorated the long relationship between the college and Bruton Parish Church.[85] This argument was buttressed by the fact that the cross was originally donated to the church in memory of a nineteenth-century professor at William and Mary.[86] At first glance, this claim resonates with the cultural acknowledgment approach of *Lynch*. Under this theory of permissible acknowledgment, permanent display of the cross would be justified because it furthers the secular purpose of symbolizing and celebrating the school's substantial bonds with Bruton Parish, bonds that include the many college presidents who served as rectors of that congregation.[87]

The cultural argument falters at the connection between the religious acknowledgment and its purported secular purpose. Permanent or default display of the cross on the chapel altar offered virtually no visual cues that the college intended the cross to convey a message about the school's links with Bruton Parish. Instead, the presentation indicated only that the chapel was presumptively a place of Christian worship.

Recognition of the historic and ongoing relationship between the college and Bruton Parish is a legitimate secular purpose, and the cross can be a constitutionally acceptable element in conveying that recognition. To serve as cultural or historical acknowledgment, however, the display must make the relationship between college and church more apparent, and less an afterthought to what seemed to be the reverential purpose of the display. The ultimate compromise placement of the cross, in an appropriately marked display case on the side wall of the chapel, is a far more defensible acknowledgment of history and culture than the unadorned placement on the altar.

We harbor no illusions that sorting unacceptable reverential acknowledgments from acceptable cultural ones will be easy. As we have conceptualized the inquiry, its focus is the purpose of government's claims and

---

85. John Kennedy, Against William & Mary, American Conservative Union Foundation, *available at* http://www.acuf.org/issues/issue90/commentsmary.aspWren; Cross — Point-by-Point Examination of Two Statements by President Gene Nichol, Save the Wren Cross Blog, December 19, 2006, *available at* http://savethewrencross.blogspot.com/2006/12/wren-cross-point-by-point-examination.html.

86. Lupu and Tuttle, *The Cross at College*, at 952-53.

87. *Id.* at 952.

actions, not simply their effect, although the latter frequently will provide good evidence of the former. In addition, our view supports an inquiry into the history and process of decisions, by the relevant government actors, whether or not to sponsor displays. If that history and process support the notion that other, nonmajority religious communities have had reasonable opportunity to achieve cultural acknowledgment of their holidays by the government, the likelihood that the government is intending to engage in reverential acknowledgment of any faith, including that of the majority, is significantly reduced.

Because the inquiry is purpose-driven, the age of the display may be of particular importance — sometimes the purpose of long-standing messages may be lost in time's mist. As the *Lynch-Allegheny* sequence reveals in overly exquisite detail, the full context of displays may render them subject to varying interpretation. And, as shown by the *McCreary County–Van Orden* pairing, the statements of public officials may aggravate (or, as we discuss below, ameliorate) the reverential effect of certain messages. Officials ignorant of the law, or looking for the political credit that may inure to those responsible for reverential acknowledgments, may well make statements that effectively incriminate the entire enterprise.[88] Others, crafty and well advised, may find ways to cloak reverential messages in a cultural patina. Moreover, those with private and public motives that incline them toward reverential acknowledgments will almost always be equally enthusiastic about their cultural counterparts.

Close cases are thus inevitable, and we see precisely how gaps in proof and appropriate notions of institutional restraint will let some reverential acknowledgments slip by as acceptable cultural ones. In this regard, Justice Breyer's focus in *Van Orden* on the age of the display makes complete sense. In close cases, challengers may find it quite difficult to prove that the government intended a display to serve reverential rather than cultural purposes.

If a secular government may act for cultural but not for reverential purposes, striking down every cultural acknowledgment that has an arguably reverential component would be an overenforcement of the constitutional norm. In some constitutional circumstances, a theory of prophylaxis can justify invalidation of practices taken for both constitutionally licit and illicit

---

88. The story of the Ten Commandments in McCreary County reflects some of this flavor. 545 U.S. at 851-858. See also *Green v. Haskell*, 568 F. 3d 784 (10th Cir. 2009), *reh'g denied*, 574 F. 3d 1235 (10th Circuit 2009) (upholding a finding that county commissioners were motivated by reverential religious purposes in approving a request to erect a Ten Commandments monument on the lawn of the county courthouse).

reasons.[89] But the context of passive government displays is much softer[90] than that of government-sponsored active worship, especially among children in public schools, where considerations of coercion buttress concerns about the government's secular character. So, in a setting where enforcement cannot be precise, and the choice is between underenforcement and overenforcement of the Establishment Clause, we have trouble seeing the case for the latter.[91] As a result, judges should appropriately give other branches the benefit of credible doubts.

Legislative Prayer Revisited — *Town of Greece v. Galloway*

In the spring of 2013, the Supreme Court agreed to hear *Town of Greece v. Galloway,*[92] a case in which the Second Circuit held unconstitutional the particular practices of prayer at the opening of monthly meetings of the town board. The case presents an opportunity for the justices to reshape the law governing Establishment Clause challenges to government-sponsored religious messages. Moreover, it offers us an especially useful vehicle for exploring the concepts of historical, reverential, and cultural acknowledgment.

Disputes about legislative prayer have been roiling the lower courts over the last several years.[93] *Marsh v. Chambers* created deep uncertainty about the constitutional boundaries of legislative prayer. *Marsh* relied heavily on the fact that the first Congress hired chaplains, who delivered prayers in both the House and the Senate. The concept of historical acknowledgment, however, does not save legislative prayer. In *Town of Greece* and many similar

89. See, e.g., *Hunter v. Underwood,* 471 U.S. 222 (1985) (invalidating provision in Alabama Constitution that disenfranchised those who committed specified felonies, on the ground that enactment of the provision had been motivated by a desire to exclude African Americans from voting).

90. See Steven Smith, *Constitutional Divide: The Transformative Significance of the School Prayer Cases,* 38 Pepperdine L. Rev. 945 (2011).

91. For a somewhat different approach to the problem of Establishment Clause underenforcement, see Richard Schragger, *The Relative Irrelevance of the Establishment Clause,* 89 Texas L. Rev. 583 (2011).

92. *Town of Greece v. Galloway,* 681 F. 3d 20 (2nd Cir. 2012). See appendix for an update, in which we reflect on the Supreme Court's decision, announced May 5, 2014, in the *Town of Greece* case.

93. *Pelphrey v. Cobb County,* 547 F. 3d 1263 (11th Cir. 2008); *Turner v. City Council,* 534 F. 3d 352 (4th Cir. 2008); *Hinrichs v. Speaker of the House of Representatives,* 506 F. 3d 584 (7th Cir. 2006).

cases, plaintiffs challenge government-sponsored statements of belief. These statements are not only factual assertions of what earlier Americans claimed to believe, or ceremonial repetitions of a long-standing solemnizing message, such as "God save the United States and this Honorable Court."

In *Marsh,* the Court noted with apparent approval that, over time, the Nebraska legislative chaplain changed the prayer from explicitly Christian to generically monotheistic in character. And, in an oft-cited footnote, the Court added that "the content of the prayer is not of concern to judges where, as here, there is no indication that the prayer opportunity has been exploited to proselytize or advance any one, or to disparage any other, faith or belief. That being so, it is not for us to embark on a sensitive evaluation or to parse the content of a particular prayer."[94] That appraisal is internally contradictory, because judges must parse the prayer or pattern of prayers to decide if the practice is designed to proselytize, advance, or disparage any faith tradition. The *Marsh* footnote is also deeply ambiguous. Although most prayers do not explicitly proselytize or disparage, most prayers advance some faith. In lower court decisions after *Marsh,* legislative bodies that have sponsored prayer in repeatedly and explicitly Christian language have not fared well in court.[95] In contrast, legislative bodies that have adopted policies that promote a widely diverse range of prayer givers and prayers have tended to succeed.[96]

Against this backdrop, *Town of Greece v. Galloway* offers the Court, with four justices appointed since the Ten Commandments cases, the opportunity to both clear up the ambiguities left by *Marsh* and provide some useful new direction in cases involving government-sponsored religious messages. As the Second Circuit analyzed the problem, the court was obliged to evaluate the town's practices in light of the "totality of the circumstances." Rather than evaluating the content, one by one, of particular prayers, the appeals court examined the town's process of selecting prayer givers, the distribution among various faiths of the prayers, and the content included in the prayers most frequently offered.

That examination led the appeals court to conclude that the practice, viewed as a whole, affiliated the town with Christianity and therefore did not fall under whatever safe harbor *Marsh* had provided.[97] Unlike

94. *Marsh v. Chambers,* 463 U.S. 783, 794 (1983).

95. See, e.g., *Joyner v. Forsyth County,* 653 F. 3d 341 (4th Cir. 2011); *Wynne v. Town of Great Falls,* 376 F. 3d 292 (4th Cir. 2004).

96. See, e.g., *Turner v. City Council of Fredericksburg,* 534 F. 3d 352 (4th Cir. 2008); *Simpson v. Chesterfield County Board of Supervisors,* 404 F. 3d 276 (4th Cir. 2005).

97. The full opinion can be found at 681 F. 3d 20 (2nd Cir. 2012). All the facts recited in the next few paragraphs are described in that opinion.

the Nebraska legislature in *Marsh,* the town board of Greece (a suburb of Rochester, New York) did not have a long-standing practice of opening its monthly deliberations with prayer. The board instituted the practice in 1999, at the direction of the town supervisor. The board invites the prayer giver for each meeting. Monthly meetings begin with calling the roll of board members, followed by a recital of the Pledge of Allegiance by the board and the audience. Then the supervisor introduces the month's designated prayer giver (its "chaplain of the month," as described by the supervisor), who faces the audience and delivers the prayer over a public address system. As the court described the practice, "[p]rayer givers have often asked members of the audience to participate by bowing their heads, standing, or joining in the prayer."

From the inception of the practice in 1999, employees of the Town Office of Constituent Services invited clergy to deliver these monthly prayers. The first employee to handle this responsibility called all the religious organizations in the town's community guide (published by the local chamber of commerce). She then compiled a list of "Town Board Chaplains," individuals who had accepted invitations to give prayers. Each month she and her successors used this list, updating it occasionally, to find someone willing to give the prayer.

From 1999 until 2008, when the first objections to the prayer practice surfaced, the town board chaplain list contained only Christian organizations and clergy. This appeared to reflect the town's religious demography. All houses of worship in Greece, population approximately 100,000, are Christian. There are a few Jewish synagogues just outside town, but they were not listed in the community guide. After Susan Galloway and Linda Stephens, both town residents, complained about the prayer practice, a Wiccan priestess and a lay Jewish man delivered a few prayers. Each did so, however, only after inquiring about the opportunity to do so; the town did not invite them. The town did invite the chairman of the local Baha'i congregation to deliver a prayer. These three non-Christians were added to the list of town board chaplains.

As the Second Circuit described the 121 prayers in the record, "a substantial majority . . . contained uniquely Christian language. Roughly two-thirds contained references to 'Jesus Christ,' 'Jesus,' 'Your Son,' or the 'Holy Spirit.' Within this subset, almost all concluded with the statement that the prayer had been given in Jesus Christ's name."[98] The other one-third "spoke in more generally theistic terms."

98. 681 F. 3d at 24.

Writing for the Second Circuit,[99] Judge Calabresi said that the case fell between *Marsh v. Chambers* and *County of Allegheny v. ACLU*. Calabresi noted that the Court in the latter had refused to follow *Marsh* in relying on historical practice, because the nativity scene, unlike the prayers in Nebraska, showed "the government's allegiance to a particular sect or creed."

Reasoning from these decisions, Calabresi concluded that the practices in the town of Greece, viewed in their totality by a reasonable observer, "conveyed the view that the town favored or disfavored certain religious beliefs," and therefore "established particular religious beliefs as the more acceptable ones."[100] Calabresi based this conclusion on all the circumstances of the practice — choosing prayer givers from a list derived only from places of worship within the town, without regard for whether some residents worshiped in different ways; failing to publicly solicit volunteer prayer givers or publicize the opportunity to deliver invocations at board meetings to all, without regard to religious beliefs; and operating for years in a manner that systematically produced explicitly Christian prayers. Following *Marsh,* the appeals court said it would be inappropriate to evaluate the content of any single prayer. And it likewise ruled out a constitutional requirement that the town open its meetings either with nondenominational prayers or no prayers at all. To require exclusively nondenominational prayers, the court said, would represent an unconstitutional establishment of nondenominational religion.

Judge Calabresi's analysis of the problem resonates considerably with our approach to the Establishment Clause. Significantly, his treatment of *Allegheny County* diverges from the premises of the "endorsement" theory adopted in that decision. As we have explained, that theory rests on the concern that citizens will experience religious alienation as a result of a government-sponsored religious message. Accordingly, judges who rely on the "endorsement" theory ask whether the government intended to create favored and disfavored classes of citizens based on religion, or whether an "objective observer" would perceive the government display as having that effect.

Although Calabresi does rely on the viewpoint of "an ordinary, reasonable observer," he appears to be using the concept of reasonable observation in a quite different way. Calabresi's observer does not ask whether it is reasonable to feel alienated by the town's expression of a religious identity. Instead,

---

99. The district court had ruled for the town. *Galloway v. Town of Greece,* 732 F. Supp. 195 (W.D.N.Y. 2010).

100. 681 F. 2d at 29-30. Judge Calabresi also relied on other appeals, court decisions that had ruled on issues of legislative prayer.

his observer asks whether it is reasonable to see the town as affirming, and therefore establishing, a particular religious tradition. How the observer feels is irrelevant. What the town has done, understood objectively in light of all the circumstances, is what controls.

Seen in this light, the town's practices violate the Establishment Clause. The town made no attempt to distance itself from the choices of prayer offered by the legislative chaplains, and it made little effort to ensure any sort of religious diversity among those choices. In addition, the integration of the prayer with the Pledge of Allegiance, the use of the board's public address system, and the participation of the board and members of the audience all supported an inference that the town had established Christianity as its official religion.

If the Supreme Court holds that the board's prayer practice violates the Establishment Clause, the town still could proceed in a number of constitutionally acceptable ways. Obviously, it could dispense entirely with prayer at board meetings. In addition, the Constitution still leaves open two paths for the town to follow in creating a solemn invocation before its meetings. First, the town could issue a set of guidelines to invited "chaplains," directing them to deliver a nondenominational, nonproselytizing prayer. This was precisely what the Court approved in *Marsh,* and many state legislatures currently do exactly this in issuing invitations to guest clergy. *Marsh* makes this traditional and historically validated practice a cultural rather than a reverential acknowledgment.

Second, consistent with the Constitution's requirement that the government not act reverentially, the town could create a more open process, designed to distance itself from the content of invocations as well as to produce a variety of them. Such a process might include a broad outreach, in which town residents are invited to offer a solemnizing message, religious or secular, prior to a board meeting. A process that encourages a wide variety of invocations helps to limit the possibility that the government is expressing its reverence through any of them. The practices that emerge would not align the town with any faith tradition. Instead, the practices would over time express the varying views of religiosity and cultural solemnity held by the people of the town.

To be sure, a heterogeneous community can far more readily achieve this kind of pluralism than a religiously homogeneous one. In a town where almost everyone shares a particular faith, the religiosity of the people may be expressed in a uniform way. Even under those circumstances, town officials can explicitly state that the "chaplains" are speaking for themselves, not for the town. If they do so, they can avoid "the impression that town officials themselves identify with the sectarian prayers and that residents in attendance are expected to participate in them."[101]

As shown by *McCreary County,* where county officials repeatedly emphasized and claimed credit for the reverential purposes of displaying the Ten Commandments, government officials can aggravate the Establishment Clause problems of religious displays. The government, however, may also ameliorate Establishment Clause problems with appropriate disclaimers, and other ways of signaling cultural acknowledgment rather than reverential affirmation of a religious message. Like the age of the display as a potential source of distance, disclaimers should only work in otherwise close cases. We don't think that a town can put a Latin cross or Star of David on the roof of town hall and then avoid a constitutional violation with a sign asserting that the symbol is not intended to mark the town's religious identity. In a legislative prayer case, however, an official, public, and regular assertion that the prayer giver is speaking as an individual rather than for the town might make a considerable difference. Whatever the actual mix of prayers, a good faith effort at pluralism in choice of speakers, coupled with such a disclaimer, should be enough to prevail. (See appendix for an update, in which we reflect on the Supreme Court's decision, announced May 5, 2014, in the *Town of Greece* case.)

Disclaimers might also make a constitutional difference in cases involving permanent monuments. Because these disclaimers will be passive (like the monuments themselves) and not spoken, their size and placement will always be significant. Consider, for example, how a disclaimer might have functioned in *Van Orden,* if Justice Breyer had voted against the state. Instead of being limited to the remedial choice of removing the monument, with all the attendant controversy, the parties might have agreed that the state would post a disclaimer next to the monument. That disclaimer could read: "This monument to the Ten Commandments was donated to the State of Texas by the Fraternal Order of the Eagles, and the State has accepted and displayed it solely for the secular reason of discouraging crime by juveniles and others." Mr. Van Orden's lawyers might have proposed an even more aggressive disclaimer, such as "The State of Texas hereby acknowledges that the text of the Ten Commandments displayed here is a version of the commandments that appears in the Bible's Book of Exodus, and the State neither affirms nor denies the divine authority of these commandments." The latter form of disclaimer

101. *Id.* at 33.

would change the display from an apparent claim by the state that God has commanded humans to act in a certain way, to a much less constitutionally troublesome claim that many people, through long-standing cultural sources, associate these commandments with divine authority.

This reorientation of Establishment Clause concerns might extend to other kinds of cases, and widely alter the path of decisions. For example, courts might be far more willing to confront the constitutional problem presented by inclusion of the words "under God" in the Pledge if, rather than facing an all-or-nothing choice to validate or invalidate the Pledge, courts could order schools to provide obligatory explanations of the Pledge as well as regular reminders that students have the right to opt out of the Pledge altogether.[102] In at least some cases, the possibility of nuanced remedies will eliminate the all-or-nothing choices that drive courts to bad decisions on the constitutional merits.

Conclusion

We confess that we have no simple and easily applied theory for resolving the problems identified in this chapter. Going forward, decisions like *Allegheny County* and *McCreary County* have put some checks on the authority of government to exhibit a religious character or engage in activities of worship. But it's not hard to see that the trend line in the Supreme Court is to limit those decisions, and perhaps even to overrule them on general principle. In *Town of Greece v. Galloway,* the Court may well jettison the "endorsement" test. Justice O'Connor, that test's author and strongest proponent, is gone; her replacement, Justice Alito, has signaled a far more deferential attitude toward government religious displays.[103] We nevertheless hope that the Court will ultimately articulate a theory of permissible and impermissible forms of religious acknowledgment, because such a theory promises to reground the Establishment Clause in original and powerful considerations of government's limited character.

102. As Christopher Eisgruber and Lawrence Sager suggest, officials might also be ordered to inform students that they may substitute other specified words, such as "under law," for "under God." Sager and Eisgruber, *supra* note 23, at 152.

103. *Salazar v. Buono,* 130 S. Ct. 1803, 1821-1824 (2010) (Alito, J., concurring).

PART III

Government and the People's Religious Liberty

In prior chapters, we have emphasized the secular character of American government, and explored the various limitations that the Establishment Clause imposes on government in order to maintain that character. But what about the liberty of a "religious people"? How does the Constitution protect the freedom of the people to pursue their own forms of religious belief, worship, and practice?

Over the past fifty years, those most interested in the subject of religious liberty have stressed the central importance of exemptions. Under what circumstances does someone have a right to be excused from complying with a legal rule because of a religious objection? Take, for example, the story made famous in the Supreme Court's 1990 decision in *Employment Division v. Smith*. In that case, a substance-abuse treatment center fired two Native American counselors after they tested positive for use of peyote, a hallucinogenic substance. The state determined that the counselors had been terminated for "work-related misconduct," and thus denied them unemployment insurance benefits. The counselors acknowledged that use of illegal substances would constitute such misconduct, but they asserted a religious excuse. They claimed they had used peyote for sacramental purposes in the Native American Church. Because their use of the drug was religious, the counselors argued that the Free Exercise Clause entitled them to exemption from any legal penalties associated with that use.

The Supreme Court rejected the counselors' claim. Since that decision, the subject of religious liberty has been bogged down in a fruitless conversation about the justification and scope of religious exemptions from general laws. In this chapter and the one that follows, we suggest that the search for a theory of religious exemptions is misguided. Religious freedom in America is not, and never has been, the consequence of special treatment for religion. Instead, that freedom — which is unrivaled in the world — is the product of a constitutional strategy aimed at limiting the state in more general ways. That strategy, which has functioned for nearly a century, is designed to (1) guarantee the secular character of the state and (2) advance norms that protect religious freedom and religious minorities in the same ways they protect secular causes and groups. The Constitution does not protect religion through a strategy of religion-specific norms. It protects religious freedom through a set of far more general rights, which encompass most of what religion needs to thrive.

To many critics, the Court's *Smith* ruling stripped the Free Exercise Clause of constitutional force. The critics are correct that *Smith* has had a very real effect on the law of free exercise, and on the general perception of that law among lawyers, judges, and concerned citizens. But even if the critics are not entirely wrong, they are strikingly myopic. Our view is historically longer, substantively richer, and considerably more panoramic in scope. The regime of religious liberty that has developed in the United States over the past century is robust indeed, and it protects strenuously — though not perfectly — the rights of the people to maintain their own choices of religious character. That regime is both enhanced and limited, however, by the restraints and disabilities that flow from the government's secular character.

Chapter 6 focuses on the many ways in which the Constitution protects religious liberty. Importantly, nearly all these protections extend to both religious and analogous nonreligious activities. Chapter 7 turns to the discretion that the Constitution vests in secular government to accommodate the religious character of the people. Although the Constitution grants generous authority to make such accommodations, that power is limited by a variety of considerations, including the state's secular character.

CHAPTER 6

The Core of Religious Liberty

Consider what most Americans — lawyers or otherwise — would agree are the key principles of religious freedom: (1) the right to worship as one chooses; (2) the right to be free of compulsion to worship — or to support worship — contrary to one's own beliefs; (3) the right to prepare and disseminate writings that contain materials for religious persuasion, contemplation, and worship; (4) the right to assemble with others for the purpose of worship; (5) the right to proselytize to others about one's religious convictions; (6) the right of parents and guardians of children to direct and control the religious upbringing of children in their custody; and (7) the right of religious sects and denominations to be treated equally with others under the law.

We hope that our readers, even as they nod to each item on this list, ask themselves about its constitutional source. This chapter's answers would be relatively straightforward but for the Supreme Court's wobbly and misleading pattern of decisions about the independent force of the Free Exercise Clause. For all but about a quarter-century (1963-1990) of our constitutional history, the Court's Free Exercise decisions have followed a reasonably consistent path. The clause enriches and informs other constitutional liberties, like freedom of speech and association, and protects all faiths from intentionally discriminatory treatment (as compared with other faiths) by the government. Except for that quarter-century, the clause has not supported a constitutional right to exemption from the general regulation of conduct that is within the state's power to control.

The Sources of Religious Liberty

Most of the core of religious liberty in contemporary America — the items on the list above — has been internalized in our culture and customs, and hardly needs the protection of law. Indeed, this core is so ingrained that Americans tend to be shocked or surprised when they learn that other, ostensibly democratic societies do not respect all its key principles, such as the right of individuals to choose their own form of worship, or that of groups to proselytize through personal persuasion or dissemination of their own sacred writings. When antireligious bigotry rears its head — as occurred in some quarters against Muslims after 9/11 — political leaders from across the spectrum in America are quick to condemn it.

The primary wellspring of religious freedom in America is disestablishment of religion, and the space created by that disestablishment.[1] Once the state vacates the arena of religious policy and practice, wholly private religious communities have room to flourish. Consider why this is the case. An established church — certainly, the English establishment from which the United States self-consciously broke — tends to exhibit core elements. Recall, from the introduction, the ways in which a strong form of established church inhibits religious liberty. Under threat of criminal penalty, the state compels attendance at worship in the official church. The state defines the content of orthodox beliefs and forms of acceptable worship, such as that specified in the Church of England's *Book of Common Prayer.* The government regulates the ministry by selecting, paying the salaries of, and exercising control over clergy and others in the religious hierarchy. Taxpayers are compelled to provide financial support for the property and personnel of the established church. Moreover — and central to understanding the connection between disestablishment and the resulting freedom to exercise religion — the government's promotion of an official church is frequently accompanied by varying degrees of suppression of rival faiths. In England, and in some of its colonies in the New World, laws prohibited publication of unapproved religious texts, public preaching by those who did not have an official license, and unauthorized assembly for worship.

To put the matter more succinctly, a strong form of established church represents a government-sponsored monopoly, backed by coercive force, over the means of organized worship. Disestablishment broke that monopoly, and transformed the market into one that invites free entry and open com-

---

1. We develop this argument in more detail in chapters 1 and 2.

petition. In America, once that coercive monopoly collapsed, rivals became free to compete strenuously for religious adherents. In a way that is perhaps unique to the American experience, the liberating effects of the end of the coercive monopoly included what Madison referred to as "a multiplicity of sects"[2] and involved a profound affirmation of what we now see as the core principles of religious freedom.

Disestablishment in Virginia — and in America

However much historians and scholars dispute the lessons of disestablishment in Virginia in the 1780s, the particular and powerful linkage between disestablishment and affirmation of private religious freedom is bold and undeniable. When Governor Patrick Henry's proposed assessment for the support of religious teachers and houses of worship was undone by a political campaign, most prominently marked by dissemination of James Madison's "Memorial and Remonstrance,"[3] the Virginia legislature instead enacted Thomas Jefferson's Bill for Religious Freedom: "Be it . . . enacted by the General Assembly, That no man shall be compelled to frequent or support any religious worship, place, or ministry whatsoever, nor shall be enforced, restrained, molested, or burdened in his body or goods, nor shall otherwise suffer on account of his religious opinions or belief; but that all men shall be free to profess, and by argument to maintain, their opinions in matters of religion, and that the same shall in no wise diminish, enlarge, or affect their civil capacities."[4]

The first part of Jefferson's bill affirms what we would now call a nonestablishment sensibility. That is, it repudiates state-compelled attendance at, and financial support for, "any religious worship." The part that follows, quite logically to the founding generation, reinforces what contemporary lawyers would call a free exercise sensibility — that "all men shall be free to profess, and by argument to maintain, their opinions in matters of religion." Both simply and profoundly, the Virginia bill ends state-established worship and embraces private freedom to worship, or

2. Federalist Papers, nos. 10, 51.

3. James Madison, "Memorial and Remonstrance against Religious Assessments" (1785), reprinted in the appendix to the dissent of Justice Rutledge, *Everson v. Bd. of Educ.,* 330 U.S. 1, 63-71 (1947).

4. The full text of Jefferson's bill is reprinted in the supplemental appendix to the dissent of Justice Rutledge, *Everson v. Bd. of Educ.,* 330 U.S. 1, 72-74 (1947).

not, as each chooses, and private freedom to present and defend "opinions in matters of religion."

When we focus on both the history and the current status of these principles, three phenomena are striking. First, all these rights are extremely well protected in American constitutional law. Indeed, we think it fair to say that — with the one great and disturbing exception of the federal campaign against the Mormons in the late nineteenth century — most of these principles have rarely been subject to serious challenge, even at the margin, throughout the history of federal constitutional law.

Second, the development of these rights through Supreme Court adjudication has unfolded through a conceptual strategy of protecting analogous secular concerns. These include freedom of speech, press, and association; parental rights; and the equality rights of unpopular social groups, including those with a religious character. A strategy of mandatory religious exemptions, which we reject, puts religionists and secularists at war with one another, with the former claiming a right to be free from laws that the latter must obey. By contrast, a strategy of protecting religion under broader umbrellas of rights and immunities makes religionists and secularists into partners in developing a workable theory of the limited state. What broadens the freedom of some will inevitably enhance the comparable freedom of all.

Third, our constitutional history reveals that, for many years, religiously motivated claims were at the cutting edge of constitutional freedoms, and pulled analogous secular claims along in their wake. As America has grown more secular, the reverse phenomenon has begun to appear — the courts have frequently extended secular freedoms to their religious counterparts. Only when equal treatment of religious and secular interests threatens the secular character of the state, as is sometimes true in government funding of private religious experience, has the Constitution forced different treatment of religion and its secular counterparts.

Foundational Moves in the Judicial Strategy
for Protection of Religious Liberty

The Rejection of Religion-Only Exemptions

Federal constitutional adjudication of religious liberty questions was extremely rare in the nineteenth century. Most such questions arose at the state or local level, and the Free Exercise Clause originally applied to the federal government alone.[5] Moreover, there is little evidence that state courts in the nineteenth century were sympathetic to claims of mandatory religious exemptions from general laws.[6] The dominance of a common Protestant ethos in nineteenth-century America meant that general laws typically reflected the values of that ethos, so exemption claims were rarely asserted and even more rarely accepted.[7]

The Supreme Court's only nineteenth-century encounters with such questions arose out of conflicts between the United States and the communities of Mormons in the western territories, particularly Utah and Idaho. The Court's decision in *Reynolds v. United States*,[8] which upheld a federal ban on plural marriage in the territories, offers an understanding of religious liberty that is quite consistent with the argument we present in this work. That is, the Court in *Reynolds* rejected the constitutional strategy of exemptions for religiously motivated conduct. In so doing, it upheld a general prohibition on plural marriage and refused to entertain the argument that a religious community — by declaring which laws endanger the salvation of its members — can effectively create exemptions from general laws regulating the conduct of all. "To permit this," Chief Justice Waite wrote, "would be to make the professed doctrines of religious belief superior to the law of the land, and in effect to permit every citizen to become a law unto himself. Government could exist only in name under such circumstances."[9]

Had the nineteenth-century law of religious freedom started and

5. See *Barron v. Baltimore*, 32 U.S. (7 Pet.) 243 (1833) (Bill of Rights applies only to the federal government); *Permoli v. New Orleans*, 44 U.S. (3 How.) 589 (1845) (following *Barron* in holding that the Free Exercise Clause of the First Amendment applies only to the federal government, and not to states or units of local government).

6. The leading contenders in the historical debate over the question of mandatory free exercise exemptions from otherwise general laws include Philip Hamburger, *A Constitutional Right of Religious Exemption — an Historical Perspective*, 60 Geo. Wash. L. Rev. 915 (1992) (arguing that there is no historical support for such mandatory exemptions, state or federal), and Michael W. McConnell, *The Origins and Historical Understanding of Free Exercise of Religion*, 103 Harv. L. Rev. 1410 (1990) (arguing that the American history of religious liberty supports such exemptions).

7. A rare exception involved cases of conflict with Saturday Sabbatarians; see *Stansbury v. Marks*. 2 Dall. 213 (Pa. 1793) (civil case involving a Jewish witness who refused to testify on a Saturday). But disputes about the relationship between religious conviction and the calendar, which arise in virtually all religiously heterogeneous societies, do not involve basic norms of right versus wrong behavior, or matters of what the founding generation would have called "civil peace."

8. *Reynolds v. United States*, 98 U.S. 145 (1878).

9. 98 U.S. at 167.

stopped there, it would have laid down one marker of an effective strategy for dealing with such questions — they must be treated as more general questions of state authority and personal freedom. If the state may restrict legal marriage to monogamous arrangements, it may do so for all persons, regardless of faith.

But the conflicts between the United States and the Mormons went further and became uglier. Two cases, decided twelve years after *Reynolds* — *Davis v. Beason*[10] and *The Late Corporation of the Church of Jesus Christ of Latter-Day Saints v. United States*[11] — moved well beyond the rejection in *Reynolds* of religion-based exemptions from general laws. *The Late Corporation* upheld an act of Congress that repealed the corporate charter of the church and seized the church's property. In that decision, the Court asserted that the LDS church did not further a legitimate "religious or charitable purpose" because it advanced the doctrine of plural marriage. *Davis* upheld an Idaho territorial law that required each prospective voting registrant to take an oath that he is not (among other things) a member of an organization or association that "teaches, advises, counsels or encourages its members . . . to commit the crime of bigamy or polygamy."[12] *Davis* thus permitted the territory to condition one basic right — participation in the democratic process — on surrender of others, including the right to belong to a particular religious community.[13]

In both *The Late Corporation* and *Davis*, the Court grounded the decision in a finding that the corporation's support of plural marriage was "contrary to the spirit of Christianity." This rationale is nothing less than a state proclamation of the true character of "Christian civilization" and Christian marriage. These decisions thus explicitly affirm a coercive preference for orthodox Christian teaching over competing religious principles, and offend the contemporary constitutional principle that law must eschew religious judgments.

10. *Davis v. Beason*, 133 U.S. 333 (1890).

11. *The Late Corporation of the Church of Jesus Christ of Latter-Day Saints v. United States*, 136 U.S. 1 (1890).

12. 133 U.S. at 346-347.

13. *Davis* is quite inconsistent with later First Amendment decisions involving the question of guilt by association; to establish culpability for membership in an unlawful association, the state today must demonstrate that a group has unlawful aims, and that a particular member knows of those aims and has a specific intent to further them. See, e.g., *Scales v. U.S.*, 367 U.S. 203 (1961); see also *McDaniel v. Paty*, 435 U.S. 618 (1978) (Free Exercise Clause forbids excluding clergy from the right to hold state legislative office).

The Rise of the General Strategy for Protecting Religious Liberty and Equality

Early in the twentieth century, religious liberty began to recover from its debilitating encounter with Mormonism and to assume the pattern we describe. That is, considerations of religious liberty informed more general claims of personal liberty, instead of creating religiously exclusive rights.

The earliest example of this tendency arose in the germinal decisions protecting the right of parents to direct and control their children's education. The first two decisions in this line explicitly involved religious entities. In *Meyer v. Nebraska* (1923),[14] the Court invalidated a Nebraska law outlawing instruction in modern foreign languages prior to the eighth grade. Meyer was a teacher of the German language in a Lutheran parochial school. In *Pierce v. Society of Sisters* (1925),[15] the Court struck down an Oregon compulsory education law that required minor children to attend public school. The plaintiffs included a private military academy and the Society of Sisters of the Holy Names of Jesus and Mary, a religious order that operated a parochial school. In a justly famous passage, the Court in *Meyer* said this about the meaning of "liberty" in the Due Process Clause of the Fourteenth Amendment (and, by necessary implication, in the identical clause in the Fifth Amendment):

> While this Court has not attempted to define with exactness the liberty thus guaranteed, the term has received much consideration. . . . Without doubt, it denotes not merely freedom from bodily restraint but also the right of the individual to contract, to engage in any of the common occupations of life, to acquire useful knowledge, to marry, establish a home and bring up children, to worship God according to the dictates of his own conscience, and generally to enjoy those privileges long recognized at common law as essential to the orderly pursuit of happiness by free men.[16]

These words vividly describe the general strategy, as distinguished from the exemption strategy, for protecting religious freedom. The Court did not create a constitutionally mandated exemption from the Nebraska statute for the teaching of language in a religious school or setting. Instead, the Court

---

14. *Meyer v. Nebraska*, 262 U.S. 390 (1923).
15. *Pierce v. Society of Sisters*, 268 U.S. 510 (1925).
16. 262 U.S. at 399 (citations omitted).

protected religious and other freedoms from unjustified intrusions. To be sure, *Meyer* and *Pierce* both arose during the period in which the Supreme Court was strenuously protecting economic rights as part of that general strategy. That is why the opinions include a concern for Meyer's occupational rights and, in *Pierce,* for the school's proprietary interests in delivering education for a price.

Despite the dramatic erosion of the constitutional concern for economic freedom after 1937, however, the decisions in *Meyer* and *Pierce* continue to be lynchpins of constitutional law — not as decisions about religious exemptions from otherwise acceptable norms, but rather as decisions about protecting the right of parents to direct their children's education. More recently, and in wholly secular settings, the Supreme Court has steadfastly reinforced the legacy of *Meyer* and *Pierce* as foundational decisions about parental rights,[17] and not as decisions about religion-specific freedoms.

The constitutional strategy suggested by *Meyer* and *Pierce* has proliferated in modern constitutional law. Consider the problem of control over religious proselytizing. This is a sensitive issue in a number of countries around the world, especially those with a state church or dominant religious tradition. In such circumstances, both religious and political authorities frequently act with hostility toward the work of missionaries, who strive to win adherents away from the faith held by the majority and protected by the state.[18] In such societies, religious proselytizing tends to be tightly regulated. Among other restrictions, religions frequently have to be recognized and registered by the state, and even then, have to operate under severe restrictions in their effort to win converts.[19]

17. In *Farrington v. Tokushige,* 273 U.S. 284 (1927), the Court applied the doctrine of parental rights to a Hawaiian territorial law that outlawed "foreign language schools"; Hawaiians of Japanese, Chinese, and Korean descent operated such schools in order to teach their language and ancestral culture to their children. *Wisconsin v. Yoder,* 406 U.S. 205 (1972), extends this theme in an opinion that appears to rest on the Free Exercise Clause alone, but *Smith* rerationalized *Yoder* as a case involving hybrid right of religious and parental freedom, 494 U.S. at 881, and more recent cases protect parental rights in a wholly secular context. See, e.g., *Troxel v. Granville,* 530 U.S. 57 (2000) (invalidating law that required custodial parents to permit child visitation by grandparents).

18. See the opinion in *Kokkinakis v. Greece,* European Court of Human Rights, App. No. 14307/88 (May 25, 1993), reprinted in part in W. Cole Durham Jr. and Brett G. Scharffs, *Law and Religion: National, International, and Comparative Law Perspectives* 30-36 (Aspen Publishers, 2010).

19. See materials on the requirements that religious organizations must officially register with the governments of Russia and China in Durham and Scharffs, *supra* note 18, at 438-449.

In the United States, the legal approach to religious proselytizing crystallized, during the late 1930s and early 1940s, in a series of decisions involving the Jehovah's Witnesses. The Witnesses engaged in door-to-door proselytizing, as well as preaching on the streets of cities and towns. Through both the overtly anti-Catholic content of their message and the aggressive manner of its delivery, the Witnesses generated significant public opposition, which led to official restrictions.

In response to prosecution for violating these restrictions, the Witnesses raised constitutional defenses, and a number of these cases reached the Supreme Court. The Court did not view the cases as involving specifically religious messages or speakers. Instead, the Court framed the issues in more general terms, and focused on constitutional control over the discretionary power of local officials to favor or disfavor particular causes. Accordingly, the Court used these cases to establish a set of enduring principles about the rights of political, social, or religious proselytizers to be free of such censorial discretion.

In *Lovell v. Griffin*,[20] the Supreme Court held invalid, as a violation of the freedom of speech, a local ordinance that required any person seeking to distribute literature to first obtain a permit from a city official, who had complete discretion to grant or deny the request. This, the Court recognized, effectively made the local official a censor over all attempts to reach the local citizenry through pamphlets or other written material. Although *Lovell* involved proselytizing by a Jehovah's Witness, the opinion gave no special consideration or weight to the religious character of the speech.

Soon thereafter, in *Cantwell v. Connecticut*,[21] the Court decided that the Free Exercise Clause — together with the free speech clause — rendered invalid a conviction for common law breach of the peace by a street proselytizer for the Witnesses who played a phonograph record attacking the Roman Catholic Church. More recent decisions make explicit what was clear from the Court's rhetoric from the outset — that the right of proselytizing door-to-door or in the streets is not limited to efforts at religious persuasion.[22]

---

20. *Lovell v. Griffin*, 303 U.S. 444 (1938).

21. *Cantwell v. Connecticut*, 310 U.S. 296 (1940). This decision is noteworthy because it's the first time the Court says the Free Exercise Clause applies to the states. See also *Murdock v. Pennsylvania*, 319 U.S. 105 (1943) (invalidating a fee for a license to distribute literature as a forbidden flat tax on the exercise of religion). The tax would be equally unconstitutional as applied to a distributor of political literature.

22. See, e.g., *Hynes v. Mayor of Oradell*, 425 U.S. 610 (1976) (political canvassing by candidate for office); *Staub v. Baxley*, 355 U.S. 313 (1958) (labor union canvassing).

Moreover, in the same era as *Lovell* and *Cantwell,* a comparable strategy appeared in the famous footnote 4 to the Court's opinion in *United States v. Carolene Products Co.*[23] The footnote's third paragraph emphasizes the need for courts to protect "discrete and insular minorities" from unfriendly legislation directed against them as a result of prejudice.[24] In the list of those minorities, which include racial and ethnic groups, religious groups come first. As the law has developed, the Court has relied on the religion clauses to protect religious minorities against discrimination,[25] while it has typically relied on the equal protection clause to protect racial and ethnic minorities.[26] Nonetheless, the underlying theories of judicial intervention overlap considerably.[27]

The most dramatic episode in the tension between religion-specific exemptions from general laws and a theory that folds religion into a wider set of constitutional rights involved efforts to compel public school students to recite the Pledge of Allegiance to the American flag. In *Minersville School District v. Gobitis,*[28] the Supreme Court rejected a free exercise claim that a school district must exempt religiously motivated children from the duty of all public school children to salute the American flag. The majority opinion, written by Justice Frankfurter for eight justices, emphasized the power of the state to promote patriotism and national unity, even in the face of conscientious religious objection.[29]

Just three years later, after the United States had entered the Second

23. *United States v. Carolene Products Co.,* 304 U.S. 144 (1938).

24. "Nor need we inquire whether similar considerations enter into the review of statutes directed at particular religious . . . or national . . . or racial minorities . . . : whether prejudice against discrete and insular minorities may be a special condition, which tends seriously to curtail the operation of those political processes ordinarily to be relied upon to protect minorities, and which may call for a correspondingly more searching judicial inquiry." *Id.* at 152, note 4 (citations omitted).

25. See *Church of the Lukumi Babalu Aye, Inc. v. Hialeah,* 508 U.S. 520 (1993); *Larson v. Valente,* 456 U.S. 228 (1982).

26. *Brown v. Board of Education,* 347 U.S. 483 (1954) (invalidating de jure racial segregation in public schools); *Hernandez v. Texas,* 347 U.S. 475 (1954) (protecting Mexican Americans against discrimination in jury selection).

27. See, e.g., *Church of the Lukumi Babalu Aye, Inc. v. Hialeah,* 508 U.S. 520 (1993) (Free Exercise Clause forbids targeting the religious practices of a particular religious sect).

28. *Minersville School District v. Gobitis,* 310 U.S. 586 (1940).

29. Justice Stone, the author of the famous footnote 4 in *Carolene Products,* was the sole dissenter in *Gobitis,* and he relied explicitly on that footnote's invocation of concern for religious minorities, as originally expressed in decisions like *Meyer* and *Pierce.* 310 U.S. at 606.

World War, the Court, in *West Virginia Board of Education v. Barnette*,[30] up-ended *Gobitis*. From our perspective, the approach taken in *Gobitis* differs in essence from that embraced in *Barnette*. In *Gobitis* the students requested an exemption, and the Court rejected their claim. A student may not rely on a religious objection to escape an otherwise enforceable duty to recite the Pledge. In *Barnette* the students asked the Court to bar enforcement of the mandatory salute statute, and the Court agreed.[31] The Court held that all students have the right to refuse to utter a state-compelled affirmation of political loyalty.

Thus, for nearly a century, religious liberty and other forms of liberty have exerted a considerable and salutary influence on one another. The core principles of expressive liberty, associational liberty, parental freedom, and constitutional norms of equality form a broad shield, under which religious liberty has found strenuous protection. When the Supreme Court in *Employment Division v. Smith* refers to cases like *Cantwell* as involving a "hybrid situation" of rights,[32] the reference is precisely to this proud and exact jurisprudential tradition.[33]

---

30. *West Virginia Board of Education v. Barnette*, 319 U.S. 624 (1943). See also *Wooley v. Maynard*, 430 U.S. 705 (1977).

31. Remarkably, the concurring opinions of Justices Black and Douglas, and the dissenting opinion of Justice Frankfurter, treat the problem presented by *Barnette* as if it involved the exemption question decided in *Gobitis*. The Black-Douglas opinion emphasizes that "religious faiths . . . do not free individuals from responsibility to conduct themselves obediently to laws which are . . . imperatively necessary to protect society . . . from grave and pressingly imminent dangers," and in rhetoric foreshadows the strenuous exemption standard that would later appear and disappear. 319 U.S. at 643-644. This approach builds on earlier free speech precedents, which had invoked the test of "clear and present danger" to justify control of the content of speech. See *Schenck v. U.S.*, 249 U.S. 47 (1919).

The Frankfurter dissent in *Barnette* — full of distress over the rapid undoing of the *Gobitis* result — devotes considerable space to arguing against the concept that religious children (or their parents) should be entitled to religious exemptions from duty, and appears to miss altogether that the *Barnette* opinion does not require any such exemptions. In light of the Court's abrupt turnaround between 1940 and 1943, perhaps the failure of the various opinions to join issue more precisely is understandable. What deserves particular emphasis, however, is that *Barnette* did not reject the antiexemption stance adopted in *Gobitis*. Instead, *Barnette* embraced the general constitutional strategy of locating a right that could be exercised for either religious or secular reasons — in this context, a right to be free from state-compelled affirmations of political loyalty. This protected the acute needs of the Jehovah's Witnesses for such a freedom for their children, without privileging religious concerns in any way.

32. *Employment Division v. Smith*, 494 U.S. 872, 882 (1990).

33. That is, the reference to hybrid rights is not an attempt to craft or suggest some elusive and seemingly arbitrary new trigger for protecting religious freedom only when it

The reasons why the general constitutional strategy has triumphed over the exemptions strategy are deep and significant. First, the secular claims that are analogous to the protected religious claims — for example, the secular right to proselytize for political and social causes — have constitutional force equal to and independent of that presented by assertions of religious rights. To put the point from the other direction, the law has consistently developed in ways that refuse to privilege religious speakers, associations, parents, or conscientious objectors[34] over their nonreligious counterparts.[35]

In addition to the general force of nonreligious rights to free speech, association, and equality, we want to emphasize another set of reasons why religion-based rights tended for many years to quickly or immediately become assimilated with their secular analogues. Although many of the doctrines that protect religious liberty first appeared in a setting where the claimants were religiously motivated and raised religion-specific objections, the resulting legal norms do not require courts or other institutions to evaluate questions of religiosity. Such questions might include whether the claim truly has a religious character,[36] or whether the belief underlying the claim is held with religious sincerity.[37] Far more problematically, these questions might also include whether the claim has deep or shallow significance to individuals or a faith community — that is, whether the religious practice at issue is central or peripheral, obligatory or customary, subject to rewards or pains in the hereafter, and so on.

At the heart of our argument in this work as a whole is the proposition

---

is conjoined with an element, however flimsy, of other constitutionally protected concerns. Rather, it is a reference to situations in which religious freedom is subsumed in other, more general rights.

34. This phenomenon is especially visible in the context of statutory exemptions for conscientious objectors from military conscription. *United States v. Seeger,* 380 U.S. 613 (1965); *United States v. Welsh,* 308 U.S. 333 (1970).

35. The earliest post-*Smith* account of this phenomenon is William P. Marshall, *In Defense of Smith and Free Exercise Revisionism,* 58 U. Chi. L. Rev. 308 (1991). This theme is reinforced in *Christian Legal Society v. Martinez,* 130 S. Ct. 2971 (2010), in which the Court rejected a claim by a religious group of law students that its rights to freedom of association entitled it to ignore restrictions on exclusions from membership, applicable equally to all student groups at the law school. As the Court saw the problem, the claim in *Martinez* was one of religious privilege, not associational equality. For elaboration of this point, see William P. Marshall, *Smith, Christian Legal Society, and Speech-Based Claims for Religious Exemptions from Neutral Laws of General Applicability,* 32 Cardozo L. Rev. 1937 (2011).

36. See *Africa v. Pennsylvania,* 662 F. 2d 1025 (3rd Cir. 1981) (holding that MOVE is not a religion, so its "naturalist minister" is not entitled to special diet in prison).

37. *U.S. v. Ballard,* 322 U.S. 78 (1944).

that official judgments about "ecclesiastical questions" are beyond the competence of government. By this we do not mean that they are beyond human reason. Instead, we refer to the constitutional competence of a government limited to matters of temporal and secular concern.

This idea is far from new, though it has rarely been fully explicated. Indeed, as we trace in earlier chapters, the basic prohibition on religious judgments by government has been embedded in our law for many decades. In cases involving disputes over church property,[38] and in disputes over the employment status of clergy,[39] courts have long been explicit about the constitutional necessity of judicial abstention from questions that involve religious commitments, obligations, and performances. The Supreme Court has recently traced this "hands-off" doctrine to the combined operation of the Free Exercise Clause and the Establishment Clause.[40] Without regard to the question of which clause imposes the limitation, courts have consistently ruled that agents of the state lack authority to decide questions such as who is qualified for ministry or which faction is more faithful to the original teachings of the church.

These two powerful and persistent themes — the tendency to generalize back and forth between religious liberty and its secular analogues, and the requirement of state abstention from deciding questions of religious significance — animate and constrain both the judicial protection of religious freedom and the scope of permissive accommodation of religion by legislatures and government administrators. Before spelling out those institutional connections in detail, however, we must track the detour taken by the Supreme

---

38. See, e.g., *Jones v. Wolf*, 443 U.S. 595 (1979); *Presbyterian Church v. Mary Elizabeth Blue Hull Memorial Presbyterian Church*, 393 U.S. 440 (1969); *Watson v. Jones*, 80 U.S. (13 Wall.) 679 (1871). See generally Kent Greenawalt, *Hands Off! Civil Court Involvement in Conflicts over Religious Property*, 98 Colum. L. Rev. 1843 (1998).

39. See, e.g., *EEOC v. Hosanna-Tabor Evangelical Lutheran Church & School*, 132 S. Ct. 694 (2011); *Serbian E. Orthodox Diocese v. Milivojevich*, 426 U.S. 696 (1976); *McClure v. Salvation Army*, 460 F. 2d 553 (5th Cir. 1972). Almost every circuit court has followed the ministerial exception from civil rights actions created in *McClure*, and none have rejected its approach. See Ira C. Lupu and Robert W. Tuttle, *Courts, Clergy, and Congregations: Disputes between Religious Institutions and Their Leaders*, Georgetown J. L & Pub. Pol'y 119, 123-128 (2009).

40. *EEOC v. Hosanna-Tabor Evangelical Lutheran Church & School*, 132 S. Ct. 694 (2011). See also *EEOC v. Catholic Univ. of America*, 83 F. 3d 455 (D.C. Cir. 1996); see generally Lupu and Tuttle, *supra* note 39, 119, 123-128. Professor Garnett attributes the doctrine to both clauses. See Richard W. Garnett, *Do Churches Matter? Toward an Institutional Understanding of the Religion Clauses*, 53 Vill. L. Rev. 273 (2008). Professor Kathleen Brady rests her understanding of these doctrines on the Free Exercise Clause alone. Kathleen Brady, *Religious Organizations and Free Exercise: The Surprising Lessons of* Smith, 2004 BYU L. Rev. 1633.

Court between the early 1960s and 1990, in which the Court first appeared to make and then ultimately broke the troublesome promise of constitutionally mandated, religion-specific exemptions from general legal obligations.

Sherbert, Yoder, and the Temporary Rise of the Model of Mandatory Religious Exemptions

The Supreme Court's first signs of attraction to an exemption model came in a case that posed the perpetually difficult question of a religious calendar. Virtually every religiously heterogeneous society faces calendar questions, because majorities inevitably design the calendar around their own customs and practices. Accordingly, the days of special religious observance — including Sabbaths, for faiths that observe such weekly rituals — of religious majorities will be favored in calendar design over the comparable days of religious observance in minority faiths. In the United States and Europe, for example, states historically treat Sundays with the same special concern and respect that Israel affords to Saturdays, and a variety of Muslim-majority nations give to Fridays. Those who celebrate an uncommon Sabbath in such countries frequently find themselves at a significant disadvantage.

The quarter-century of flirtation with the exemption model in the United States originated, quite ambiguously, in a set of calendar problems. Although many lawyers would date the beginnings of that regime to the Supreme Court's decision in *Sherbert v. Verner*,[41] the Court planted the seeds of *Sherbert* one year earlier in *Braunfeld v. Brown*,[42] which rejected a claim by Orthodox Jewish shopkeepers for an exemption from Pennsylvania's Sunday closing law. The merchants argued that this law disadvantaged them, because they were obliged by the state to close on Sundays and by their faith to close on Saturdays. Accordingly, they asked to be free to remain open on Sundays — that is, to be exempt from the state law obligation to close on that day. In a companion case, *McGowan v. Maryland*,[43] the Court upheld the Sunday closing law against an Establishment Clause challenge, on the ground that the state had secular reasons for insisting on a uniform day of rest. That in turn led the Court in *Braunfeld* to reject the free exercise exemption claim, in part on the grounds that the shopkeepers — who remained completely free

---

41. *Sherbert v. Verner,* 374 U.S. 398 (1963).
42. *Braunfeld v. Brown,* 366 U.S. 599 (1961).
43. *McGowan v. Maryland,* 366 U.S. 420 (1961).

to observe their own Saturday Sabbath — suffered only an economic burden rather than a conflict between their legal and religious obligations.

Although *Braunfeld* rejected the merchants' claim, the opinion included some unfortunate language in its evaluation of their argument. The Court said that if the law had the indirect effect of impeding the merchants' religious exercise, enforcement of the law against them would be unconstitutional if "the State may accomplish its [secular] purpose by means which do not impose such a burden."[44] The Court in *Braunfeld* ruled that the state did not have any readily available alternative, because administering an exemption from the Sunday closing law for Saturday Sabbatarians would be quite difficult. Among other possibilities, the economic advantages of being open on Sunday when most stores were closed would create incentives for insincere religious claims to the exemption.

The suggestion in *Braunfeld* that the state may deny religious accommodations only when it lacks feasible alternatives set the stage for the decision in *Sherbert v. Verner* just two years later. In *Sherbert,* the Court ruled that South Carolina could not disqualify Adele Sherbert from unemployment compensation on grounds of "unavailability for work without good cause" as a result of her observance, as a Seventh-Day Adventist, of a Saturday Sabbath. As the Court noted, South Carolina law protected Sunday Sabbatarians from this kind of coercive pressure to work on their Sabbath.[45] The Court should have made this discrimination between Saturday and Sunday Sabbatarians its exclusive ground of decision, thus permitting the state the future choice to treat either all or no Sabbath observance as "good cause" to be unavailable for work at particular jobs. Instead, the Court mentioned that discrimination only in passing,[46] and rested its decision on the "substantial burden" imposed

44. *Id.* at 607. Here, the Court cited *Cantwell v. Connecticut,* which involved religious proselytizing, and hence a conjunction of free speech with free exercise concerns. The mistake in this dictum in *Braunfeld* was the extension of the concept that the state must choose policy alternatives that minimize indirect burdens on religion from a speech-centered context to one in which religious practice was not subsumed in another, more general constitutional right.

45. As the Court described the situation in *Sherbert,* "When, in times of 'national emergency,' the textile plants are authorized by the State Commissioner of Labor to operate on Sunday, 'no employee shall be required to work on Sunday . . . who is conscientiously opposed to Sunday work, and if any employee should refuse to work on Sunday on account of conscientious . . . objections, he or she shall not jeopardize his or her seniority by such refusal or be discriminated against in any other manner.'" 374 U.S. at 406, *citing* S.C.Code, §64-4.

46. 374 U.S. at 406 (expressing the view that the "unconstitutionality of the disqualification of the [Saturday] Sabbatarian is thus compounded by the religious discrimination which South Carolina's general statutory scheme necessarily effects").

on Mrs. Sherbert by the South Carolina policy — a burden that the Court described as the equivalent of a fine (measured by the value of lost unemployment benefits) on her choice of Saturday worship. The state could justify the imposition of such a burden only by showing that it was necessary to achieve some very important goal. South Carolina could not make that showing in this case, and thus had to recognize Saturday worship as a good cause for Mrs. Sherbert's unwillingness to accept a job that required Saturday work.

Sherbert thus stands for the principle that general laws might violate the Free Exercise Clause when they impose burdens on people who have religious motivations for not complying with those laws. It is vital to see that this principle had never before appeared in our constitutional law. Decisions like *Pierce, Cantwell,* and *Barnette* rested on broader and general theories of constitutional rights, available to those with or without religious motivation for their conduct. Moreover, *Reynolds, Gobitis,* and several other decisions[47] explicitly rejected the exemption model on which *Sherbert* rested.

Had *Sherbert* been decided exclusively on a theory of interfaith discrimination — that is, a state preference for Sunday Sabbatarians over those who observed a Sabbath on other days of the week — the decision would have fit comfortably with well-established antidiscrimination norms. And the remedy would have involved the classic choice mandated by equality principles — pay all or pay none. *Sherbert's* broader rationale, however, based on a concern for protecting religion against "substantial burdens," is quite different, and raises profound questions about (1) the legitimacy of privileging religiously motivated conduct over its secular analogues, and (2) the state's competence to decide the significance of burdens on religiously motivated behavior. Other justices in *Sherbert* raised the question of religion's privileged position.[48] The concern about secular judicial competence was barely visible in *Sherbert,* perhaps because the religious imperative of Sabbath observance is so widely understood. As other claims for religious privilege worked their way through the judicial system in the years to follow, however, *Sherbert's* more troubling implications began to take hold.

The starkly unambiguous invocation of the model of free exercise exemptions in the Supreme Court arrived with its 1972 decision in *Wisconsin v.*

47. *Hamilton v. Regents of the University of California,* 293 U.S. 245 (1934); *Prince v. Massachusetts,* 321 U.S. 158 (1944).

48. 374 U.S. at 415 (Stewart, J., concurring) (asserting that the Court's Establishment Clause precedents barred the state from treating Saturday Sabbath observance more favorably than a desire to watch Saturday television programs).

Yoder.[49] *Yoder* involved a group of Old Order Amish who asserted the right to remove their children from school at the age of fourteen, rather than sending them until they were sixteen, as the law required. Unlike *Sherbert,* in which the discrimination against Saturday Sabbatarians suggested a plausible account of the decision apart from the exemptions model, *Yoder* straightforwardly applied the exemptions model of religious liberty. In explicit terms, the Court asserted that those who suffered government-imposed substantial burdens on religious freedom were entitled to exemptions unless the government could demonstrate that denial of such exemptions was necessary to achieve highly important interests.

In applying this doctrine, the Court emphasized the longevity and seriousness of communal religious purpose revealed by the history of the Old Order Amish. Applying the rules of the exemption model to the record made in the Wisconsin courts, the Supreme Court ruled that (1) continued attendance at the public schools by children fourteen or older would work a significant harm to the long-term continuation of the Amish community, and (2) the state did not have a strong interest in denying the exemption, because the state's concern for the independence and self-sufficiency of its citizens was fully satisfied by the substitute training as Amish farmers and housewives that the community would offer its fourteen- and fifteen-year-olds.

Contemporary criticism of *Yoder* tended to focus on the issues that Justice Douglas raised in his dissent — that is, whether the ruling gave too little weight to the independent interests of Amish teenagers, who might wish for an education that would liberate them to pursue opportunities for a life other than one of agrarian simplicity and rigid gender roles. When viewed in light of that child-focused concern, the religious exemption–based theory of *Yoder* tended to minimize the harm. The rights protected by *Yoder* were limited to those parents with a religious basis for withdrawing children from school. Chief Justice Burger's opinion made this quite explicit: "Thus, if the Amish asserted their claims because of their subjective evaluation and rejection of the contemporary secular values accepted by the majority, much as Thoreau rejected the social values of his time and isolated himself at Walden Pond, their claims would not rest on a religious basis. Thoreau's choice was philosophical and personal rather than religious, and such belief does not rise to the demands of the Religion Clauses."[50]

In other words, reading *Yoder* on its own terms — as a unique claim of

49. *Wisconsin v. Yoder,* 406 U.S. 205 (1972).
50. 406 U.S. at 216.

communitarian religious privilege, and not as a general right of all parents and custodians to home-educate their children as a way to separate them from the influences of the dominant culture — kept the decision in a seemingly narrow channel, and did not threaten the general regime of compulsory education for children up to the age of sixteen.

But experience and reflection soon revealed that this view of *Yoder,* however much it may have ameliorated a more general threat to the well-being of children, produced a profound problem for constitutional adjudication and theory. If, as *Yoder* suggested, courts should strenuously test the application of laws that "substantially burdened" religious freedom, enforcement of all sorts of laws that apply generally and do not target religion for disfavored treatment would be brought under a constitutional cloud. For example, laws regulating the use of drugs, and laws regulating child welfare outside the context of education, might frequently come into conflict with religiously motivated practices.

In *Yoder's* immediate wake, the lower courts managed to find ways to keep religious exemption claims in check.[51] Moreover, the Supreme Court engaged in its own persistent campaign to create increasingly forceful and sharp boundaries on the scope of the exemption model. Between 1972 and the Court's 1990 decision in *Smith,* the only successful free exercise claims involved either open discrimination against religion[52] or, like *Sherbert,* the terms of unemployment compensation.[53] In all other contexts, the Supreme Court found abundant ways to either avoid or weaken the rule in *Yoder.* It held that the *Yoder* rule did not apply in the armed forces[54] or in prison,[55] and that the rule required actual conflict between legal and religious duties, and thus did not provide grounds to question the government's insensitivity to the religious concerns of Native Americans.[56] In addition, the Court held that *Yoder's* careful weighing of the harms imposed by the state and religious adherents on one another would not be replicated in the context of the need

51. The best work on the ways in which lower courts managed to do this is James E. Ryan, Note, Smith *and the Religious Freedom Restoration Act: An Iconoclastic Assessment,* 78 Va. L. Rev. 1407 (1992).

52. *McDaniel v. Paty,* 435 U.S. 618 (1978) (state may not bar clergy from elected office).

53. *Thomas v. Review Board,* 450 U.S. 707 (1981); *Hobbie v. Unemp. App. Comm'n,* 480 U.S. 136 (1987); *Frazee v. Illinois Dep't of Emp. Sec.,* 489 U.S. 829 (1989).

54. *Goldman v. Weinberger,* 475 U.S. 503 (1986).

55. *O'Lone v. Estate of Shabazz,* 482 U.S. 342 (1987).

56. *Bowen v. Roy,* 476 U.S. 693 (1986); *Lyng v. Northwest Indian Cemetery Protective Ass'n,* 485 U.S. 439 (1988).

for uniform taxation or in a case involving racial discrimination.[57] *Sherbert* and *Yoder,* despite their rhetorical force, did not unleash a wave of judicially mandated religious exemptions. By 1989, the pattern of decisions suggested that the Court had stared into the abyss of the exemptions model, and had stepped well away from its edge.

Employment Division v. Smith and the Demise of the Religious Exemptions Model

By the time *Employment Division v. Smith* arrived, the Court had significantly undermined the exemption model embraced in *Yoder* and continued to apply it vigorously only in the context of unemployment compensation. *Smith* itself involved that context, though it had a very different character than the earlier cases. In *Smith,* the challengers were denied unemployment benefits because they had engaged in work-related misconduct — they had used peyote in the religious rituals of the Native American Church. The misconduct focus of the case permitted the Court to recast the free exercise question as one involving a claim of religion-based exemption from a general rule of criminal law. Smith and his fellow employee argued that the Free Exercise Clause effectively gave them a right to use peyote in rituals of the Native American Church, without concern for either a criminal prohibition on use of the substance or the unemployment law's condemnation of illicit drug use as possible work-related misconduct. To this assertion of religious privilege, the Court in *Smith* gave the same negative answer it had in *U.S. v. Reynolds* more than a century earlier. Citing *Reynolds* and — quite appropriately, though without adequate explanation — *Minersville v. Gobitis,*[58] the *Smith* Court restored the original constitutional rule that the Free Exercise Clause does not exempt religiously motivated conduct that is otherwise subject to general regulation.

In moves that made matters more confusing, the Court did not overrule *Yoder* or the earlier decisions involving religion and unemployment compensation. It recast *Sherbert* as a case about the duty of administrators to give religious hardship claims equal treatment with comparable secular claims. And it recast *Yoder* in a way that linked it with decisions like *Pierce,*

57. *Bob Jones University v. United States,* 461 U.S. 574 (1983).

58. The Court in *Gobitis* refused to declare that religious motives justified an exemption from the duty of schoolchildren to salute the American flag. A few years later, in *Barnette,* the Court declared that the salute could not be made compulsory for any public schoolchildren, regardless of their motivation for refusing to salute.

Cantwell, and *Barnette* — that is, as involving a "hybrid situation" of rights in which a broader, secular conception of rights (speech, parental rights, etc.) does the constitutionally relevant work.[59] Put differently, the Court's opinion in *Smith* rejected the exemption model entirely, and returned the law of religious liberty to the general strategy that we have described in this chapter.

To those who favored the exemption model, the general sweep of the decision in *Smith* produced political outrage, and eventually led to the adoption of religious liberty legislation at both federal and state levels. We will say more about the forms of that legislation in the following chapter. But the tendency of the *Smith* opinion to shatter prior understandings, built from the decisions in *Sherbert* (1963) and *Yoder* (1971), deserves close attention.

First, the roller-coaster ride that the doctrine of free exercise exemptions experienced between 1963 and 1990 reveals that the American view of what religious liberty requires had subtly changed with time, immigration patterns, and culture. Claims to free exercise exemptions were, as a historical matter, at the periphery of religious liberty concerns, perhaps because at the founding, Protestant religious liberty offered the defining framework. In that religious tradition, worship and belief focused on inward experience of the divine. When religious practices were of special importance, such as the observance of a Sunday Sabbath, the relevant customs tended to be widely shared and hence routinely protected in the law. In such a world, religious exemptions from general duties would rarely if ever seem necessary.[60]

In contemporary America, the combination of wide-ranging religious pluralism,[61] extending far beyond Protestant Christianity, and the far-reaching expansion of government has created many more occasions for conflict between

59. Whether *Yoder* is correct when it is so recast is a different question. See Note, *Yoder Revisited — Why the Landmark Amish Schooling Case Could — and Should — Be Overturned,* 97 Va. L. Rev. 681 (2011).

60. Saturday Sabbatarians occasionally presented such a problem, even at the time of the framing. See *Stansbury v. Marks,* 2 Dall. 213 (Pa. 1793). And the question of Sunday mail delivery generated a significant conflict in the early American republic. See the discussion of the "Sunday Mail Controversy" in Michael W. McConnell, John H. Garvey, and Thomas C. Berg, *Religion and the Constitution* 70 (Aspen, 2nd ed., 2006). For rather different views of the broader historical record with regard to accommodations, compare Philip Hamburger, *A Constitutional Right of Religious Exemption — an Historical Perspective,* 60 Geo. Wash. L. Rev. 915 (1992), with Michael W. McConnell, *The Origins and Historical Understanding of Free Exercise of Religion,* 103 Harv. L. Rev. 1410 (1990).

61. Kenji Yoshino, *The New Equal Protection,* 124 Harv. L. Rev. 747 (2011) (discussing the relationship between the outcome in *Smith* and the explosion of religious pluralism in America).

religious practice and government policy. Accordingly, the conventional boundaries of religious liberty claims have moved from the core of inward-focused belief and worship to a periphery of less-common but publicly visible religious practices. Of course, from the perspective of those who make practice-related claims, they may be anything but peripheral. Such claims (about clothing, grooming, diet, particular days for worship, use of mind-altering substances as a sacrament, etc.) may be quite central to the religious lives of those who assert them. The intensity of believers' commitment to such practices is precisely why the ruling in *Smith* has produced a firestorm over the past two decades.

The state's interest in regulating these practices, however, typically emerges from secular concerns, and is not directed at the religious basis for the regulated practice.[62] The secular analogues of the religious conduct at issue — for example, the use of mind-altering substances, or dietary choices — do not involve constitutionally protected activity. As a result, the constitutional strategy of protecting both religion and its secular analogues by finding their common, constitutionally privileged elements, such as freedom of speech or association, is not available. In such cases, the demand for exemption or accommodation is frequently limited to religiously motivated practice alone.

Our angle of vision on the state's role, however, suggests that some forms of practice-related demands for religious accommodations are constitutionally problematic, because they require the government to evaluate the religious significance and impact of government policy. Of course, religion is a category of activity identified by the Constitution itself, as well as by a variety of statutory schemes,[63] so determinations by government agents of what constitutes religious activity are inevitable. The government faces no constitutional impediment to deciding whether an activity is religious, or whether the activity has been burdened in some legal sense.[64] But secular government lacks the jurisdictional competence to determine the religious significance — the substantiality — of the alleged burden.

---

62. In cases where the state's interest does involve religious judgment, the *Smith* rule does not apply, and the practices are protected against hostile state regulation. *Church of the Lukumi Babalu Aye, Inc. v. Hialeah*, 508 U.S. 520 (1993).

63. Section 501 (c)(3) of the Internal Revenue Code, for example, authorizes tax-exempt status for entities organized for charitable, religious, educational, scientific, and literary purposes, among others.

64. For analysis of what should count as a legally cognizable burden, see Ira C. Lupu, *Where Rights Begin: The Problem of Burdens on the Free Exercise of Religion*, 102 Harv. L. Rev. 933 (1989) (identifying legal coercion, discrimination, loss of entitlements, and interference with legally protected interests as qualitative measures of what should qualify as a burden).

We recognize that several generations of religious liberty lawyers have become accustomed to arguing in terms of the substantiality of burdens on religion. From the early 1960s until 1990, the law of the Free Exercise Clause invited this. After 1990, legislatures (federal and state) enacted various religious liberty statutes that required precisely such a determination as a trigger of protection. To these lawyers, our argument that this conventional (if unfortunate) category of inquiry is constitutionally inappropriate may seem quite alien. But these lawyers and their academic defenders, eager to protect religious freedom, have lost sight of the basic lesson that the secular state respects religious judgments by abstention rather than participation. These judgments are left to religious communities or individuals, subject to law that respects relevant constitutional norms.

The hazards of official religious judgments are multifold, and were repeatedly exhibited in the Supreme Court's pre-*Smith* decisions. Consider the relevant legal dynamics when the question of religious significance is put in play. Whether or not the state has a persuasive reason for refusing to exempt the practice from its general laws, the government, acting through a prosecutor or a lawyer defending the state's bureaucracy, will typically assert that a particular religious practice is trivial, or nonobligatory, or capable of being replaced by a substitute practice — say, the use of grape juice instead of wine in Christian communion or in the blessing of the Jewish Sabbath. The defender of the practice will thus be driven to take the other side and claim that the practice is religiously mandatory, crucial, and irreplaceable. As a result, the state's judges will be required to make religious appraisals, a type of judgment that the Establishment Clause has removed from the authority of the state.

The problem of judicial competence does not exhaust the dangers of particular state judgments about the significance of religious experience. These evaluations also present hazards of favoritism and official approval for some faiths, and inevitable disapproval of others.[65] In *Wisconsin v. Yoder*,[66] for example, Chief Justice Burger's opinion commended at length the simple

65. See, e.g., *Bob Jones University v. United States,* 461 U.S. 574 (1983) (holding that IRS may treat religious beliefs on race relations as contrary to public policy and therefore undeserving of tax-exempt status). Scholars have expressed concern that tax officials may strip tax-exempt status from those who hold religious beliefs against same-sex marriage; see, e.g., Douglas W. Kmiec, *Same-Sex Marriage and the Coming Anti-Discrimination Campaigns against Religion,* in *Same-Sex Marriage and Religious Liberty: Emerging Conflicts,* ed. Douglas Laycock, Anthony R. Picarello, and Robin Fretwell Wilson (Rowman and Littlefield, 2008), though there are as yet no examples of such official action.

66. *Wisconsin v. Yoder,* 406 U.S. 205 (1972).

virtues of the way of life pursued by the Old Order Amish,[67] and the likely impact on those virtues if Amish children were obliged to remain in school until age sixteen.[68] In dissent, Justice Douglas wondered how other religious denominations, including his own, would fare under a judicial appraisal of their record for virtue.[69]

His concerns proved prophetic. In the wake of *Yoder*, lower courts found themselves measuring claims by families in other Christian denominations seeking to remove their children from school. Applying *Yoder*, those courts closely scrutinized the content of claimants' religious beliefs, the role of those beliefs in the claimants' way of life, and the durability of the beliefs and life patterns when pressed by the demands of compulsory education laws.[70] Courts invariably found that the claimants fell short when measured against the standards of the Amish.[71]

Moreover, the exemption model depends on an inherently arbitrary calculus. Judges must first determine the weight — the religious substantiality — of the practice at issue, and then decide how that weight balances against the state's competing interests.[72] In *Smith*, for example, the dissenting opinion focused — in part, in expressly theological terms — on the harm imposed on the Native American Church and its members by the state's ban on peyote.[73] Although Justice O'Connor agreed about this appraisal of religious harm, she concurred in the result because she believed that the state's antidrug interests were sufficient to justify such damage to the Native American Church.[74]

67. *Id.* at 209-212, 216-217.

68. *Id.* at 210-213, 218-219.

69. *Id.* at 246 ("I am not at all sure how the Catholics, Episcopalians, the Baptists, Jehovah's Witnesses, the Unitarians, and my own Presbyterians would make out if subjected to such a test").

70. See, e.g., *Johnson v. Charles City Community Board of Educ.*, 368 N.W. 2d 74, 83-84 (Iowa, 1985) (holding that fundamentalist Baptist parochial school is not entitled to a statutory or constitutional exemption from state accreditation standards because, inter alia, "exposure to the more general American culture [does not] pose such an immediate threat to plaintiffs' mode of living as is the case with the Amish"). *Id.* at 84.

71. It is quite different for scholars — exercising intellectual judgment rather than state authority — to speculate on the relationship between the state's law and the survival of the cultural commitments of religious communities. See, e.g., Robert Cover, *The Supreme Court, 1988 Term, Foreword: Nomos and Narrative*, 97 Harv. L. Rev. 4 (1989).

72. Native Americans are still waiting for any such judgments to run in their favor. See *Employment Division v. Smith*, 494 U.S. 872 (1990); *Lyng v. Northwest Indian Cemetery Protective Ass'n*, 485 U.S. 439 (1988); *Bowen v. Roy*, 476 U.S. 693 (1986).

73. 494 U.S. at 913-916 (Blackmun, J., joined by Brennan and Marshall, JJ., dissenting).

74. *Id.* at 903-906 (O'Connor, J., concurring).

The outcome in *Employment Division v. Smith* is thus best defended on the primary ground that government agents are constitutionally incompetent to decide questions of religious significance, because of the absence of constitutionally acceptable standards to do so.[75] In other contexts, government officials frequently weigh present and future costs and benefits. No one believes that the science of that weighing is exact, but the process represents a standard move for the secular state, devoted to the temporal well-being of its citizens and operating under conditions of empirical uncertainty. By contrast, questions about the religious costs of compliance with law cannot be squeezed into any rational and generalizable cost-benefit equation.

The Court's opinion in *Smith* explicitly recognizes this problem of official competence: "Repeatedly and in many different contexts," Justice Scalia wrote, "we have warned that courts must not presume to determine the place of a particular belief in a religion or the plausibility of a religious claim."[76] In the Supreme Court's decisions since *Smith*, the long-standing constraint on judicial evaluation of "the place of a particular belief in a religion" has remained fully intact. Over the past twenty years, the lone victory for a free exercise claim in the Supreme Court occurred in *Church of the Lukumi Babalu Aye, Inc. v. Hialeah*,[77] in which the Court found that the city council had singled out for prohibition a particular religious sect's practice of animal sacrifice. Nothing in the decision required any evaluation of the religious significance of animal sacrifice.[78]

75. The analogy between this theme and the doctrine of political questions, which precludes decision of certain constitutional issues because of "a lack of judicially discoverable and manageable standards for resolving" them (see *Baker v. Carr*, 369 U.S. 186, 217 [1962]), should be quite evident.

76. 494 U.S. at 886-887 (citing cases concerning unemployment compensation, church property, and criminal fraud), and 887 n. 4. See also *Lyng v. Northwest Indian Cemetery Protective Ass'n*, 485 U.S. 439, 457-458 (1988) (courts are not competent to decide which beliefs and practices are central or indispensable to a particular religious faith).

77. *Church of the Lukumi Babalu Aye, Inc. v. Hialeah*, 508 U.S. 520 (1993).

78. The Court's more recent decision in *Gonzales v. O Centro Espirita Beneficiente Uniao do Vegetal*, 546 U.S. 418 (2006), does not represent a step backward from *Smith*'s prohibition on evaluating the religious significance of a practice. The unanimous opinion in *O Centro* upheld a religious community's claim for an exemption, required by the Religious Freedom Restoration Act (RFRA), from the Controlled Substances Act's prohibition on importation of hoasca tea, which the religious group used in its sacraments. As suggested above and elaborated in the following chapter, the most serious constitutional problem of RFRA is the requirement that government decision-makers determine what constitutes a "substantial burden" on religious freedom; but the government did not dispute that point in the *O Centro* litigation. Rather, the result in *O Centro* rested on the government's inability to demonstrate

We are taking the argument about government competence to decide questions of religious significance an important step beyond *Smith*. Unlike Justice Scalia, who argued in *Smith* that the central concern in the case arose from a need to separate judicial from legislative or executive power,[79] we do not believe that this disability is limited to the judicial branch. Rather, the relevant constitutional disability attaches to all branches and all levels of government. In this constitutional context, separation of powers means separating the functions of the secular state from those that are unique and distinctive to religious communities and their members.[80]

The implications of this position, rooted in the Establishment Clause, are sweeping, but they are hardly devastating to the cause of religious liberty. Instead, the post-*Smith* legal world returns to the dominant narrative of religious liberty. That narrative is not about religious exemptions. It lifts up the constitutional limits on religious judgments by the state, and the general set of rights in which religious liberty is subsumed. The narrative also highlights the question of equal treatment for religious and secular interests when they are similarly situated.

The theme of umbrella rights, under which religious liberty can find shelter, has been consistently reaffirmed in the past twenty years. Just as in the pre-*Smith* era, courts have continued to find common elements between religious liberty and its secular constitutional analogues. When these analogues involve substantive liberties like freedom of speech, freedom of association, and parental rights, the dynamics of adjudication are easy enough to see. Religious elements may color the narrative of the claim, as was the situation in *Barnette*, but these elements do not change the claim's substantive weight.[81] Similarly, for

---

that the exemption threatened its interests in public health or the interdiction of drug trafficking. *Id.* at 430-437. Similarly, the question of government competence to decide questions of religious significance did not arise in *Cutter v. Wilkinson*, 544 U.S. 709 (2005), which upheld on their face the inmate-protection provisions of the Religious Land Use and Institutionalized Persons Act, but did not purport to evaluate the burden on religious freedom with respect to any particular practice.

79. *Employment Division v. Smith*, 494 U.S. at 890 (suggesting that claimants seek legislative rather than judicial accommodations for religious practices).

80. Without elaborating the point, the late John Hart Ely described the Establishment Clause in precisely these terms. John Hart Ely, *Democracy and Distrust* 94 (Harvard University Press, 1980) ("The First Amendment's religious clauses . . . make sure the church and the government [give] each other breathing space: the provision thus performs a structural or separation of powers function").

81. Similarly, the religious character of the speech by members of the Westboro Baptist Church is part of the narrative in *Snyder v. Phelps*, 131 S. Ct. 1207 (2011) (freedom of

the past thirty years, decisions such as *Widmar, Pinette,* and *Good News Club*[82] have consistently ruled in favor of equal access to public forums for speakers with a religious perspective. Thus, free speech principles that condemn viewpoint discrimination in the operation of such forums have done the important constitutional work of protecting religious speech and association.[83]

The Court's decision in *Christian Legal Society v. Martinez*[84] is completely in keeping with this understanding. A policy of the Hastings College of Law required all student groups seeking school recognition, and the attendant benefits, to be open to all students. The national organization of the Christian Legal Society (CLS) required the voting members and officers of each chapter to subscribe to a statement of beliefs and a code of conduct prohibiting "unrepentant homosexual conduct" and other sexual relations outside of heterosexual marriage. The college refused to recognize the Hastings chapter of CLS, because those requirements were inconsistent with the policy of allowing all students to be eligible to join all recognized student groups.

In a 5-4 decision, the Court upheld the requirement that recognized student groups accept "all comers" as a reasonable condition of access to the college's speech forum. To the argument that the all-comers policy violated CLS's freedom of expressive association, the Court responded by distinguishing access to a subsidy, which the forum provided, from the basic right to exclude those who do not share a group's beliefs. CLS, acting privately, had that right to exclude, including on the basis of beliefs about sexual orientation. But when CLS participated in the college forum, it lost that unfettered right

---

speech protects church members from tort liability for inflicting emotional distress on father of deceased soldier), but has no consequence for the ultimate disposition of the case. Secular speech with the same effect would be treated identically for constitutional purposes.

82. We address several of these decisions in more detail in chapter 4.

83. The latest, and as yet unresolved, conflict in this long line is represented by *Bronx Household of Faith v. Bd. of Educ. of the City of New York,* 650 F. 3d 30 (2nd Cir. 2011) (New York City may exclude "religious worship services" from the community events otherwise allowed on school premises during nonschool hours, because the city reasonably believes that allowing such worship services on public property would violate the Establishment Clause), *cert. denied,* 132 S. Ct. 816 (2011). Despite the apparent finality of the disposition of the case in favor of the city, the district court judge who earlier had ruled against the city has ordered the city to permit continued worship services by the Bronx Household of Faith on public school premises, 2012 U.S. Dist. LEXIS 23385 (S.D.N.Y., Feb. 24, 2012), and the litigation continues. The Supreme Court has rejected the Establishment Clause–related defense offered by the city in all the other cases in which the government has sought to exclude private religious speech from a public forum of any kind.

84. *Christian Legal Society v. Martinez,* 130 U.S. 2971 (2010).

to exclude, because the all-comers policy was a reasonable way of promoting tolerance among students.

On the facts as the Court had them,[85] the outcome in *Christian Legal Society v. Martinez* dovetails perfectly with the approach to rights suggested in this chapter. CLS has no special, religion-based rights to an exemption from the rules governing access to the speech forum operated by Hastings law school. If the all-comers policy was unreasonable, it would be an unconstitutional limit on access to the forum with respect to all student groups, religious or not. Because the Court found that policy to be sufficiently reasonable, groups with a religious character like CLS were not entitled to different and favorable treatment.

Had the CLS case involved an attempt by the state to punish wholly private acts of expressive association, the outcome would have been different. For an extreme example, imagine an attempt to criminalize the exclusion of openly gay persons by private associations committed to moral or religious principles against same-sex intimacy. Such a law would violate the First Amendment's freedom of expressive association. This result would be the same for secular groups as for religious ones. Constitutional law strenuously protects the right of individuals to join and associate with private groups that exclude on bases that are typically seen as invidious — for example, exclusions based on race, sex, religion, politics, sexual orientation, or any other personal characteristic. Of course, this protection of associational freedom is never unlimited. Government and commercial enterprises do not enjoy that constitutional liberty. Although difficult questions arise about whether the excluding group is authentically private, the scope of the right of associational freedom never turns on the question of the association's religious character.[86]

---

85. The parties stipulated that Hastings had an all-comers policy, applicable to all recognized student organizations. CLS attempted thereafter to raise questions about the authenticity and application of that policy, but the Court majority refused to permit the stipulation to be questioned at the Supreme Court phase of the proceedings. 130 S. Ct. at 2982-2984.

86. See, e.g., *Terry v. Adams,* 345 U.S. 461 (1953) (ruling that the Texas Jaybird Democratic Association could not exclude African American voters from its political primaries, because those primaries effectively chose the nominee of the Democratic Party and, because Texas was a one-party state, effectively chose the ultimate holder of state office). See *Runyon v. McCrary,* 427 U.S. 160 (1976) (freedom of association does not protect private school against civil action for refusing to admit African American students); *Roberts v. U.S. Jaycees,* 468 U.S. 609 (1984) (freedom of association does not protect the all-male Jaycees from antidiscrimination suit based on gender, because the state has a strong interest in access of women to such social organizations, and the Jaycees did not have an official message of the importance of gender exclusion).

Similarly, a decision to cohabit intimately with more than one partner should have exactly the same degree of protection for religious polygamists and polyandrists as for their secular counterparts. The scope of that liberty is a question about the boundaries of the right of intimate association, as defined primarily by the Court's decision in *Lawrence v. Texas*.[87] But here, too, the scope of the liberty does not turn on the religious or nonreligious motives for the conduct.

Thus, for almost a century, religious liberty in America has been protected through a broader strategy of marking off certain domains as presumptively outside of state control. These domains encompass both religious and nonreligious acts, beliefs, expressions, and associations. Judicial protection of these domains does not require distinctions between religious and nonreligious enterprise, or evaluation of the impact of state policies on religious belief or experience. When religious activity falls within these domains, it is fully protected. When it does not, the state's power to regulate comes into play, without regard to the religious character of what is regulated.[88]

The paradigm of equality among faith groups, and the more complex idea of equality between religious causes and their secular counterparts, represents the other primary element of the dominant narrative. In some of the early decisions about assimilating religious liberty to liberty generally, one sees an undercurrent of protecting vulnerable religious groups against sectarian animus. There is every reason to believe that the Court perceived nativist, anti-Catholic animus in the Oregon law, struck down in *Pierce v. Society of Sisters*,[89] that required all children to attend public schools. More recent decisions that invoke the theme of equality among religious sects are more explicit about protecting minority religions against political hostility.

In *Larson v. Valente*,[90] for example, the Court struck down a portion of Minnesota's regulation of charitable fund-raising, because the Court perceived that the scheme was designed to favor long-standing religious interests over those of the Unification Church. Similarly, in *Church of the Lukumi*

87. *Lawrence v. Texas*, 539 U.S. 558 (2003).
88. We do not read the Supreme Court's opinion in *EEOC v. Hosanna-Tabor Evangelical Lutheran Church & School*, 132 S. Ct. 694 (2011) as being to the contrary of what we say. The Hosanna-Tabor case is not about constitutionally unique rights of religious entities; rather, it is about the state's constitutional incompetence to decide for a religious group who is fit for religious ministry, and the corresponding immunity that flows from recognition of that incompetence.
89. *Pierce v. Society of Sisters*, 268 U.S. 510 (1925).
90. *Larson v. Valente*, 456 U.S. 228 (1982).

Babalu Aye, Inc. v. Hialeah,[91] the Court focused on the city's thoroughly undisguised hostility to the Santerian practice of ritual sacrifice. In these cases, the government engaged in impermissible judgments that a particular faith, its adherents, and its practices did not deserve respect equal to that afforded other faiths.[92]

The more difficult set of questions raised by the paradigm of equality involves the state favoring or disfavoring religion generically, rather than singling out particular sects for disfavored treatment. May the state, for example, provide certain exemptions or funding opportunities for secular entities or causes without affording the same opportunities to religious entities or causes? When the relevant goods are matters of constitutional right — for example, the rights to freedom of speech, association, or privacy — the state is under a strenuous constitutional duty to treat religion identically with its secular counterparts.

When, however, the state is engaged in distributing constitutionally gratuitous goods, such as public financial support for private activity or constitutionally discretionary exemptions, the narrative grows more complex. For reasons that we have developed throughout this book, religion is constitutionally distinctive in some ways. The state must steer clear of religious judgments and may not promote the people's spiritual welfare. Accordingly, unlike the constitutional strategy for protecting the people's religious freedom through obliging the state to provide full and equal respect to the general rights involved in religious expression and association, the strategy of nonestablishment pushes the other way. It requires the state to keep its distance from religious experience, and thus to treat religion differently than its secular analogues. For example, as we explain in chapter 3, the state is obliged to exclude teachers of religion from a program that pays the salaries of private school teachers.

What remain are difficult situations in which the state generically treats religious activities differently than secular ones, in contexts in which the Constitution commands neither mandatory equal treatment for religion nor mandatory exclusion of it from certain kinds of state support. These situations include cases in which (1) the state excludes religious activities from a generally available benefit; (2) the state affords one or more secular exemp-

---

91. *Church of the Lukumi Babalu Aye, Inc. v. Hialeah*, 508 U.S. 520 (1993).

92. See also *Bd. of Ed. of Kiryas Joel Village Sch. Dist. v. Grumet*, 512 U.S. 687 (1994) (state may not favor religious sect with grant of special school district status for the community in which it is the dominant group). We discuss the *Kiryas Joel* decision, which rests on the Establishment Clause rather than the Free Exercise Clause, in the following chapter.

tions from a general obligation without any corresponding religious exemption; and (3) the state affords religious exemptions, only without any corresponding secular exemptions. We address the third category in the following chapter. But the first two categories of discretionary, unfavorable treatment for religion deserve attention here. Why don't such measures violate the mandate of equality between secular and religious activities that operates in the realm of substantive rights like speech and association?

In the first category, consider *Locke v. Davey*,[93] in which the Supreme Court rejected the argument that Washington State had violated the Free Exercise Clause by excluding from a state scholarship program students who were pursuing degrees that would prepare them for a career in religious ministry. The state claimed that including such students in the scholarship program might violate the state constitution, even if it would not violate the First Amendment's Establishment Clause. The Court, by a 7-2 majority, ruled for the state, on the theory that there should be "play in the joints" between the kind of state support for religion that the Establishment Clause forbids and the kind of nondiscrimination that the Free Exercise Clause requires. The Court concluded that Washington was permitted to exclude ministerial candidates from the state scholarship program because state payment for that education was reasonably close to the constitutional danger zone of control over education for ministry.

Locke seems to us quite sound. As we argue in the next chapter, the Constitution creates significant discretion to accommodate religious experience beyond what the core of religious liberty requires. Similarly, the Constitution should be read, as *Locke* interprets it, to create a substantial zone of discretion to refuse to support religious experience when that support seems uncomfortably close to the edge of the state's constitutional disability in religious matters. As we hope this book reveals, that disability is easier to conceptualize in general terms than it is to apply in concrete situations. When the state declines to fund religious activities, or confronts public school teachers who are arguably engaged in religious indoctrination of their students, the state should have authority to make policies that will move it away from the danger zone. If it did not, every state action regarding religion would involve constitutional mandates. Such a legal regime would be rigid, unresponsive to ordinary political pressures, and subject to judicial control in every minute aspect. The interplay between a secular government and a religious people will operate far more efficiently

93. *Locke v. Davey*, 540 U.S. 712 (2004).

if political actors have some discretionary authority to accommodate the relevant, competing concerns.[94]

In the second category — exclusion of optional religious exemptions when constitutionally optional secular exemptions are provided — the Supreme Court has had less to say, but the lower courts and commentators have approached this set of questions in a variety of ways. Some have argued that the presence of a secular exemption requires the state to have a very strong reason to refuse a religious exemption. Those who take this position argue that *Smith* focuses on "generally applicable" rules, and that a rule with significant secular exemptions is not "generally applicable."

To take a famous example, may a city enforce a rule prohibiting beards against officers under a religious obligation to wear them, while simultaneously exempting officers who are undercover or cannot shave for health-related reasons? The issue presented by this policy, invalidated under the Free Exercise Clause in an opinion by Judge Alito for the Third Circuit in *Fraternal Order of Police v. Newark,*[95] is exquisitely poised between the model of religious-specific exemptions, which *Smith* rightly rejects, and the model of secular and religious equality, which the Constitution to some extent embraces.

The Newark policy and others like it might be analyzed in a number of ways. Under the pre-*Smith* exemption model, judges would have asked if that policy substantially burdens Muslim officers, religiously obligated to wear beards, and, if so, whether the government has a compelling interest in denying an exemption to such officers. For all the reasons we have suggested in this chapter, we think the Constitution bars inquiry into the "burden" question.

Second, under the dominant paradigm of constitutional equality, which condemns sectarian animus, judges should ask whether the policy intentionally targets Muslims, or any other religiously obligated beard wearers, for disfavored treatment. Of course, the secular exceptions for undercover work or

94. For a more critical view of *Locke* and the potential dangers of government discretion of this sort, see Thomas C. Berg and Douglas Laycock, *The Mistakes in* Locke v. Davey *and the Future of State Payments for Services Provided by Religious Institutions,* 40 Tulsa L. Rev. 227 (2004).

95. *Fraternal Order of Police v. Newark,* 170 F. 3d 359 (3rd Cir. 1999). For an incisive discussion of the *Fraternal Order of Police* decision and the more general problem of when regulations should be considered "generally applicable" under *Smith,* see James M. Oleske Jr., Lukumi *at Twenty: A Legacy of Uncertainty for Religious Liberty and Animal Welfare Laws,* 19 Animal L. Rev. 295 (2013), available at http://papers.ssrn.com/sol3/papers.cfm?abstract_id=2216207.

avoiding shaving for health reasons do not provide any direct evidence of hostility to any particular sect, or even a more general hostility to religious custom. Unlike most police assignments, undercover work may be facilitated by wearing a beard. Moreover, a health exception may be required by federal law on discrimination against people with disabilities. So the secular exemptions do not necessarily manifest any animus toward religious experience, even though the overall policy is not sympathetic to that sort of experience.

Third, we might ask, as Alito did, whether the challenged policy is "generally applicable" in the sense used by the Supreme Court in *Smith*. Alito concluded that the existing exceptions made the policy not generally applicable. Having made some arguably discretionary exceptions, the city lacked a constitutionally sufficient reason to exclude religiously motivated beard wearers. This approach, under which any secular exception invites a religious exception, eliminates the need for proof of intentional discrimination against religion. Thus, the approach is far more hospitable to religious freedom than the no-targeting rule of *Lukumi* and *Larsen*.[96]

Despite the normative attraction of Alito's sensitivity to religious freedom, his stance is not required by the Constitution. The government quite frequently, and for a wide variety of reasons, exempts certain conduct from particular policies. Sometimes the reasons for doing so are a matter of substantive sympathy. Other times the pattern of exemptions and nonexemptions may be more a matter of administrative ease or, as in health exceptions, required by other law. In short, there is no reason to believe — as a categorical matter — that the government infringes religious liberty every time it makes a secular exemption and fails to make a religious exemption.

To be sure, a rule that mandates religious exemptions whenever government makes comparable secular exemptions does not raise the problems of constitutional competence about religious questions. Courts deploying such a strategy would not have to evaluate the significance of the religious claim. Rather, they would have to decide whether the claim for religious exemption is sufficiently analogous to the existing secular exemption to justify a presumptive demand for equal treatment.

96. In the litigation filed by religious institutions against the federal Department of Health and Human Services with respect to mandatory coverage of pregnancy prevention services in employer-provided health insurance, the argument that this particular mandate is not "generally applicable" is a key part of the constitutional argument that the mandate violates the Free Exercise Clause. See, e.g., Complaint in *Colorado Christian University v. Sebelius*, U.S. Dist. Ct. District of Colorado, Pars. 33-43; 51-52; 114-115, available at http://www.becketfund.org/wp-content/uploads/2011/12/CCU-v-Sebelius-Complaint-final.pdf.

The leading academic advocates for such a strategy are Christopher Eisgruber and Lawrence Sager. In their provocative and important book on religion and the Constitution,[97] they argue against the idea of religious privilege suggested by the pre-*Smith* norms of free exercise. For reasons different from those we have given, they believe that the Court correctly decided *Smith*. They argue, however, that the Constitution requires the government to give religious commitments respect equal to that afforded other deep concerns and commitments of the citizenry. As this chapter explains, when the underlying activity involves substantive constitutional rights independent of religion, such as speech or association, this concern for equal constitutional regard is already built into the relevant norms.

When, however, the underlying activity — like using peyote or wearing a beard — is not constitutionally guaranteed, the project of equal treatment for religious practice inevitably presents a number of difficult problems. Religious commitments are not readily comparable to other needs and preferences, such as physical health. Can the possibility of skin irritation or damage from shaving really be equated with a sense of defying God's will from the same act, so that exemption of either requires exemption of the other? The problem of comparison cuts more deeply when complainants argue that legislatures have provided exemptions for analogous religious practices but have failed to exempt the practice of their faith. For example, state legislatures during the Prohibition era exempted religious use of wine by churches and synagogues. Should that exemption require the legislature to exempt from criminal prohibition the sacramental use of peyote by the Native American Church?[98]

We are quite sympathetic to the impulse that gives rise to such an assertion. But, like other critics,[99] we do not understand how judges can in a disciplined way ascertain when policies burdensome to a religious minority would or would not be applied to analogous but not identical practices of other faiths. At best, the enterprise seems riddled with indeterminate predictions about the political strength of various faiths to succeed in conflicts where the underlying policy issues may be quite different in one case from

97. Christopher L. Eisgruber and Lawrence G. Sager, *Religious Freedom and the Constitution* (Harvard University Press, 2007).

98. *Id.* at 92-93.

99. Michael W. McConnell, *The Problem of Singling Out Religion*, 50 DePaul L. Rev. 1 (2000); Andrew Koppelman, *Is It Fair to Give Religion Special Treatment?* 2006 Univ. of Ill. L. Rev. 571; Thomas Berg, *Can Religious Liberty Be Protected as Equality?* 85 Texas L. Rev. 1185 (2007).

the next. At worst, reasoning in this fashion invites something quite akin to the very judgments, about religious weight and significance, against which we have been arguing. Unless the exclusion of a religious exemption is demonstrably the product of animus against a particular faith, the choice to create only secular exemptions — or even other religious exemptions — should withstand constitutional review.

Of course, the core of religious liberty analyzed in this chapter is only part of the scope of accommodations that the nonjudicial branches of government may offer to religious practice. Such accommodations are permissive, not mandatory. These discretionary accommodations must respect appropriate constitutional limits, including the basic jurisdictional prohibition on governmental appraisals of questions of religious significance. Many accommodations respect the relevant limits, but others do not. The next chapter explores the forms and limits of such permissive regimes of accommodation.

CHAPTER 7

Government Responsiveness to a Religious People —
Forms and Limits

The preceding chapter addressed the constitutional core of religious liberty, and explained that virtually all of it is a product of the space created by non-establishment norms, as well as more general constitutional concerns involving expression, association, privacy, and equality. The government's ability and authority to accommodate the religious needs of its people are not limited, however, to that universe of constitutional mandates. Beyond those basic requirements of the Constitution, government responds in many different ways to the demands and concerns of a religious people.

Unlike the relatively short-lived regime of mandatory exemptions for religiously motivated behavior under the Free Exercise Clause, various other forms of government responsiveness to religious concerns are long-standing. Both before and after the ratification of the Constitution, for example, several American colonies and states chose to accommodate a variety of religious minorities, including Quakers and members of other faith groups who would not bear arms in defense of the state.[1] These exemptions could not plausibly

1. For a concise account of the relevant history of controversies over exemptions from the obligation to bear arms, see Michael W. McConnell, *The Origins and Historical Understanding of Free Exercise of Religion,* 103 Harv. L. Rev. 1410, 1468-1469 (1990). Similar controversies broke out in the colonies and states with respect to the taking of oaths by witnesses in court and government officers. See *id.* at 1467-1468. The U.S. Constitution would address this problem directly by requiring all officers of state and local government to bind themselves "by Oath or Affirmation, to support this Constitution." U.S. Const., Art. VI, cl. 3. See also Art. I, §3, cl. 6 (senators "shall be on Oath or Affirmation" when sitting as a court of impeachment; U.S. Const., §1, cl. 8) (requirement of presidential "Oath or Affirmation" prior to entering "Execution of his Office"). Those options for government officers are constitutionally mandatory; the right of conscientious objection to bearing arms is discretionary, and depends upon legislative acts.

be seen as government promoting or sponsoring its own religious identity. In these situations, the state had expressed its own need for men to bear arms, but it nevertheless saw the justice and utility of responding to the conscientious concerns of a religious minority.

Over the past few centuries, government has found many ways to accommodate the people's religious needs. The most frequent mode is noninterference. That is, the government recognizes that an obligation it seeks to impose will conflict with the religious beliefs of individuals or communities, and so it creates some form of exemption from that obligation. For example, the state may exempt certain religious groups from rules of road safety[2] or restrictions on the use of controlled substances.[3] In such situations, the state simply moves out of the way and allows the religiously motivated practice to proceed.

At the other end of the spectrum, the government responds by affirmatively providing opportunities for worship or religious experience to people who are under the government's care or control. For example, the government provides chaplains in the armed forces, state universities, public hospitals, and prisons. In these contexts, the government is not merely removing impediments to private choices of religious experience. Rather, it recognizes that people in certain circumstances have very limited or no opportunity to pursue religious experience, and fills that gap with government-provided resources. This kind of affirmative responsiveness is, at first glance, in the sharpest tension with the ideal of a secular government, because it involves the state providing places of worship space and paying clergy — acts that would otherwise violate core principles of nonestablishment. We take up this kind of responsiveness in detail in the book's final chapter.

Between these poles of noninterference and affirmative provision lies a wide variety of policies that involve discretionary government responsiveness to the people's religious needs. Consider, for example, the context of employment, both public and private. Acting as an employer, the state may accom-

---

2. For example, a Kentucky law enacted in 2012 gives the owners of horse-drawn buggies the alternative to use lanterns and white reflective tape instead of the orange triangle — the standard slow-moving vehicle symbol — to which the Amish have religious objections. http://religionclause.blogspot.com/2012/04/kentucky-governor-signs-into-law-bill.html.

3. The United States protects members of the Native American Church from legal bans on the use of peyote. 42 U.S.C. §1996a(b)(1) provides: "Notwithstanding any other provision of law, the use, possession, or transportation of peyote by an Indian for bona fide traditional ceremonial purposes in connection with the practice of a traditional Indian religion is lawful, and shall not be prohibited by the United States or any State."

modate religious employees whose practices conflict with various workplace rules about uniforms or physical appearance.[4] Similarly, the state may choose to adjust the work schedules of employees who observe religious holidays, including a weekly Sabbath. Doing so may of course inconvenience others. Moreover, in important ways, government extends its concern about religion in the workplace to the private sector as well. Title VII of the 1964 Civil Rights Act, for example, forbids religious discrimination in the workplace,[5] and as part of that regime requires private as well as public employers to make reasonable accommodations for the religious needs of employees.[6]

This chapter focuses on those kinds of government responsiveness that are not mandated by the Constitution. However uncharitable this may seem, the core of religious liberty described in the prior chapter requires none of these accommodations. Accordingly, these practices are completely discretionary, and they raise some of the most difficult and important questions for our approach to the religion clauses. On the one hand, secular government may not respond to religious needs as a way of promoting religious faith or experience, favoring some faith traditions over others, or expressing the government's own religious identity. On the other hand, within the limits generated by those prohibitions, government should be free to recognize and respond to the deeply held and widely varying religious commitments of its people. If government were not free to do this, but remained free to respond to other needs of its citizens — say, for recreation or art — it might fairly be accused of unjustifiable hostility to religious experience. In this chapter, we explain which discretionary responses are constitutionally appropriate and which are forbidden by the nonestablishment norm.

4. After the Supreme Court ruled in *Goldman v. Weinberger,* 475 U.S. 503 (1986), that the First Amendment did not protect the right of religious members of the armed forces to deviate from prescribed requirements of dress and uniform, Congress enacted a discretionary accommodation, permitting members to wear "neat and conservative" religious apparel, subject to military regulation and control. See 10 U.S.C. [sec.] 774 (2005).

5. Section 703 (a) (1) of the Civil Rights Act of 1964, Title VII, 78 Stat. 255, 42 U.S.C. sec. 2000e-2 (a) (1), makes it an unlawful employment practice for an employer to discriminate against an employee or a prospective employee on the basis of his or her religion.

6. Congress included the following definition of religion in the 1972 amendments to Title VII of the 1964 Civil Rights Act: "The term 'religion' includes all aspects of religious observance and practice, as well as belief, unless an employer demonstrates that he is unable to reasonably accommodate an employee's or prospective employee's religious observance or practice without undue hardship on the conduct of the employer's business." §701 (j), 42 U.S.C. §2000e (j).

The Model of Equal Treatment

Most instances of discretionary government responsiveness to religious needs appear in circumstances in which government treats comparable secular needs in identical ways. These responses, though not required by the Constitution, nevertheless involve the broad variety of mechanisms and institutions through which the government helps to facilitate the flourishing of the people's civic, social, and spiritual lives. For a prime example, one of the earliest challenges in the Supreme Court to a legislative accommodation of religious entities occurred in *Walz v. Tax Commission,*[7] in which challengers attacked New York City's exemption from taxation for "properties used solely for religious worship." One of the Court's principal justifications for rejecting this attack was that the city had singled out neither one faith nor churches as such for the exemption. Instead, the Court wrote, the city "has granted exemption to all houses of religious worship within a broad class of property owned by nonprofit, quasi-public corporations which include hospitals, libraries, playgrounds, scientific, professional, historical, and patriotic groups."[8]

This characterization of this tax exemption reflects, in a discretionary setting, the Constitution's generic strategy for respecting rights: the government treats religion in ways identical to its secular counterparts, neither favoring nor disfavoring any nonprofit entity because of its religious character. Indeed, it would be difficult to justify, on constitutional or policy grounds, a rule that excluded religious nonprofits from a property tax exemption available to secular nonprofit organizations.[9] As the Court suggests in *Walz,* any attempt to tax property used "solely for religious worship" would require the government to appraise what constitutes such a use and the extent to which the property is devoted to such a use. Imagine, for example, that a house of worship makes a meeting room available several evenings a week for a twelve-step program,[10] open to all, to fight substance abuse. Appraisals of the

7. *Walz v. Tax Commission,* 397 U.S. 664 (1970).

8. *Id.* at 673-674.

9. In some circumstances, however, the nonestablishment principle permits — or even requires — distinctive treatment of religious organizations. For example, in *Locke v. Davey,* 540 U.S. 712 (2004), Washington State successfully defended its policy of not permitting state-sponsored college scholarships to fund studies in preparation for religious ministry. The Supreme Court agreed that this exclusion was justifiable in light of the state's policy of keeping its distance — neither supporting nor regulating — from the enterprise of ministry.

10. Four of the twelve steps in the Alcoholics Anonymous program make explicit reference to God (see http://www.aa.org/en_pdfs/smf-121_en.pdf), though each reference invokes

extent of explicitly religious activity in a twelve-step program could produce a form of interaction that would itself be constitutionally troublesome,[11] with tax auditors tempted to make suggestions about revising the steps in order to preserve a tax exemption.

This model of equal responsiveness to both secular and comparable religious interests is replicated over and over, at all levels of government. Consider, as a brief set of examples, (1) exemption for nonprofit entities from federal and state income tax;[12] (2) permitted absences from school, a setting in which reasons of health, family emergency, and religious need (among others) will be afforded equal respect; and (3) historically recognized military draft exemptions, which at various times have included health, family needs, and educational commitments as well as religiously based pacifism.[13] Whenever the government responds to religious needs as part of a broader class of concerns, the government does not make those religious needs a matter of its own ends or identity. Instead, it recognizes that many of its people will make those concerns a central part of their own life projects. With respect to affording relief from general obligations, the Supreme Court has never expressed any serious constitutional doubt about forms of responsiveness that treat religion equally with its secular counterparts.[14]

---

the participant's personal understanding of God. See *id.,* step 3: "3. Made a decision to turn our will and our lives over to the care of God *as we understood Him.*"

11. In *Walz* and elsewhere, the Court has expressed concern that the state not become "excessively entangled" in decisions about what actions do or do not have a religious character. 397 U.S. at 674-675. See also *Lemon v. Kurtzman,* 403 U.S. 602 (1971) (scheme for aiding religious schools deemed unconstitutional because enforcing restriction of financial support to secular instruction only would cause "excessive entanglement").

12. See, e.g., U.S. Internal Revenue Code, section 501 (c)(3) (exemption of charitable organizations, including those with a religious character, from federal taxation of income).

13. See 50 USCS Appx §456, "Deferments and Exemptions from Training and Service."

14. Affirmative government provision of resources necessary to facilitate religion in state-run institutions and enclaves, like prisons, state hospitals, military bases, and public universities, might also be understood through the model of equal treatment. Whenever government provides the resources for religious experience, it always provides comparable resources for other kinds of experience — for example, athletic facilities, forms of secular entertainment, educational opportunities, forums for social interaction, and the like. If the model of equal treatment were always a constitutional safe harbor for state provision of religious resources, chaplaincies and state-run houses of worship would be unproblematic. As revealed by the earlier chapter on government financial support for religious experience, however, the model of equal treatment cannot be mechanically applied to affirmative government facilitation of religious experience. Instead, even in contexts in which norms of equal treatment are satisfied, this sort of affirmative provision must be separately justified by other considerations, typically

Religious Distinctiveness and Government Responsiveness

As a number of prior chapters have argued, religion is constitutionally distinctive in certain respects. This distinctiveness, which derives from concerns about government power, responsibility, and identity, plays out in matters of civil authority over disputes involving religious organizations; government financing of religious experience; the place of religion in public education; and state-sponsored displays of religious messages. In all these contexts, the distinctiveness of religion forces government to refrain from supporting religious causes or resolving ecclesiastical questions.

In some circumstances, however, the government has asserted the distinctiveness of religion as justification for special treatment. When government responds specially to the needs of religion, the situation is the perfect reverse from those we analyzed at the end of the last chapter, in which government responds to secular needs but not to religious ones. Imagine, for example, that the city of Newark had exempted from its "no beards" policy only those police officers who had religious reasons to wear a beard, and had not exempted those with health-based reasons not to shave. Would such a "religion-only" exemption represent the kind of favoring, subsidy, promotion, or sponsorship of religion that the Establishment Clause condemns?[15]

This question is more difficult to answer than it first appears. After all, government regularly recognizes what Kant called the "crooked timber of humanity."[16] At times, rules that apply generally, have overall positive utility, and do not inflict significant burdens on most addressees may impose severe hardship on others. Because nonreligious practices or groups can seek specific forms of responsiveness in their favor, a categorical ban on relief that is targeted to religion would effectively and unjustifiably disfavor religion. More fundamentally, excluding the possibility of all forms of religion-specific relief would interfere with secular government's appropriate role of respecting the religiosity of the people.

---

involving government responsibility to make special provision for religious experience when government's own institutions have limited the access to it. We will revisit these questions in the book's concluding chapter. See also Ira C. Lupu and Robert W. Tuttle, *Instruments of Accommodation: The Military Chaplaincy and the Constitution*, 110 W. Va. L. Rev. 89 (2007).

15. Chris Eisgruber and Larry Sager describe this precise scenario as "an exceptionally difficult case." Christopher L. Eisgruber and Lawrence G. Sager, *Religious Freedom and the Constitution* 117–118 (Harvard University Press, 2006).

16. Immanuel Kant, *Idea for a General History with a Cosmopolitan Purpose* (1784), Proposition 6, "Out of the crooked timber of humanity, no straight thing was ever made."

Once the Court in *Everson* (1947) ruled that the Establishment Clause applied to the states, questions inevitably arose as to the validity of various state and local measures that responded to asserted religious needs. The Supreme Court's earliest encounters with such measures were not completely up to the task. In 1948, the Court in *McCollum v. Bd. of Education*[17] held unconstitutional a program of religious instruction by sectarian school instructors on public school premises during public school hours. The Court viewed the program as impermissibly identifying the state as a sponsor of religious instruction, rather than as a response to parental needs to find a time in the educational day for religious training. After intense public criticism for acting in a way that some viewed as hostile to religion, the Court in *Zorach v. Clauson* (1952)[18] upheld New York State's program of released time from compulsory public school hours for religious instruction off the premises.

Zorach seems poorly reasoned. The hours of the public school day imposed no burden at all on religious instruction that parents might desire for their children; such education could readily be made available before school, after school, or on weekend days. Even if the encumbrance on time represented by the hours committed to the normal school day were a burden on the religious freedom of parents, that encumbrance equally burdened parents who wanted their children to have more time for sports, scouting, musical training, or any other extracurricular activity. Singling out religion alone for released time, without offering the same response for secular activities, cannot be justified by any distinctive burden imposed on religion through the operation of normal school hours.

It was not until a trilogy of decisions in the 1980s that the Supreme Court significantly clarified the principles applicable to religion-specific acts of government responsiveness.[19] In *Estate of Thornton v. Caldor*,[20] decided in 1985, the Court invalidated under the Establishment Clause a Connecticut law that required all employers, public and private, to set up work schedules in a way that allowed all employees to observe their weekly Sabbath. In a somewhat cryptic opinion, Chief Justice Burger described the "absolute" character of the scheme as its chief constitutional flaw. Because the law permitted no

17. *McCollum v. Bd. of Education*, 333 U.S. 203 (1948).

18. *Zorach v. Clauson*, 343 U.S. 306 (1952).

19. The Court's opinion in *Trans World Airlines, Inc. v. Hardison*, 432 U.S. 63 (1977), which limited the scope of employers' duty to accommodate the religious practices of employees, was an earlier signal of the concern about the tendency of religiously distinctive responsiveness to shift costs unreasonably to third parties.

20. *Estate of Thornton v. Caldor*, 472 U.S. 703 (1985).

exceptions, it effectively transferred all the costs of accommodation of Sabbath observance to employers and fellow employees, whose schedules would have to change to allow Sabbatarians their preferred day off. In the doctrinal language of the time, this meant that the "primary effect" of the scheme was the advancement of religion. Concurring in *Caldor*, Justice O'Connor emphasized a different vice of the scheme; it singled out Sabbatarians for unique protection, and therefore revealed what O'Connor called an endorsement of Sabbath-observing faiths over all others.[21]

Two years later, in *Corporation of Presiding Bishops v. Amos*,[22] the Court upheld an exemption for religious organizations from federal law's prohibition on religious discrimination in employment. The prohibition on religious discrimination, the Court recognized, would uniquely burden religious organizations, because organizations devoted to a secular ideology are under no comparable restriction on their ability to choose employees who are devoted to their mission. Thus, the exemption permits religious entities to prefer coreligionists for employment, enabling those entities to control their religious messages, and use their power to hire as an instrument for building and maintaining a cohesive religious community. The religion-specific exemption upheld in *Amos* thus responded in perfect proportions to what would have been a distinctive burden on religious institutions. This is why, we suspect, the Court in *Amos* was unanimous.

The trilogy concludes with the decision in *Texas Monthly v. Bullock* (1989),[23] in which the Court invalidated an exemption from the Texas sales tax for religious publications sold by nonprofit religious organizations. The Court reasoned that liability for sales taxes, equal to that imposed on for-profit and nonprofit organizations alike with respect to other publications, did not distinctively burden religion. Accordingly, the benefit provided an unconstitutional subsidy for religion.[24] Moreover, this subsidy functioned to advantage religious expression over other publications, and consequently offended a separate, overarching norm of evenhandedness of state policy toward both secular and religious expression.[25]

Thus, just before the Court rejected the doctrine of mandatory exemptions in *Smith*, the trilogy suggested three principles to assess the validity of discretionary exemptions for religion. First, such acts must be designed

---

21. 472 U.S. at 711.
22. *Corporation of Presiding Bishops v. Amos*, 483 U.S. 327 (1987).
23. *Texas Monthly v. Bullock*, 489 U.S. 1 (1989).
24. 489 U.S. at 14-17.
25. 489 U.S. at 26 (White, J., concurring in the judgment).

to relieve, and be reasonably proportionate to, burdens distinctively experienced by religion. This standard fit the Title VII exemption upheld in *Amos* but could not be applied successfully to the tax exemption in *Texas Monthly* or the absolute preference for Sabbath observance in *Caldor*. Second, the government's response must not have an unreasonably large impact on third parties. The scheme condemned in *Caldor* is an obvious example of one that forces third parties — employers and fellow employees — to bear a disproportionate share of the costs of the accommodation. Third, as suggested by Justice O'Connor's concurring opinion in *Caldor*, such acts must be available on a denominationally neutral basis. Government may not give relief to some faith groups while denying the same relief to others. Special rights for Sabbatarians, for example, as Connecticut afforded in *Caldor*, could not be seen as evenhanded toward faiths that celebrated religious holidays but did not observe a weekly Sabbath.

These three principles — denominational neutrality, the presence of religion-distinctive burdens to justify religion-distinctive responsiveness, and the concern for the impact of such measures on private third parties — all deserve careful explication. The neutrality principle seems doctrinally and theoretically obvious, but raises subtle questions of application. The second and third principles have been significantly undertheorized, and a closer look at both will shed considerable light on the tensions between the idea of secular government and the mission of responsiveness to a religious people.

Denominational Neutrality

Acts of government responsiveness must be available on a denominationally neutral basis. That is, they may not favor some faiths over others. If such favoritism is overt, the government will have effectively proclaimed the superiority of, or sense of desert in the members of, a particular faith or set of faiths. There can be no reason that government could offer, consistent with the secular jurisdictional limitation, to justify such a preferential accommodation — say, for Christians and Jews, but not others, to be released early from school for religious instruction.

Some responsive acts are quite easy to frame in a way that is transparently and obviously neutral among sects. For example, the requirement in Title VII of the 1964 Civil Rights Act that employers make reasonable accommodations for the religious practices of their employees protects workers of all faiths. Likewise, the Religious Land Use and Institutionalized Persons Act includes the religious practices of all incarcerated persons, and protects all houses of worship in the land use process.

Just as obviously, other responsive acts are defective under this principle. For example, the employment law of South Carolina at the time of *Sherbert* protected Sunday Sabbatarians but no others against pressure to work on their chosen day of prayer and rest.[26]

Even where the denominational preference is more subtle, the Supreme Court has been sensitive to the dangers of responsive measures that are available only to politically popular or influential sects. For example, in *Board of Education of Kiryas Joel Village School District v. Grumet*,[27] the Court invalidated a school district for a village occupied almost entirely by a particular Orthodox Jewish community. The legislature had created the district because some children in the community were disabled, and therefore entitled to state-provided financial support that constitutionally could not be funneled through the village's private religious schools. These children, because of their unusual modes of dress and other customs, had been the targets of derision in the nearby public schools of another community. Despite these plausible reasons for the state to respond to the plight of these particular children, the Court struck down the law creating a public school district for the village, because New York law had no established process through which faith groups (or any discrete social groups) in other communities might obtain a similar designation as a school district.[28]

Denominational neutrality or its absence is almost always easy to identify as a formal matter, and in that sense this principle is the easiest for lawmakers to confidently satisfy. At times, however, the forms and content of religious accommodations make this principle somewhat difficult to apply. The three most difficult problems of application involve (1) intentional religious gerrymanders, in which what seems a faith-neutral response is designed to protect one group and not others; (2) the existence of arguably analogous religious practices to which government does not offer similar protection; and (3) the affirmative provision of government resources, such as paid chaplains. We defer discussion of the third set of issues to the book's next and final chapter.

26. *Sherbert v. Verner*, 374 U.S. 398, 406 (1963).

27. *Bd. of Ed. of Kiryas Joel Village Sch. Dist. v. Grumet*, 512 U.S. 687 (1994).

28. Justice Scalia dissented. See *id.* at 745-747 (Scalia, J., dissenting) (arguing that the Court inappropriately assumed that the state would act unconstitutionally if faced with a similar community's request for such an accommodation). For more detailed discussion, see Ira C. Lupu, *Uncovering the Village of Kiryas Joel*, 96 Colum. L. Rev. 104 (1996).

Intentional Gerrymanders

Without question, some acts of government responsiveness will help some faiths more than others. When government facilitates the observance of religious holidays, for example, those faiths with more holidays than others may benefit disproportionately. Similarly, religious exemptions from laws concerning banned substances, such as alcohol or peyote, will help only those groups that use those particular substances in their rituals or sacraments. The requirement of denominational neutrality is not offended by the uneven distribution of the consequences of such exemptions, because any and all faith groups may modify their practices or beliefs to take advantage of them. Only the intentional favoring or disfavoring of particular groups in the distribution of benefits raises constitutional problems. This is just the flip side of the Court's ruling in the Church of the Lukumi case,[29] in which the Court held that Hialeah violated the Free Exercise Clause by singling out for prohibition the Santerian practice of animal sacrifice. The government also offends this principle when it intentionally favors certain faith groups by providing accommodations that are not available to others.

A nice example of the gerrymander problem is the Internal Revenue Code's exemption for certain self-employed individuals from the tax imposed by the Federal Insurance Contribution Act in order to finance old age, survivors, and disability insurance. To qualify for the exemption, a person must be "a member of a recognized religious sect . . . and [an] . . . adherent of established tenets or teachings of such sect . . . by reason of which he is conscientiously opposed to acceptance of the benefits of any private or public insurance which makes payments in the event of death, disability, old-age, or retirement or makes payments toward the cost of, or provides services for, medical care."[30] The exemption accommodates self-employed members of the Old Order Amish, who reject the idea of government responsibility for their community's well-being and maintain their own system of care for their dependent members.[31]

At first glance, it appears that the criteria to qualify for the exemption are formally neutral among faiths, and groups other than the Amish might qualify. The exemption is limited, however, to groups that the com-

29. *Church of the Lukumi Babalu Aye, Inc. v. Hialeah,* 508 U.S. 520 (1993).

30. 26 U.S.C. sec. 1402(g)(1).

31. In *United States v. Lee,* 455 U.S. 252 (1982), the Supreme Court ruled that the Free Exercise Clause did not require that the same exemption be afforded Amish employers with respect to their Amish employees.

missioner of Social Security finds "ha[ve] been in existence at all times since December 31, 1950."[32] Although no members of groups other than the Amish have ever challenged this particular limitation, it would seem to be especially vulnerable to constitutional challenge. Perhaps Congress included the closing date in the exemption scheme as an antifraud device, aimed at blocking members of newly formed, and perhaps religiously insincere, groups from claiming the exemption from self-employment tax. Congress could have addressed that concern, however, through a requirement that claimants show a sincere and continued commitment to self-sufficiency. But a closing date in the past for the group's formation effectively makes this exemption not sect-neutral, because it excludes new groups that have identical religious commitments.[33]

Different Treatment of Analogous Practices

The second, and perhaps more common, problem that arises from the requirement of denominational neutrality is unequal responsiveness to analogous practices. For example, consider a jurisdiction that exempts sacramental uses of alcohol from a more general prohibition on use of that substance, but fails to exempt sacramental use of peyote or some other banned substance from its general laws on the subject of hallucinogenic drugs. Is such disparate treatment constitutionally permissible? On this question, our view is much like the one we expressed in analyzing the Newark Police Department's partial exemption from the requirement that its officers not wear beards. When the conduct for which a new exemption is claimed presents a different set of secular risks, costs, and benefits from that for which an exemption is allowed, the government retains its discretionary power to make distinctions on secular grounds. Government should have the opportunity to show that the use of peyote does not present the same set of concerns as the use of alcohol, in terms of frequency of use, the hazards of intoxication or addiction, patterns of illicit distribution, and effects on physical or mental health. If such dif-

32. 26 U.S.C. sec. 1402(g)(1)(E).

33. Native American religions may involve a special case, in which historic relations between the tribes and both federal and state governments may permit unique forms of responsiveness to Native American faith communities. See, e.g., *Peyote Way Church of God v. Thornburgh*, 922 F. 2d 1210 (5th Cir. 1991) (state may exempt Native American Church from ban on peyote without extending the exemption to other faiths, not populated primarily by Native Americans, that seek to use peyote in their sacraments).

ferences exist, government should be free to exempt religious use of either alcohol or peyote without constitutional compulsion to exempt the religious use of the other.[34]

Our conception of denominational neutrality, like the Supreme Court's, depends strongly on formality and bright lines. We reject as unworkable the theory advanced by Douglas Laycock and Thomas Berg that the government must be substantively neutral between religion and irreligion, and among sects.[35] By substantive neutrality, Professors Laycock and Berg mean that government should be under a duty to minimize any incentives or disincentives for the people to be religious or not, to follow any particular faith, or to maintain any particular faith practices.

In a polity in which the government must maintain a secular identity, however, the government will inevitably take responsibility for the promotion of secular values and not religious ones. And the government will, with equal inevitability, forbid certain conduct because of perceived secular harms. In a world so circumscribed, it will be impossible for the government to remain substantively neutral. The government will always be promoting or discouraging various practices toward which some or all religions will be differently inclined. A doctrine of substantive neutrality would force the government into perpetual attentiveness to religious commitments and practices. For reasons that protect rather than undermine liberty in general, our constitutional tradition has rightly rejected both that requirement of religious attentiveness and the mandates (and perpetual arguments about those mandates) that would follow from such an obligation.

Religion-Distinctive Burdens

A key component of the 1980s trilogy on the validity of religion-specific acts of government responsiveness is the requirement that such acts respond to burdens that are distinctive to religion. The sales-tax exemption in *Texas Monthly* failed because it could not meet that test. In contrast, the Title VII exemption for coreligionist hiring, upheld in *Amos,* meets

34. See discussion in chapter 6 of our disagreement with Chris Eisgruber and Larry Sager on this point.

35. The germinal piece on the difference between substantive and formal free exercise neutrality, described in those terms, is Douglas Laycock, *Formal, Substantive, and Disaggregated Neutrality toward Religion,* 39 DePaul L. Rev. 993 (1990). See also Thomas C. Berg, *Religion Clause Anti-Theories,* 72 Notre Dame L. Rev. 693, 703-707 (1997).

it perfectly. The rationale for this requirement seems obvious enough. If government relieves religious entities of burdens that equally afflict their secular counterparts, government would be expressing a forbidden preference for religious institutions over others. So, to add another example, a state law that exempted from health and safety requirements only child care centers owned and operated by religious entities could not be justified. The need for health and safety standards is uniform across the population of children, and the standards rarely, if ever, impose any distinctive burden on religious operators.

Between *Texas Monthly* and *Amos* are a host of situations in which the question of a unique or distinctive burden on religion might be difficult. For example, the Religious Land Use and Institutionalized Persons Act (RLUIPA) relieves prison inmates of some burdens on their freedom that may not be distinctive to religion — for example, restrictions on access to particular reading materials. The Supreme Court in *Cutter v. Wilkinson*[36] upheld the "institutionalized persons" provision from a constitutional attack by the state of Ohio, and in doing so emphasized the requirement that religion-specific measures respond to religion-specific burdens — in that case, the wide scope of restrictions in prisons on religious practices.[37] The opinion in *Cutter* thus seemed to be influenced by a quantitative appraisal of the burdens that emerge from the experience of incarceration. Looked at practice by practice, however, the relief given to inmates by this act might not be so readily justifiable as a response to a distinctive burden on religion. Prison diets, for example, may burden religious freedom, but may also impose burdens on prisoners with diet-related health problems.

Consider as well the long-standing controversy about the "parsonage exemption" in the Internal Revenue Code.[38] The exemption authorizes clergy

36. *Cutter v. Wilkinson*, 544 U.S. 709 (2005).

37. In *Cutter*, the Supreme Court held that RLUIPA §3 rests on a reasonable legislative judgment that the religious exercise of institutionalized persons has suffered distinctive burdens, such as discrimination and arbitrary limitation. 544 U.S. 709, 720 (2005) ("RLUIPA's institutionalized persons provision . . . alleviates exceptional government-created burdens on private religious exercise"). The Court has not yet considered a facial challenge to §2, but we think it would similarly conclude that a legislative record of distinctive harms to religious land uses justifies the grant of special protections for such uses. Lower courts have uniformly rejected such challenges to the land use provisions. See, e.g., *Westchester Day Sch. v. Vill. of Mamaroneck*, 504 F. 3d 338, 355-356 (2nd Cir. 2007); *Midrash Sephardi, Inc. v. Town of Surfside*, 366 F. 3d 1214, 1235-1237 (11th Cir. 2004); *Guru Nanak Sikh Soc'y v. County of Sutter*, 456 F. 3d 978, 992-995 (9th Cir. 2006).

38. The exemption, which appears in Internal Revenue Code §107, has been declared

to exclude from taxable income the value of housing, or a housing allowance, provided to them by religious organizations. When originally enacted, the exemption reflected a traditional practice of building a parsonage adjacent to the church. The church-provided housing was designed to supplement the traditionally low salaries paid to ministers, but also afforded congregation members immediate access to their cleric. Over time, however, the exemption expanded to include housing allowances for homes regardless of ownership by or proximity to the church. Moreover, the exemption was claimed by a wide variety of clergy, many of whom were otherwise quite adequately paid.[39] Under current circumstances, it is very hard to see why the more general requirement — that the provision of housing or a housing allowance to employees be treated as taxable income — should not be applied to clergy in the same way as all other employees.[40] In its current scope, the parsonage exemption no longer responds to any distinctive burden on religious entities, and is therefore constitutionally questionable. The parsonage exemption could be saved by widening it to include secular nonprofits, but such a change would constitute a large and quite unjustifiable tax expenditure in favor of high-level employees of nonprofit organizations.

unconstitutional by a federal district court in Wisconsin. See *Freedom from Religion Foundation v. Lew,* 2013 U.S. Dist. LEXIS 166076 (W.D. Wis., Nov. 22, 2013). The case is now on appeal in the U.S. Court of Appeals for the 7th Circuit.

39. For example, Rick Warren — author of *The Purpose-Driven Life* and pastor of Saddleback Church — claimed the parsonage exemption for his entire annual church salary, which exceeded $75,000. See *Warren v. Commissioner,* 114 T.C. 343 (2000) (ruling that parsonage exemption should be limited to the fair market rental value of the property). The litigation between Pastor Warren and the IRS was ultimately resolved by a statute, the Clergy Housing Allowance Clarification Act of 2002. For more on this dispute, see Edward Zelinsky, *Do Religious Tax Exemptions Entangle in Violation of the Establishment Clause? The Constitutionality of the Parsonage Allowance Exclusion and the Religious Exemptions of the Individual Health Care Mandate and the FICA and Self-Employment Taxes,* 33 Cardozo L. Rev. 1633 (2012).

40. For all nonclergy employees, and for all employers, the value of lodging provided by an employer to an employee is excluded from taxable income if the lodging is for the convenience of the employer, and the employee "is required to accept such lodging on the business premises of his employer as a condition of his employment." U.S. Internal Revenue Code, section 119 (a).

State Competence to Appraise Religious Burdens

Beyond questions of distinctiveness and proportionality lurks a separate question that runs through other parts of this book — the state's constitutional competence to evaluate the extent of any asserted burden on religious experience. As we have argued throughout this work, the Establishment Clause limits the state's assertion of religious authority. The state is not jurisdictionally competent to make religious decisions, such as what constitutes the most faithful interpretation of religious texts, the fitness of a person for religious ministry, or the relative religious significance of particular beliefs or conduct.

Moreover, this limitation applies equally to legislators and administrators as to judges. Legislators and administrators considering responsive measures, especially those that are religion-specific, may take account of the frequency and intensity of preferences for such measures, but they may not independently weigh their religious significance.

Although the 1980s trilogy generated fairly stable criteria for deciding whether a religion-specific response unconstitutionally promotes or favors religion, the Supreme Court has never directly considered whether particular religious accommodations push government officials beyond their constitutional competence. Several legislative responses to *Employment Division v. Smith*[41] offer particularly detailed and important contexts in which to explore this underappreciated question.

Following the Supreme Court's decision in *Smith,* a coalition of religious and civil rights organizations succeeded in urging passage of the Religious Freedom Restoration Act (RFRA) of 1993.[42] RFRA purports to codify the Court's pre-*Smith* standard for free exercise exemptions. Under the statute, if a government policy (at any level of government in the United States) "substantially burdens" a "sincerely-held" religious belief or practice, burdened adherents are entitled to relief from the application of the policy to them unless such action is the "least restrictive means" of achieving a "compelling government interest."[43] RFRA's expansive reach did not endure for very long. In 1997 the Supreme Court held in *City of Boerne v. Flores*[44] that the RFRA was unconstitutional as applied to state and local governments, because it

41. *Employment Division v. Smith,* 494 U.S. 872 (1990).
42. 42 U.S.C. §2000bb.
43. *Id.*
44. *City of Boerne v. Flores,* 521 U.S. 507 (1997).

exceeded Congress's enforcement power under section 5 of the Fourteenth Amendment.[45]

After a failed attempt to enact another comprehensive religious accommodation statute (the Religious Liberty Protection Act)[46] that would remedy the defects identified in *Boerne,* Congress in 2000 passed the Religious Land Use and Institutionalized Persons Act (RLUIPA).[47] The contexts of land use and corrections permitted Congress to avoid the constitutional defects in RFRA,[48] and steered around divisive social issues that had strained the RFRA coalition.[49]

For several reasons, RLUIPA offers an especially illuminating opportunity to explore government responsiveness to religion-specific burdens. First, the statute offers far more robust protection for religious exercise than the Constitution demands for those activities.[50] Any protection that exceeds the constitutional mandate of free exercise is by definition a discretionary form of responsiveness. Second, RLUIPA employs a variety of standards, each of which presents a subtly different form of response. We focus primarily on the part of the act that governs restrictions on the religious activity of institutionalized persons, because that part of the scheme — calling for an appraisal of whether the government has "substantially burdened" religious freedom[51] — raises the jurisdictional problem most acutely.

In the context of religious land use,[52] the statute deploys five distinct standards for judicial review of land use restrictions. Most of the land use

45. *Id.* at 532-534.

46. Religious Liberty Protection Act of 1998, 105th Congress, H.R. 4019 and S. 2148.

47. 42 U.S.C. §2000cc *et seq.*

48. RLUIPA, 42 U.S.C. §§2000cc(a)(2), 2000cc-1(b) (listing jurisdictional bases for statute).

49. See C. Canady, *New Legislation on Religious Liberty,* 117 Christian Century, no. 22, p. 786 (Aug. 2, 2000); 146 Cong. Rec. S7, 778-779 (daily ed. July 27, 2000) (statement of Sen. Reid) (during the RLUIPA debate, discussing obstacles to enactment of RLPA).

50. Even under pre-*Smith* Free Exercise jurisprudence, the incarcerated did not enjoy robust rights of religious accommodation. *O'Lone v. Estate of Shabazz,* 482 U.S. 342 (1987) (prison restrictions on religious liberty will be upheld if the restrictions are reasonably related to legitimate penological considerations).

51. 42 U.S.C. §2000cc-1(a).

52. Religious institutions had only minimal success in claiming exemption from land use regulations before *Smith,* although courts purported to apply the *Sherbert-Yoder* strict scrutiny standard. See, e.g., *Lakewood, Ohio Congregation of Jehovah's Witnesses, Inc. v. City of Lakewood,* 699 F. 2d 303 (6th Cir. 1983). See generally Robert W. Tuttle, *How Firm a Foundation? Protecting Religious Land Uses after Boerne,* 68 Geo. Wash. L. Rev. 861, 871-880 (2000) (discussing pre-*Smith* federal and state court decisions in land use disputes that involved religious institutions).

provisions focus on discrimination against religious uses or exclusion of such uses,[53] but the most controversial and constitutionally vulnerable part of the scheme is triggered by the same "substantial burden" standard that governs the claims of institutionalized persons.[54] In both contexts, requiring government decision makers to assess the religious significance of state-created restrictions or obligations raises serious constitutional difficulties.

RLUIPA-Institutionalized Persons

Persons in government-run institutions are subject to elaborate restrictions on their freedom, including their religious freedom. Congress, in attempting to prohibit unreasonable restrictions, legislated in very general terms, and delegated the particulars of judgment to prison administrators and judges reviewing their actions. Section 3 of RLUIPA provides:

> (a) General rule. No government shall impose a substantial burden on the religious exercise of a person residing in or confined to an institution, as defined in section 2 of the Civil Rights of Institutionalized Persons Act (42 U.S.C. 1997), even if the burden results from a rule of general applicability, unless the government demonstrates that imposition of the burden on that person
>
> (1) is in furtherance of a compelling governmental interest; and
>
> (2) is the least restrictive means of furthering that compelling governmental interest.[55]

This provision adopts a standard derived from the Supreme Court's interpretations of the Free Exercise Clause in *Sherbert* and *Yoder,* and makes that standard applicable to governmentally operated hospitals, nursing homes, and all types of adult and juvenile correctional facilities.[56] The correctional context accounts for virtually all the extraordinarily large number of reported cases applying this provision.[57] The Supreme Court has twice heard disputes over

53. 42 U.S.C. §2000cc(b).

54. 42 U.S.C. §2000cc(a)(1).

55. 42 U.S.C. §2000cc-1.

56. See the definition of "institution" in the Civil Rights of Institutionalized Persons Act, 42 U.S.C. §1997.

57. A recent LEXIS search for reported decisions applying RLUIPA §3 produced over a thousand cases.

this part of RLUIPA. In *Cutter v. Wilkinson*,[58] the Court rejected a state's claim that the statute violated the Establishment Clause by promoting religion. Later, in *Sossamon v. Texas*,[59] the Court ruled that RLUIPA does not authorize courts to award claimants money damages from the state for violations of the statute. Neither the Supreme Court nor the lower federal courts have considered, however, the problem we have identified in this chapter. Section 3 of RLUIPA presents that problem in its starkest form. In disputes arising under this provision, prison officials and courts are routinely called upon to make religious judgments.

Consider just a few examples of litigation under section 3. In *Luke v. Williams*,[60] a court determined that a Wiccan prisoner's religious exercise was not substantially burdened by the state's restriction on his practice of faith outdoors and use of certain religious artifacts. The court rejected the inmate's claim because prison officials had consulted with an expert on Wiccan practice, who opined that practice of the faith did not require what the prisoner sought.[61] In *Sayed v. Proffitt*,[62] a court ruled that a Muslim prisoner's religious exercise was not substantially burdened by the state's refusal to allow him to perform "full ablution" (a shower) before weekly prayer service. The court agreed with prison officials, who in turn relied on an authority on Islam in concluding that partial ablution was an adequate substitute.[63] And in *Vigil v. Jones*,[64] a prisoner claimed to believe in "Judeo-Christianity," and said that his religious exercise was substantially burdened by the prison's designation of him as a Protestant. That designation prohibited him from taking part in Jewish worship services.[65] The court rejected his claim, and held that Protestant worship gave the claimant "a reasonable opportunity to participate in prison sponsored ceremonies that observe Judeo-Christian values."[66]

58. *Cutter v. Wilkinson*, 544 U.S. 709 (2005).

59. *Sossamon v. Texas*, 131 S. Ct. 1651 (2011).

60. *Luke v. Williams*, 2010 U.S. Dist. LEXIS 123752 (D. Or., Nov. 19, 2010).

61. *Id.* at *8 ("Defendants also consulted with multiple Wiccan clergy members, one of whom stated that 'Wiccan ceremonies are very personal and can be purely meditative; no special property is needed for this' ").

62. *Sayed v. Proffitt*, 2010 U.S. Dist. LEXIS 109221 (D. Col., Sept. 27, 2010).

63. *Id.* at *17-*20 (including detailed description of religious authority's explanation of ablution requirement).

64. *Vigil v. Jones*, 2010 U.S. Dist. LEXIS 95104 (D. Col., Aug. 9, 2010).

65. *Id.* at *14-*21.

66. *Id.* at *22. See also *Wares v. Simmons*, 524 F. Supp. 2d 1313, 1317-1318 (D. Kan. 2007) (officials relied on rabbis' determination that certain religious books were not important for claimant).

In each of these disputes, a government official concluded that the claimant's religious exercise was not substantially burdened because the claimant had reasonable alternative means to practice his faith. In the context of land use, questions about alternatives frequently focus on secular considerations of location, cost, and characteristics of land. In prisons, however, the reasonableness of alternatives is defined entirely in religious terms — that is, by what officials deem religiously sufficient for the claimant. Such judgments inevitably require officials to exercise religious decision-making authority.[67] Officials cannot avoid this problem by deferring to the judgment of religious experts. Such deference simply transfers the same concern to the state's determination of who is qualified to speak as an expert on the claimant's faith.

Perhaps the ubiquity of this problem in prison disputes can be explained by the unique institutional setting. As the Court noted in *Cutter,* "the government exerts a degree of control unparalleled in civilian society and severely disabling to private religious exercise."[68] Corrections officials may restrict the possession of sacred texts and objects,[69] assembly with other believers,[70] and access to religious leaders and worship experiences,[71] as well as choices about grooming, attire, and diet.[72] For the incarcerated, these core elements of religious liberty depend on government permission. It is easy to see how exercise of the power to grant or withhold that permission may lead officials to a substantive assessment of the religious reasons for the request.

Moreover, the apparent frequency of official religious judgments may be due to the government's role as affirmative provider of religious experi-

67. If the statute incorporates the Supreme Court's pre-*Smith* Free Exercise jurisprudence, the use of religious authority to deny a claim would be in tension with the Court's decision in *Thomas v. Review Bd.,* 450 U.S. 707, 715 (1980) ("Intrafaith differences . . . are not uncommon among followers of a particular creed, and the judicial process is singularly ill equipped to resolve such differences in relation to the Religion Clauses").

68. *Cutter v. Wilkinson,* 544 U.S. 709, 720-721 (2005).

69. *Mauwee v. Palmer,* 2010 U.S. Dist. LEXIS 131704 (D. Nev., Nov. 29, 2010) (possession of eagle talon for religious ritual); *LaPointe v. Walker,* 2010 U.S. Dist. LEXIS 96776 (S.D. Ill., Sept. 15, 2010) (rug for prayer).

70. *Ahmad v. Thomas,* 2010 U.S. Dist. LEXIS 100866 (S.D. Tex., Sept. 23, 2010) (worship services).

71. *Young v. Erickson,* 2010 U.S. Dist. LEXIS 134606 (E.D. Wis., Dec. 20, 2010) (access to worship services and religious leader).

72. *Sylvian v. Florida Department of Corrections,* 2010 U.S. Dist. LEXIS 115183 (N.D. Fla., Oct. 29, 2010) (grooming standards); *Jones v. Hobbs,* 2010 U.S. Dist. LEXIS 105799 (E.D. Ark., Oct. 1, 2010) (vegan meals required by religious beliefs); *Reeder v. Hogan,* 2010 U.S. Dist. LEXIS 105024 (N.D. N.Y., Sept. 29, 2010) (meals during Ramadan); *Miller v. Wilkinson,* 2010 U.S. Dist. LEXIS 103364 (S.D. Ohio, Sept. 30, 2010) (grooming standards).

ence. Because of correctional authorities' control, prisoners depend on government to facilitate their religious exercise by providing chaplains, worship space and time, and other aspects of religious life.[73] These practices may be permissible responses to the circumstances of incarcerated persons, but the context alone does not eliminate concerns about governmental competence in matters of faith. In the government's delivery of religious services, some recipients inevitably complain about the quantity, quality, or timing of the services provided.[74] Resolution of such complaints — like the grant of permission to engage in religious exercise — inevitably leads to a substantive consideration of whether the provided services are adequate.

It is easy to understand why conversations about permission or provision may lead to an assessment of religious reasons, especially when correctional facilities have easy access to experts in religious matters — prison chaplains. Prison chaplains and other experts play vital roles in helping to identify and meet the religious needs of the incarcerated, and that includes helping prisoners to appreciate the reasons for a particular accommodation. Experts may even have a role in helping prison officials to determine whether a particular claim reflects a sincerely held religious belief. But their expertise in religion should not be the source of a legal determination that a claimant's religious burden is insubstantial. That religious judgment is outside the competence of state officials, including government-employed chaplains.

The government's interest in prison administration does not confer a competence that the Establishment Clause puts off-limits to the state. Problems of administering RLUIPA in prison are best solved under the approach favored by the Supreme Court in *Cutter*, which is largely silent on the question of how to determine the substantiality of a burden but offers a contextual interpretation of the compelling interest standard. Quoting from the legislative history of RLUIPA, the court said that lawmakers "anticipated that courts would apply the Act's standard with 'due deference to the experience and expertise of prison and jail administrators in establishing necessary regulations and procedures to maintain good order, security and discipline, consistent

73. *Cutter v. Wilkinson*, 544 U.S. at 720-721.

74. See, e.g., *Oliverez v. Albitre*, 2010 U.S. Dist. LEXIS 128243 (E.D. Cal., Dec. 6, 2010) (provision of oil for Wiccan ritual); *Planker v. Ricci*, 2010 U.S. Dist. LEXIS 116083 (Nov. 1, 2010) (worship schedule for Odinist services); *Soria v. Nevada Department of Corrections*, 2010 U.S. Dist. LEXIS 116866 (D. Nev., Oct. 19, 2010) (outdoor space and materials to erect sukkah for Jewish ritual); *Green v. Werholtz*, 2010 U.S. Dist. LEXIS 102867 (D. Kan., Sept. 28, 2010) (dispute over kosher meals); *Muwwakkil v. Johnson*, 2010 U.S. Dist. LEXIS 95143 (W.D. Va., Sept. 13, 2010) (adequacy of worship schedule, among other claims).

with consideration of costs and limited resources.'"[75] Those are secular standards, and they fall squarely within the competence of officials and courts. Permitting prisoners to self-declare the substantiality of the burden on their religious exercise, and simultaneously giving prison officials wide authority to assert concerns of safety, security, and limited resources as reasons to deny the claimed accommodation, represents the appropriate solution to the problems of impermissible religious judgments.[76]

Impacts on Third Parties

The third theme that emerges from the 1980s trilogy is that religion-specific responses by government must not impose unreasonable burdens on third parties. On several occasions the Court has applied this principle to limit or strike down an accommodation but has never adequately explained the principle. In *TWA v. Hardison*,[77] for example, the Supreme Court narrowly construed the requirement in federal employment law that employers make reasonable accommodation of their employees' religious practices. The Court said that the obligation does not require employers to make accommodations that would impose more than a *de minimis* burden on the employer or fellow employees. Any more substantial burden would cause "undue hardship" to the employer. *Hardison* involved an airline employee who wanted to be free from Saturday work so that he could observe that day as his Sabbath. If TWA had accommodated his religious schedule, the airline's other employees would have been forced to work more Saturdays. Moreover, the accommodation of Hardison — a more junior employee — would have compromised the seniority system that the airline and the union had in place. That, the Court concluded, would have caused undue hardship to TWA.

In *Estate of Thornton v. Caldor*,[78] the first of the 1980s trilogy, the Court

---

75. *Cutter v. Wilkinson,* 544 U.S. 709, 722-723 (2005) (quoting S. Rep. 103-111, p. 10 [1993]).

76. The story of RLUIPA's land use provisions is far more textured, because it involves a mixture of quite permissible considerations under some parts of the scheme, which focus on equal treatment of religious and secular uses, with highly questionable concerns in others, which require an assessment of the burden imposed on religious entities by local land use policies. For extended treatment of these issues, see Ira C. Lupu and Robert W. Tuttle, *The Forms and Limits of Accommodation: The Case of RLUIPA,* 32 Cardozo L. Rev. 1907 (2011).

77. *TWA v. Hardison,* 432 U.S. 63 (1977).

78. *Estate of Thornton v. Caldor,* 472 U.S. 703 (1985).

constitutionalized the concerns expressed in *Hardison* about the transfer of hardships from religious employees to others. The Court's brief opinion in *Caldor* invalidated, under the Establishment Clause, a Connecticut state law that required all employers to accommodate the Sabbath observance of all employees, regardless of the inconvenience or cost such accommodation might impose on the employer or other employees. The Court emphasized the "absolute" quality of the required accommodation in concluding that, however benign its religion-protecting purposes, its "primary effect" unconstitutionally advanced religion.

More recently, the decision in *Cutter v. Wilkinson,*[79] upholding the prison provisions of RLUIPA, also referred to the potential burdens on third parties associated with accommodating religious needs of prisoners. In *Cutter,* the Court tied this concern both to the *Caldor* problem of costs borne by private third parties (other inmates and prison guards, whose safety might be at stake) and to the state's own interests, subsumed in RLUIPA's compelling interest defense, in protecting those third parties from harm. *Cutter* indicated that prison officials and courts, in applying the compelling interest test, should be especially sensitive to the burdens that an accommodation might impose.[80]

Why should the kind and degree of cost shifting in cases of religious accommodation be so problematic? After all, government frequently shifts to employers the costs of accommodating various employee concerns — for example, those involved with alleviating the risk of injury,[81] the hazards of unpredictable unemployment,[82] the obligation of military service,[83] the problems of disability,[84] or the need for leave for medical or family-related reasons.[85] In all these contexts, government at times forces employers to reallocate responsibilities or resources in ways that are costly to employers and, in some cases, to other employees.

79. *Cutter v. Wilkinson,* 544 U.S. 709 (2005).

80. A similar approach by zoning authorities and courts is constitutionally appropriate in applying the land use provisions of RLUIPA. When officials deviate from otherwise applicable land use criteria in response to claims based on religious exercise, the normal concerns for the interests of abutters, neighbors, and others in the community affected by land use decisions take on constitutional dimensions.

81. This is the object of workers' compensation schemes, which produce compensation for employee injuries that arise out of and in the course of employment.

82. The risk of involuntary unemployment is the standard concern of unemployment insurance, which all states maintain.

83. Soldiers and Sailors Civil Relief Act, 50 U.S.C. secs. 501 *et seq.*

84. See, e.g., the Americans with Disabilities Act, 42 U.S.C. secs. 12101 *et seq.*

85. See, e.g., the Family and Medical Leave Act, 29 U.S.C. secs. 2601 *et seq.*

Two lines of thought may help explain the special constitutional concern about the impact on third parties from religious accommodations. The first is the prohibition on government compulsion of anyone to support religion. Viewed through this prism, any cost imposed on third parties is a form of exaction, akin to a tax assessed for the specific benefit of religious beneficiaries.

This theme, though appealing on the surface, does not explain why the concern about impact on private third parties is focused on the degree of compelled subsidy, rather than the pure fact of it. A tax imposed for the direct support of religion, no matter how small or diffused throughout the set of taxpayers, would violate the Establishment Clause.[86] In contrast, a government accommodation that has a small and highly diffused impact is not likely, on those grounds alone, to be constitutionally suspect. This is true of the religious accommodations under Title VII that may impose *de minimis* costs on employers and other employees. Likewise, the statutory right of religious institutions to hire only members of their own communities imposes small and diffuse costs on prospective employees, who may be shut out of some work opportunities.[87] The Court in *Amos* did not suggest that the imposition of those costs represented an Establishment Clause vice, necessitating narrow construction, as in *Hardison,* or requiring invalidation, as in *Caldor.*

Recognizing that the concern for third-party impacts is a matter of degree, and not of kind, both limits the doctrine and makes it unpredictable in application. It is very difficult to specify how much impact is too much. And, of course, schemes like RLUIPA impose their own impacts on private third parties in the context of both prisons and land use. This is one of the reasons why the Supreme Court's opinion in *Cutter,* upholding the provision of the act relating to institutionalized persons, admonished the lower courts to be mindful of the effects of prisoners' religious practices on guards and other inmates.

The Court's interpretation of the duty of reasonable accommodation in *Hardison* offers a strong clue to the second, and more persuasive, theme that animates the concern over third-party impacts — unjustifiable govern-

---

86. *Everson v. Bd. of Educ.,* 330 U.S. 1, 16 (1947) ("No tax in any amount, large or small, can be levied to support any religious activities or institutions, whatever they may be called, or whatever form they may adopt to teach or practice religion").

87. There is also a cost to religious organizations' present employees, who face the risk of losing their position if they cease to be members in good standing of the employing organizations. Indeed, that was precisely the setting of *Corporation of Presiding Bishops v. Amos,* 483 U.S. 327 (1987).

ment favoritism for religion. Even when burdens are religiously distinctive, government must respond to them in ways that do not effectively favor them over all contrary interests that might be affected or interposed. As Justice White said in *Hardison,* requiring an employer to take elaborate steps to allow an employee to have every Saturday (or Sunday) off for Sabbath observance overpowers every competing claim to the day, and compels those who do not observe a weekly Sabbath to subsidize those who do.[88] Similarly, forcing communities to allow religion-based land uses without regard to the impacts on adjacent landowners and other neighbors subordinates all other land uses to religious uses. This in itself is a form of unconstitutional favoring of religion. Thus, in the interpretation of statutes like the institutionalized prisons or land use provisions of RLUIPA, courts should weigh the interests of other, affected private parties very heavily in determining whether the relevant authorities have a "compelling interest" in refusing the requested religious use.

An additional example may help clarify this difficult set of questions. In the 1990s, a number of people who filed for personal bankruptcy invoked the Religious Freedom Restoration Act (RFRA) as a defense to a bankruptcy trustee's attempt to bring monies tithed to a church back into the bankrupt's estate. In a prominent decision, the Eighth Circuit ruled that RFRA protected the tithers, and the church to which the monies had been paid, against a clawback of the proceeds into the bankrupt's estate.[89] The Eighth Circuit ruled that, in RFRA's terms, the loss of ability to tithe "substantially burdened" the bankrupt's religious freedom, and that the government did not have a compelling interest in denying religious tithers an exemption from bankruptcy rules concerning transfers harmful to creditors.

As Jonathan Lipson has pointed out,[90] a RFRA exemption in this context has an obvious, focused, and measurable impact on private creditors of the persons in bankruptcy. This impact may be a large or small dollar amount, but it is definitely a discrete private harm, and the Eighth Circuit's decision left no room to balance that private harm to creditors against religious harm

---

88. *TWA v. Hardison,* 432 U.S. at 81 ("There were no volunteers to relieve Hardison on Saturdays, and to give Hardison Saturdays off, TWA would have had to deprive another employee of his shift preference at least in part because he did not adhere to a religion that observed the Saturday Sabbath").

89. *Christians v. Crystal Evangelical Free Church (In re Young),* 82 F. 3d 1407, 1416-1417 (8th Cir. 1996), *reh'g en banc denied,* 89 F. 3d 494 (8th Cir. 1996), *cert. granted, vacated, and remanded,* 521 U.S. 1114 (1997), *aff'd,* 141 F. 3d 854 (8th Cir. 1998), *cert. denied,* 119 S. Ct. 43 (1998).

90. See Jonathan Lipson, *On Balance: Religious Liberty and Third Party Harms,* 84 U. Minn. L. Rev. 589 (2000).

to the debtor or the debtor's religious community. Instead, the Eighth Circuit concluded that the federal government did not have a compelling interest in protecting those creditors. Perhaps that is so, but it does not respond to the apparent Establishment Clause problem under *Caldor* of absolutely prefer-ring religious interests to competing secular interests, and doing so at the expense of private third parties. Moreover, under RFRA, the ability to make such charitable contributions despite competing interests of creditors was not available to those who contribute to secular charities.

After the Eighth Circuit's decision, Congress recognized both the un-fairness and constitutional vulnerability of a rule that (1) preferred those who made contributions to religious organizations to those who made comparable secular contributions, and (2) imposed no limit on the amounts that might escape the reach of bankruptcy law's protection of creditors. In the Religious Liberty and Charitable Protection Act of 1998,[91] Congress addressed the issue of charitable contributions by persons in bankruptcy. The act insulates from creditors those contributions made to any qualified religious or otherwise charitable organization, so long as the amount transferred does not exceed 15 percent of the gross annual income of the debtor, or is "consistent with the practices of the debtor in making charitable contributions."[92]

This move by Congress resonates with our analysis in this chapter, and with a variety of themes in this work as a whole. The Religious Liberty and Charitable Protection Act overrode the broad, religion-specific protections of RFRA and substituted a response to the problem of charitable contribu-tions by bankrupt debtors that equalized the treatment of religious and sec-ular donees of such contributions. This is the strategy of equal treatment of religion and its secular counterparts that we have defended in the chapters about mandatory and discretionary government responses to the needs of a religious people. The impact on private third parties remains, but it is no lon-ger religion-specific, and debtors accordingly no longer have any incentive to prefer religious charities to others as a way to funnel monies to causes other than satisfying their creditors.

The mere existence of harm to private third parties that may result from a government response to religious needs of the people is simply not an in-dependent ground for holding such a response unconstitutional. Instead, the harm must have the character of a strenuous preference for religious interests over comparable secular interests, or competing secular concerns. In light of

91. Public Law 105-183, 112 Stat. 517 (enacted June 19, 1998).
92. *Id.* sec. 3(a)(7).

the line-drawing problems presented by the question of third-party harms, this way of looking at the problem seems highly salutary as well as constitutionally sound.

The Affordable Care Act, Pregnancy Prevention Services, and Religious Liberty

The conflict over the federal mandate that health insurance policies include pregnancy preventive services offers us a rich opportunity to develop our approach to the religious liberty of the people. As the material that follows will demonstrate, opponents of the contraceptive mandate have some strong legal arguments, especially those arising from the Religious Freedom Restoration Act (RFRA). What is striking about this legal context are the ways in which limits on the secular state inevitably shape the possibilities for judicial resolution of these disputes. In particular, such disputes will implicate the limited competence of the state to answer ecclesiastical questions, and the constitutionally mandated concern over the impact of religious accommodations on third parties.

The Patient Protection and Affordable Care Act of 2010 (ACA) requires the executive branch of the federal government to specify the services that all qualified health insurance plans must include. In 2011, three executive branch agencies issued a set of proposed regulations on the subject of mandatory insurance coverage of pregnancy preventive services.[93] During the earlier period for public comment on these proposals, many commenters had urged that the regulations require employers to cover contraceptive services for all women, without any cost-sharing requirement, and without any exemption for employers with religious concerns about such services.[94] Other commenters had "asserted that requiring group health plans sponsored by religious employers to cover contraceptive services that their faith deems contrary to its religious tenets would impinge upon their religious freedom."[95]

The Obama administration initially announced that most employers covered by the ACA would be legally obligated to provide their employees with health insurance coverage for pregnancy prevention services (the "con-

---

93. U.S. Departments of the Treasury, Labor, and Health and Human Services, Group Health Plans and Health Insurance Issuers Relating to Coverage of Preventive Services under the Patient Protection and Affordable Care Act, 76 Fed. Reg. 46621 (Aug. 3, 2011).

94. 76 Fed. Reg. at 46623.

95. *Id.*

traceptive mandate").[96] The announcement proposed a narrow religious exemption, primarily for houses of worship that objected to providing these services.[97] The administration initially offered no exemption for other religiously affiliated institutions, such as schools, health care facilities, or social service providers, who had similar religious objections. Nor did the administration offer an exemption to for-profit businesses whose owners objected to the contraceptive mandate.

This announcement produced widespread and intense controversy, both political and legal. Among other religious voices, the U.S. Conference of Catholic Bishops denounced this plan, and demanded an exemption for all institutions of a religious character, as well as conscientiously objecting owners of businesses.[98]

Eventually, the Obama administration developed a compromise plan.[99] The plan simplified the criteria for complete exemption from the contraceptive mandate, although this complete exemption still extended only to houses of worship and other, narrowly defined entities devoted exclusively to religious purposes. With respect to religiously affiliated entities like universities and hospitals, the administration's revised plan allows them to maintain some distance between their participation in health coverage and the right of em-

96. 76 Fed. Reg. at 46621.

97. As if in anticipation of the Supreme Court's subsequent decision in *Hosanna-Tabor,* the departments attempted "to provide for a religious accommodation that respects the unique relationship between a house of worship and its employees in ministerial positions." 76 Fed. Reg. at 46623. As the agencies understood, this exemption would extend to houses of worship, conventions or associations of such entities, and the "exclusively religious activities of any religious order." *Id.*

98. See Comments of the U.S. Conference of Catholic Bishops, May 15, 2012, on the Advanced Notice of Proposed Rule-Making on Preventive Services, available at http://www.becketfund.org/wp-content/uploads/2012/01/ANPRM-comments.pdf; "Unacceptable," April 11, 2012, available at http://www.becketfund.org/wp-content/uploads/2012/04/Unacceptable-4-11.pdf (statement signed by over 500 religious leaders, academics, and others, asserting that the HHS policy, even as modified by the February 2012 adjustment re: who must pay the cost of pregnancy prevention services, remained a grave violation of religious freedom).

99. White House Fact Sheet: Women's Preventive Services and Religious Institutions, http://www.whitehouse.gov/the-press-office/2012/02/10/fact-sheet-women-s-preventive-services-and-religious-institutions. The final regulations on this subject are published under the title "Coverage of Certain Preventive Services under the Affordable Care Act, a Rule by the Internal Revenue Service, the Employee Benefits Security Administration, and the U.S. Health and Human Services Department, July 2, 2013," available at https://www.federalregister.gov/articles/2013/07/02/2013-15866/coverage-of-certain-preventive-services-under-the-affordable-care-act.

ployees to gain access to contraceptives as a result of the coverage. In particular, these services will not be formally covered by the insurance policy that the employer purchases. Instead, the insurer will be separately responsible for covering these services for employees of religious entities that object to coverage. With respect to for-profit businesses, however, the administration's plan created no exemption or device to enable objecting business owners to avoid or distance themselves from the contraceptive mandate.

This attempt to satisfy the competing concerns of some employers and their female employees did not come close to ending the controversy. By the end of 2012, many employers had filed lawsuits designed to block enforcement against them of the contraceptive mandate.[100] Although religiously affiliated entities filed the first round of lawsuits, these cases were on hold for some time, because the rules governing such entities had not been finalized.[101] In contrast, the contraceptive mandate has become effective against for-profit employers, and a significant number of those employers have brought lawsuits, seeking religion-based exemptions from it.[102] As of this writing, most of the decisions have found that the for-profit business owners are likely to succeed in their claims under the RFRA.[103]

100. http://www.becketfund.org/hhsinformationcentral/ (listing the courts, locations, and parties to each lawsuit).

101. See, e.g., *Persico, Roman Catholic Bishop of Diocese of Erie v. Sebelius,* No. 1:12-cv-123-sum (W.D. Pa., Jan. 22, 2013), available at http://www.leagle.com/decision/In%20FDCO%2020130123D89; *Priests for Life v. Sebelius,* No. 12-cv-753 (FB) (EDNY, April 12, 2013), available at http://docs.justia.com/cases/federal/district-courts/new-york/nyedce/1:2012cv00753/327260/56/0.pdf?ts=1365863286. The rules have now become final, and courts have begun to decide such cases. See, e.g., *University of Notre Dame v. Sebelius,* 2014 U.S. App. LEXIS 3326 (7th Cir., IN, Feb. 21, 2014).

102. In its statement of March 14, 2012, "United for Religious Freedom," available at http://www.usccb.org/issues-and-action/religious-liberty/upload/Admin-Religious-Freedom.pdf, the Administrative Committee of the U.S. Conference of Catholic Bishops expressly called for recognition of the rights of all those religiously opposed to compliance with the mandate: "The HHS mandate creates still a third class, those with no conscience protection at all: individuals who, in their daily lives, strive constantly to act in accordance with their faith and moral values. They, too, face a government mandate to aid in providing 'services' contrary to those values — whether in their sponsoring of, and payment for, insurance as employers; their payment of insurance premiums as employees; or as insurers themselves — without even the semblance of an exemption."

103. *Hobby Lobby Stores, Inc. v. Sebelius,* 2013 U.S. App. LEXIS 13316, 2013 WL 3216103 (10th Cir. Okla. June 27, 2013) (en banc), *cert. granted,* No. 13-354, U.S. Supreme Court, Nov. 26, 2013; *Tyndale House Publrs., Inc. v. Sebelius,* 904 F. Supp. 2d 106, 2012 U.S. Dist. LEXIS 163965, 2012 WL 5817323 (D.D.C. 2012); but see *Conestoga Wood Specialties Corp. v. Sec'y of the*

The political arguments in this controversy are focused on competing and apparently irreconcilable claims between the employers' religious liberty and the employees' reproductive freedom. Without question, such considerations eventually belong in any calculus of how the state should proceed. The questions posed by the lawsuits, however, cannot be resolved by some simple balancing of reproductive freedom against religious freedom. Instead, the lawsuits require inquiry into the intrinsic legal merits of the religious liberty claims themselves. If they lack intrinsic legal merits, the government need not justify its actions with any theory of countervailing values, such as reproductive autonomy or, for that matter, health care cost savings. If the religious liberty claims are intrinsically sound, however, the government will have to justify, under RFRA's very strict standards, the burden imposed on objecting employers by the contraceptive mandate.

In this chapter, we focus on the legal claims that rest on the RFRA, rather than on the Free Exercise Clause. The allegations concerning the RFRA present much more substantial legal claims,[104] as well as a stronger connection to our purposes in this chapter. The claim is stronger because RFRA, unlike the Free

United States HHS, 2013 U.S. App. LEXIS 15238, 2013 WL 3845365 (3d Cir. Pa. July 26, 2013), *cert. granted*, No. 13-356, U.S. Supreme Court, Nov. 26, 2013.

104. Outside of the special case of ministerial employees, which we discuss in detail in chapter 2, religious employers have no unique rights under the Free Exercise Clause to avoid this coverage mandate. Despite the highly general rhetoric about religious freedom and the First Amendment that has appeared from some religious bodies (see U.S. Conference of Catholic Bishops, Ad Hoc Committee for Religious Liberty, "Our First, Most Cherished Liberty: A Statement on Religious Liberty," April 12, 2012, available at http://www.usccb.org/issues-and-action/religious-liberty/our-first-most-cherished-liberty.cfm), the complaints in the lawsuits are tightly tailored to the governing law; the complaints assert that the coverage mandate is not "neutral" or "generally applicable" to all employers, and that *Smith*'s controlling rule therefore does not apply. In support of this contention, the complaints point to the various categories of employers that are not subject to this mandate, including (1) those religious employers excluded by various statutory provisions; (2) those religious employers excluded by the narrow regulatory exemption for houses of worship; (3) employers with fewer than fifty employees; and (4) employers who maintain preexisting health plans that meet specified standards of adequacy (so-called grandfathered plans). See, e.g., Complaint in *Colorado Christian University v. Sebelius et al.*, U.S. District Court for the District of Colorado, pars. 33-53; 111-125, available at http://www.becketfund.org/wp-content/uploads/2011/12/CCU-v-Sebelius-Complaint-final.pdf. This array of exclusions does not suffice to show a violation of the Free Exercise Clause. Under current interpretations of the clause, plaintiffs must demonstrate that government agencies have imposed these contraceptive coverage requirements on them out of religious animus. *Church of the Lukumi Babalu Aye, Inc. v. Hialeah*, 508 U.S. 520 (1993). In these contraceptive mandate cases, such a demonstration would be impossible.

Exercise Clause, presumptively forbids application of all federal policies that impose a "substantial burden" on religious exercise — that is, the impact of a policy on religious freedom is a sufficient trigger for application of the statute.

The first, critical question in these cases is whether the contraceptive mandate imposes the kind of burden that RFRA treats as "substantial." Through both its history and its text, RFRA instructs officials to interpret it in light of the law of the Free Exercise Clause at the time of the statute's enactment. Thus, to understand and apply the concept of "substantial burden," one must trace that concept's meaning in the law as it stood on the eve of the Supreme Court's decision in *Employment Division v. Smith*.

Parts of that law appear quite straightforward. For a burden on religion to count as legally relevant, it must involve actual conflict between a person's legal interests and his or her religious practices.[105] For an obvious example, a law that criminalizes a religious practice will always impose a legal burden on those who engage in that practice. Thus, a criminal law against use of peyote burdens Native American Church members who use peyote in the sacraments of that community. Similarly, a rule that requires people to forfeit benefits if they engage in conduct that they believe is religiously mandatory also creates a legal burden on religious exercise. That was precisely the way the Court saw the problem in *Sherbert v. Verner*, where the Court described the loss of unemployment benefits as the equivalent of a "fine imposed against [Mrs. Sherbert] for her Saturday worship."[106]

The law of what constitutes a "substantial burden" thus seems clear, but it suffers from a profound and frequently unrecognized ambiguity. What makes the burden of conflict between compliance with religious and legal obligations "substantial"? To satisfy RFRA's statutory trigger, the asserted conflict must

---

105. In contrast, a government practice that negatively affects the environment in which religious practices are performed, but does not effectively outlaw the religious practice or impose material costs on those who engage in the practice, does not constitute a burden under the law of the Free Exercise Clause. The most prominent example of this principle is *Lyng v. Northwest Indian Cemetery Protective Association*, 485 U.S. 439 (1988), in which the Supreme Court ruled that the Free Exercise Clause did not limit the authority of the United States to build a logging road on federal land in northern California, despite the effects of the construction and use of the road on spiritual sites visited by members of several Native American tribes. However grave the affective disturbance of the serenity in this location might be, the Court ruled, the government's use of its own land could not count as a legally cognizable burden on the free exercise of religion. For further discussion of Lyng, see Ira C. Lupu, *Where Rights Begin: The Problem of Burdens on the Free Exercise of Religion*, 102 Harv. L. Rev. 933 (1989).

106. *Sherbert v. Verner*, 374 U.S. 398, 404 (1963).

meet two criteria, not just one. The conflict must involve, as in *Smith* and *Sherbert*, the imposition of substantial secular costs on the religiously compliant person. However, the conflict also must involve the imposition of substantial religious costs on those who comply with secular law. The Court in *Wisconsin v. Yoder* almost exclusively emphasized this second kind of substantiality. The Court barely mentioned the five dollar fine (the secular cost) that the state might impose on the parents of children who were truant. Instead, the Court repeatedly and emphatically stressed the religious cost — a threat to the salvation of Amish parents and to the survival of the Amish community — that might have followed from compliance with compulsory education laws.

Yoder reveals the deeply troubling quality of this second side of the "substantial burden" formula. In some cases, the relevant question is religious or ecclesiastical, and the state is not competent to answer it. Of course, as a matter of common cultural knowledge,[107] as with Sabbath observance in places where that is customary, the government may choose not to dispute the religious substantiality of the burden. At other times, as a matter of litigation strategy, the state may just concede that the religious cost of legal compliance is substantial, and choose to fight on other grounds. That was the government's strategy, albeit a losing one, in the *O Centro* litigation, in which the government conceded that the prohibition on importing or using hoasca tea was a substantial burden on the religious group. But what happens when, as in the contraceptive mandate cases, the government does not concede the substantiality of the religious costs of compliance with the law?

Consider the possibilities. Employers who object to the mandate have cited a variety of reasons, as understood from within their religious tradition, as to why the mandate burdens their religious freedom.[108] They assert that the availability of such services, as a consequence of the employment relation, will implicate them in the facilitation of sin, or in scandalous association with sinful practices.[109] These practices include the avoidance of concep-

---

107. *Mack v. O'Leary*, 80 F. 3d 1175, 1178-1179 (7th Cir. Ill. 1996) (Posner, J., commenting on the problem of judges becoming arbiters of religious questions in applying RFRA, and referencing "common knowledge" as a potential source of answers to religious questions).

108. See "Unacceptable," *supra* note 98. See also Comments of the U.S. Conference of Catholic Bishops, May 15, 2012, on the Advanced Notice of Proposed Rule-Making on Preventive Services, available at http://www.becketfund.org/wp-content/uploads/2012/01/ANPRM-comments.pdf.

109. See. e.g., Complaint in *Colorado Christian University v. Sebelius*, U.S. District Court, D. Colorado, filed Dec. 21, 2011, pars. 77-88, available at http://www.becketfund.org/wp-content/uploads/2011/12/CCU-v-Sebelius-Complaint-final.pdf.

tion through medicinal intervention or, in some cases, the administration of postcoital treatments that some employers object to as abortifacients.[110] The employers insist that the burdens imposed on them by the mandate are substantial, because refusing to cover these services in an employee health plan will permit the government to impose enormous fines on the employers.[111]

The government, which cannot deny the magnitude of these fines, has responded to these arguments in a variety of ways. The Department of Justice has asserted, with very limited success, that for-profit business corporations do not "exercise religion" and therefore are not protected by RFRA. With respect to the owners of these businesses, the government concedes that they may be exercising religion in the conduct of their business affairs. But, the government argues, the connection between the owners' religious exercise and the decision by employees to make use of contraceptives is too remote and attenuated for the burden to be "substantial." That is, the employees make independent choices about the use of pregnancy prevention services.[112] The government does not force any employee to make use of such services, or to rely on insurance coverage to pay for them. Shareholders in the business entities that employ these women are therefore one or more significant steps removed from the personal decisions of female employees to take advantage of that coverage.

How should judges decide between the employers' arguments, made from within particular religious traditions, about burdens on their exercise of religion, and the government's responses to those arguments, in which the presence and weight of any such burden are contested? If we are correct that the state may not decide religious questions, the government seems stuck with the employers' self-appraisal that these burdens are substantial. Moreover, the employers' assertions that only they can judge the religious significance of a burden on religious exercise are buttressed by the Supreme

110. "Unacceptable," *supra* note 98.

111. *Hobby Lobby Stores, Inc. v. Sebelius,* 2013 U.S. App. LEXIS 13316, *15-16 (10th Cir. Okla. June 27, 2013) (en banc) (company faces fines of almost $475 million per year if it violates the contraceptive mandate).

112. The Supreme Court has relied on this kind of argument, about intervening choice as a crucial factor that alters the responsibility of the originator of funds for causing religious experience, in decisions about indirect public financing of education at religious schools. *Zelman v. Simmons-Harris,* 536 U.S. 639 (2002). The U.S. Conference of Catholic Bishops filed an amicus brief in *Zelman* in support of the constitutionality of such financing. The brief is available at http://www.usccb.org/about/general-counsel/amicus-briefs/zelman-v-simmons-harris.cfm.

Court's decision in another pre-RFRA Free Exercise case, *Thomas v. Review Board of Indiana.*[113] In *Thomas,* the Court ruled that an employee had been wrongfully denied unemployment benefits after he refused an assignment to build tank turrets in the steel fabricating plant where he worked. Thomas, a member of the Jehovah's Witnesses, asserted that his reading of Scripture made it wrong for him to produce weapons of war, even though he had earlier worked in producing rolled steel, which might be used in making weapons. The Court refused to credit contrary testimony offered by a coworker, a fellow Jehovah's Witness, who disagreed about whether producing the turrets was "unscriptural." Mr. Thomas, the Court said, had a constitutional right to draw his own lines about what his religion forbade. Similarly, in the contraceptive mandate cases, employers have argued that they, like Thomas, get to define their own religious beliefs, and to determine their own sense of the religious cost of being compelled to violate those beliefs.[114]

Taken this far, however, the *Thomas* solution saves the court from rendering religious determinations by making every RFRA claimant, in a significant respect, a judge in his or her own case.[115] Under this approach, the mere assertion that the application of a policy substantially burdens the claimant's religious freedom will force the government to either prove the claimant's insincerity or satisfy RFRA's difficult standard. Under that standard, the government must show that application of the burden to that claimant is the least restrictive way of accomplishing a compelling state interest. As suggested earlier in this chapter, allowing RLUIPA claims in prison to take this course may be pragmatically manageable, because of broad judicial deference to institutional judgments about safety and security. In society's free sectors, however, allowing all religious liberty claimants to self-declare the substantiality of the burden on their religious exercise is a recipe for a tremendous shift in legal leverage to religious claimants, unless other sensible responses by the government are available.

113. *Thomas v. Review Board of Indiana,* 450 U.S. 707 (1981).

114. Catholic critics have already responded to the assertions by the U.S. Conference of Catholic Bishops that the mandate threatens religious liberty. See, e.g., the Comments from Peter Steinfels and Cathleen Kaveny, *The Bishops and Religious Liberty,* Commonweal, June 15, 2012, available at http://commonwealmagazine.org/bishops-religious-liberty. But these critics, despite being well versed in the traditions of Catholic thought and experience, do not have authority to speak for the institutions that are claiming violations of religious liberty.

115. *Employment Division v. Smith,* 494 U.S. 872, 879 (1990) (citing *Reynolds v. United States,* 98 U.S. 145, 166-67 [1878]: "Can a man excuse his practices to the contrary [of the laws] because of his religious belief? To permit this would be to make the professed doctrines of religious belief superior to the law of the land, and in effect to permit every citizen to become a law unto himself").

We think there are two promising avenues for the government to pursue in cases where the secular cost of religious compliance is obvious but the religious cost of compliance with the law seems highly disputable. The first involves considerations of whether the claimant can easily avoid the burden by taking a different course of action. Under the ACA, employers have choices. The employer may sell or abandon the business as a way of avoiding the burden, but the costs of that method of avoidance seem quite substantial. Employers may also choose, however, to drop health coverage for employees altogether, in which case they are obliged to pay to the federal government an "assessable payment" of $2,000 per year per uncovered full-time employee.[116] That choice may actually cost employers less than they would contribute to a policy that provides all the required coverage. Employers may prefer to provide insurance rather than make this payment, but this way of avoiding the burden on their religious exercise may in some cases save them money and thus eliminate the secular costs of religious compliance.[117]

Second, courts may expand the ways that government may satisfy RFRA's compelling interest test. As the Supreme Court emphasized in the 1980s accommodation trilogy and reemphasized in *Cutter v. Wilkinson*, religious accommodation statutes should be interpreted to avoid the imposition of significant costs on third parties. These decisions teach that the Establishment Clause is a check on the extent to which accommodations may protect religious interests at the expense of competing secular interests.[118]

In the contraceptive mandate cases, the government has a strong interest in ensuring that RFRA claims by business firms (and eventually, by religious organizations) do not impose substantial secular costs on employees. In this context, however, identifying and measuring those costs are not simple. These cases present an acute problem of determining the baseline from which to measure the third-party harms caused by permissive accommodations.

In other kinds of accommodation cases, that baseline is relatively easy

116. 26 U.S.C. sec. 4980H (b)(1).

117. If employers choose this way of avoiding the burden on their religious conscience, their employees will be obliged to purchase health insurance on their own from one of the available exchanges. Any policies that they buy will include pregnancy prevention services, with no policy holder co-pays or deductibles. In addition, if the employees qualify for low-income subsidies, the United States will help cover the costs of the policies.

118. For full development of this argument in the context of the contraceptive mandate cases, see Frederick Mark Gedicks and Rebecca G. Van Tassell, *RFRA Exemptions from the Contraceptive Mandate: An Unconstitutional Accommodation of Religion*, 49 Harv. Civ. Rts.–Civ. Lib. L. Rev. — (forthcoming 2014).

to identify. For example, if a house of worship succeeds with a zoning claim under RLUIPA, and thereby expands its worship space, the question of effect on neighbors is measured by the likely change — say, in traffic, noise, or parking congestion — produced by the expansion. This is a relatively simple question of "before and after," though the "after" may be a matter of some informed conjecture.

In contrast, the employees of firms and organizations that object to covering pregnancy prevention services typically have not had such coverage from these employers in the past. Thus, the "before" and "after" are identical — no coverage of these services. Courts might view these third-party harms as zero, and therefore decline to recognize any government interest in avoiding the Establishment Clause problem of cost shifting. Alternatively, courts might view the "before" state in terms of legal entitlement rather than coverage in fact. The challenged regulations require this coverage, and a successful RFRA claim will undo that requirement. Viewed that way, the third-party harms to female employees can be measured by the value of the lost coverage, represented by the cost to the employee of self-providing (or self-insuring for) the relevant services.

Which view is sounder? We confess to some uncertainty on this point. *Sherbert v. Verner*[119] treated a lost opportunity to receive unemployment benefits as the equivalent of a fine on Mrs. Sherbert's Saturday worship. Perhaps a successful RFRA claim by an employer against the contraceptive mandate is similarly equivalent to a fine on a female employee's exercise of reproductive freedom.

In the face of such an argument, we would expect an employer to assert, under the terms of RFRA, that the government has less restrictive means to protect the interests of female employees. That is, the government can find other ways of delivering free contraceptive coverage to these employees. This move represents an effort to show that the government, rather than the employer, should take the necessary steps to eliminate the burden and thereby avoid the conflict. In response, the government will argue that any steps designed to create a separate insurer of contraceptive services, completely disconnected from the employer, are likely to be less efficient and more expensive as a way for the government to guarantee this coverage. Whether the employer or the government should have to take steps to avoid the conflict

119. *Sherbert v. Verner,* 374 U.S. 398 (1963), discussed in chapter 6, involved loss of mandatory unemployment insurance, and thus might be seen as consistent with a baseline measured by legal expectations rather than tangible circumstances.

seems a very close call. Either way, employees will bear some costs in taking advantage of the alternatives to full coverage in an employer-provided policy.

If the courts conclude that third-party harms defeat a RFRA claim by for-profit employers against the contraception mandate, is the existing, narrow exemption for houses of worship also unconstitutional, because it inflicts the same costs on employees? We think not, for two reasons. First, with respect to ministerial employees, houses of worship have the maximum constitutional latitude to set terms and conditions of employment. Second, in organizations that have exclusively religious purposes and forbid the use of contraceptives, employees have no reasonable expectation that their employers will ever facilitate the provision of such goods. The competing equities thus seem very different from the situation of a for-profit business firm, where employees fully and reasonably expect compliance with laws regulating the employment relationship.

A RFRA claim by a nonexempt religious organization, such as a university, might fall between the poles of a for-profit business and a house of worship. The practices of those employers in hiring from outside the religious community[120] might create reasonable employee expectations of treatment identical to that afforded employees of business firms. Here, too, both sides have choices. Religious institutions may proclaim their position on contraception, and may choose to hire only those who act in fidelity to that position. If they do those things, perhaps the insurance coverage of contraception will impose only a trivial burden on them. Employees who object to that position, and the insurance restrictions that accompany it, may choose to work elsewhere. Perhaps the employees can therefore avoid or minimize the costs of an accommodation. All we can confidently say about these cases is that RFRA is a clumsy and ambiguous vehicle for the government to deploy in resolving which side can force the other to make these kinds of choices.

120. As compared with for-profit employers, nonprofit religious entities have far more direct means of protecting themselves from the risk that employees will make choices that the employer considers sinful. As described earlier in this chapter, religious organizations are exempt from the prohibition on religious discrimination in Title VII of the 1964 Civil Rights Act, and are similarly exempt from such prohibitions in state civil rights laws. Accordingly, these employers may limit their workforce to people who are committed to the faith. Moreover, these employers may demand that employees respect particular teachings of the faith, and may dismiss those who violate those teachings. Thus, in providing coverage of pregnancy prevention services, government may have presented a temptation to employees, but it has not propelled employees into any sinful deeds, nor demanded that employers retain employees who engage in such deeds.

Conclusion

A secular government responds in many legitimate ways to the needs of a religious people. Some of these responses, discussed in the prior chapter, are mandatory, and many of those responses will facilitate broader causes of liberty and equality. But a secular government may also respond in many highly important and fully discretionary ways to the religious needs of its people. This chapter has sketched what we see as the appropriate forms and limits of those discretionary responses. Equalizing the response to comparable secular causes, when appropriate, and keeping the government and its agents out of the business of religious appraisals are crucial aspects of those limits.

In a society where the spirit of liberty, including religious liberty, is strong, this combination of constitutional mandates and discretionary responses can be extremely robust. And in a society where the government enforces those mandates, engages in many of those discretionary responses, and endeavors to maintain its own secular authority and identity, the combination represents the richest possible constitutional world for religious freedom. That is the society, and the Constitution, that this book has thus far described.

Others may think we have shortchanged religion by our account of the state's limited competence, and by our skepticism about religion-specific rights. For the reasons we have given, we are convinced that the themes we have emphasized will, in both the long run and the short run, protect religious freedom far better than all the rival accounts. What we have prescribed is a state with a fully secular identity, amply empowered to respond to the people's religious needs. Moreover, we have repeatedly, in both mandatory and discretionary settings, tied the interests of religion to those of its many powerful secular counterparts. Unlike the short-lived and ultimately quite fruitless state of affairs abandoned in *Smith,* the regime we have prescribed has long flourished, and seems destined to continue.

In special circumstances, however, government may respond to the religious needs of its people in more substantial and proactive ways than we have described thus far. When government induces or commands its people to locate in circumstances in which religious experience is relatively inaccessible — for example, in military service — government may take on responsibilities greater than insulating religious experience from regulation or engaging in limited forms of acknowledgment. The next and final chapter tackles the unique questions presented when the government undertakes such responsibilities.

Conclusion

CHAPTER 8

The Military Chaplaincy — a Concluding Case Study

In this book, we have explored the idea of a secular government for a religious people. We have traced that idea through a wide range of interactions between the state and religion, in its various manifestations. This final chapter focuses on the military chaplaincy — an institution that seems, at first glance, to be in substantial tension with the idea of secular government. Through the chaplaincy, the government selects, pays, and regulates clergy; erects and maintains chapels; and sponsors worship and religious instruction.[1] As we explain in the following pages, however, the military chaplaincy actually demonstrates how a secular government can fully and appropriately respond to the religious needs of the people in its service.

Through our survey of the military chaplaincy's main characteristics, we also reiterate the major themes of this book. Those themes include the government's limited competence to resolve ecclesiastical questions, the prohibition on official support for explicitly religious messages, and the scope of mandatory and discretionary protections for religious liberty. This analysis will demonstrate how our approach can help to place the chaplaincy on sound constitutional footing, as well as resolve current legal controversies involving the chaplaincy.

---

1. See generally Ira C. Lupu and Robert W. Tuttle, *Instruments of Accommodation: The Military Chaplaincy and the Constitution,* 110 W. Va. L. Rev. 89 (2007). This article provides a more detailed description of the chaplaincy, as well as a more thorough discussion of legal issues that arise in the operation of the chaplaincy.

Conclusion

The Structure of the Military Chaplaincy

The "military chaplaincy" consists of three separate institutions: the Chaplains Corps of the Army, the Chaplains Corps of the Navy,[2] and the Air Force Chaplains Corps. The regulations and practices of the three institutions vary to some degree, owing at least in part to the differing missions of the services. All three are structured by Department of Defense (DOD) regulations.[3] These regulations include two core requirements for the service chaplaincies, which are reflected in the general framework of the chaplaincies and also in the particular tasks assigned to individual chaplains. First, chaplains are commissioned to provide religious services in accordance with the tenets of the religious community that endorsed them for the chaplaincy. Second, chaplains provide commanders with advice and assistance in meeting the religious needs of all those for whom the commander has responsibility, regardless of religious affiliations. These two requirements — the particularism of a chaplain's ministry within a specific faith group, and the pluralism demanded by the obligation to assist all in need — are evident in the service of each chaplain and provide the basic framework for understanding the chaplaincy.

The military establishes the qualifications for chaplain candidates. These qualifications include a graduate degree, experience in religious ministry, and the endorsement of a DOD-approved religious organization. The endorsement certifies that the faith group recognizes the candidate as fully qualified — ordained, or its functional equivalent — for professional ministry within that faith group. Both the endorsing religious organization and the candidate must understand and accept the military's pluralistic environment, and the chaplain's role in light of that context.

To serve in a pluralistic setting, the chaplain must be willing to facilitate the religious needs of all service members. Such facilitation may include religious services provided directly by the chaplain, but may also involve the chaplain assisting the service member to obtain worship experiences or materials from other sources. Chaplains may also be assigned a number of other tasks, including supervision of other chaplains and religious facilities, counseling of individuals and families, participation in official ceremonies, and instruction in "the moral and ethical quality of leadership." Chaplains are

2. Navy chaplains also serve the Marine Corps, Coast Guard, and merchant marine.

3. Detailed sources for the description offered in the following paragraph can be found in our article on this subject, cited in note 1.

specifically forbidden by the services to undertake responsibilities that would directly involve them as combatants or in the exercise of military command.

Is the Military Chaplaincy Constitutional?

Over the last three decades a few courts and numerous commentators have considered the constitutionality of the military chaplaincy.[4] Among the various arguments offered in defense of the chaplaincy, one theme stands out — the chaplaincy exists to protect the free exercise rights of service members.[5] Although the argument has intuitive appeal, it does not hold up to legal scrutiny. As we saw in chapter 6, the Free Exercise Clause prohibits the government from directly targeting religious activity for special disability, but does not require the government to provide special treatment to religion. If the military chaplaincy disappeared, no one would have a legitimate free exercise claim to its restoration.[6]

Instead of searching for the chaplaincy's constitutional footing in the free exercise rights of service members, those who defend the institution should look to the government's power to grant discretionary religious accommodations. In chapter 7, we provide a framework for assessing the permissibility of discretionary accommodations, and identify three criteria. The accommodation must respond to a distinctive, government-imposed burden on religion; the accommodation must treat all faiths equally; and the accommodation must not impose unreasonable costs on third parties.

---

4. *Katcoff v. Marsh,* 755 F. 2d 223 (2nd Cir. 1985). The question of the chaplaincy's constitutionality has been addressed indirectly at several points during the long-running challenge to the navy's policies on hiring, promoting, and retaining chaplains. See In re Navy Chaplaincy, 534 F. 3d 756 (D.C. Cir. 2008). For the most recent development in that case, see In re Navy Chaplaincy, 2013 U.S. Dist. LEXIS 27302 (D.D.C. Feb. 28, 2013). See also Steven K. Green, *Reconciling the Irreconcilable: Military Chaplains and the First Amendment,* 110 W. Va. L. Rev. 167 (2007); Richard D. Rosen, Katcoff v. Marsh *at Twenty-Two: The Military Chaplaincy and the Separation of Church and State,* 38 U. Tol. L. Rev. 1137 (2007).

5. *Katcoff v. Marsh,* 755 F. 2d 223 (2nd Cir. 1985), provides the most prominent example of this reasoning.

6. The Religious Freedom Restoration Act (discussed in chapter 7) does not necessarily make things easier for proponents of a mandatory chaplaincy. Perhaps in a world of military conscription, failure to provide chaplains would constitute a substantial burden on religious exercise. But with a voluntary armed service, that argument is hard to maintain. Of course, members of the armed services have the right to pray and gather for worship, but those rights do not generate an obligation on the part of the military to provide paid chaplains to lead worship.

Conclusion

Response to Distinctive Burdens

The typical accommodation removes a burden imposed on a believer by a government regulation — such as the prohibition on use of hallucinogenic substances.[7] The chaplaincy represents a categorically different type of accommodation. Instead of removing obstacles to the practice of faith, this accommodation facilitates religious observance by providing the necessary resources, including ministers and worship space. This affirmative provision of resources places the chaplaincy in tension with ordinary nonestablishment norms discussed in chapter 3. To understand why the chaplaincy does not violate the ban on direct funding of religion, we need to start with the experience of military service members. Service members may be confined to remote posts for long periods, deployed at sea, or assigned to duties in hostile zones overseas. Thus, they are often isolated from ordinary opportunities to worship with their own religious community and exposed to hazards and other stresses that are rarely shared by those in civilian occupations.

The chaplaincy responds to that set of distinctive burdens imposed on members of the armed forces. The first duty of a chaplain is not to advance his or her own faith tradition. Instead, the chaplain's paramount responsibility is to assess each service member's religious needs, if any, and assist that person to find appropriate worship opportunities or other religious resources. Second, the chaplain does provide worship experiences, religious instruction, and faith-intensive counseling, but only to service members who freely choose to participate in those religious activities.[8]

Religious Neutrality

The idea of religious equality operates on a variety of levels in the armed forces and its chaplaincy. At the broadest level, the services are formally religion-neutral in their criteria for enlistment — members of any faith or none are eligible to serve their country. In an important respect, the chaplaincy facilitates that promise of equal opportunity. By providing chaplains, the military enables those who are religiously observant to serve, knowing that they will continue to have access to worship opportunities. By ensuring

---

7. See the discussion of the *Smith* decision (involving peyote use) in chapter 6, and the *O Centro* decision (involving hoasca tea) in chapter 7.

8. See Lupu and Tuttle, *supra* note 1, at 119-120.

that all religious activities are voluntary, the military offers nonbelievers an equal opportunity to serve, knowing that they will not be required to participate in religious activities as a condition of service.

The chaplaincy itself is guided by the principle of religious neutrality. As noted above, chaplains are required to assist all interested service members, of any faith tradition, in obtaining appropriate worship experience and other religious resources. Moreover, all faith groups should have an equal opportunity to provide chaplains for the armed forces. All candidates must meet basic requirements to become a military officer, but no chaplain candidate should be disqualified simply because of his or her religious affiliation.[9]

Third-Party Costs

In the context of the military chaplaincy, the primary concern about third-party burdens focuses on the risk that service members will be pressured into receiving unwanted religious experience. The concern about pressure differs from that addressed in chapter 4's discussion of religion in public schools; service members are not schoolchildren. But military life creates different types of vulnerability. The authority structure makes those in subordinate positions, if they make unpopular religious choices, susceptible to the risk of superiors' disapproval. In addition, highly stressful experiences in training or combat create their own forms of vulnerability. In light of these risks, the military chaplaincy should be especially protective of service members' voluntary choice in religious matters.

Moreover, the military should guard against improper inducements to participate in religious activity. Several years ago, soldiers at one installation were offered the choice of attending worship and daylong recreational activities at a church off base, or remaining on base and working.[10] However uncommon this practice might be, it nonetheless highlights the need to ensure that those who do not choose to participate in religious activities receive opportunities and material advantages similar to those who do.

9. See *id.* at 125, 127-132. The navy chaplaincy has been involved in a long-running litigation about the role of religious affiliation in its allocation of slots for chaplains — including hiring, promotion, and retention. See In re Navy Chaplaincy, 2013 U.S. Dist. LEXIS 27302 (D.D.C. Feb. 28, 2013).

10. ReligionClause blog, "AU Seeks Investigation of Church Program at Army Base," http://religionclause.blogspot.com/2008/07/au-seeks-investigation-of-church.html (July 24, 2008).

Conclusion

Constitutional Questions in the Practice of the Chaplaincy

Even though the military chaplaincy as an institution satisfies the standard for a permissible accommodation of religion, particular concerns about the role and conduct of chaplains remain. We noted some of these concerns, including chaplains' duty to show equal zeal in facilitating religious experience for all service members, as well as the military's need for sensitivity to the various ways service members may be impermissibly pressured into unwanted religious experience. But three other recurrent issues deserve attention, both intrinsically and because they highlight the usefulness of our approach in addressing concrete questions.

The Chaplaincy and Ecclesiastical Questions

Does the military's selection of chaplains and responsibility for worship inevitably involve the government in ecclesiastical questions? In chapter 2 we addressed the long-standing and core nonestablishment principle that bars the government from exercising religious judgment. What saves the chaplaincy from constitutional condemnation under this principle is the crucial role played by endorsing bodies — the faith community that certifies the chaplain as an ordained minister — and the chaplains' status as representatives of those bodies.

In a very important sense, military chaplains have a dual professional identity. They are commissioned officers of the U.S. government but are simultaneously authorized agents of the religious community that endorsed them. The military decides whether someone is and remains qualified to be a commissioned officer. The endorsing body, however, and not the government, determines whether someone is and remains qualified to serve as a religious leader. Ultimately, the chaplain's endorsing body has authority to evaluate the chaplain's performance in faith-group settings. If the endorsing body disapproves of the chaplain's work — perhaps because of the content of preaching or religious teaching, or the form of worship in which the chaplain participates — the endorsing body is free to revoke the chaplain's endorsement. If the chaplain is unable to find another church body endorser, he or she ceases to be a chaplain. Thus, religious bodies and their representatives determine and apply the standards for ministry and the content of faith-group worship.[11]

11. See Lupu and Tuttle, *supra* note 1, at 117.

Accordingly, the military draws a sharp distinction between the chaplain's work in a faith-group context and other parts of the chaplain's role. In the faith-group context — whether leading worship, providing religious instruction, or engaging in faith-specific counseling — the chaplain represents and serves a religious community. This religious community is not the government; it is a private body. Faith-group worship is thus an act of the people. The government certainly facilitates that worship, but it exercises no direct control over its content or the religious qualifications of those who teach or preach the group's faith.

This emphasis on the private character of faith-group worship has important implications for a number of current issues. Most prominently, some conservative religious groups have expressed concern that chaplains could be required to perform marriage ceremonies for same-sex couples. As our characterization of the chaplain's dual role demonstrates, however, the government has no authority to require a chaplain to perform any religious ceremony. Religious services are not governmental acts, and the nonestablishment principle categorically prohibits the government from exercising control over such services. A chaplain is free to decide whether or not to marry any couple, whether because of the couple's faith, prior marital status, or the chaplain's sense of their preparation for marriage. Likewise, the chaplain is free to decide whether or not to baptize or provide other religious sacraments, in accordance with the chaplain's faith tradition. Such quintessentially religious acts are not within the government's control or competence.

Prayer at Official Events

Over the past decade, perhaps the highest-profile disputes within the military chaplaincy have involved the question of prayers at official events.[12] Chaplains are frequently asked to offer prayers at public events, such as the opening of a new military hospital or a change-of-command ceremony. These events are

---

12. In *Chalker v. Gates* (D. Kansas 2010), a soldier stationed at Fort Riley complained that his rights were violated when he was required to attend "welcome home" ceremonies for his unit, recently returned from Iraq, and the ceremonies included explicitly Christian prayers. The court dismissed the suit because the soldier had not proven that he had sought remedies from within the military. See http://religionclause.blogspot.com/2010/01/challenge-to-military-prayers-dismissed.html. Other examples of such controversies can be found at the Web site of the Military Religious Freedom Foundation, www.Militaryreligiousfreedom.org/legal.

not assemblies of particular faith groups, where the government would have no responsibility for the content of any prayers offered. Instead, the military sponsors these events and frequently requires service members to attend. Although some have challenged all prayers at such events, the greatest controversies have involved prayers that make repeated faith-specific references and presume a shared faith among the audience. The most common of these disputes focus on prayer "in the name of Jesus Christ," though our analysis applies equally to any faith-specific invocation.

Some chaplains have asserted that, when called upon to pray at official events, they have a constitutional right to pray in the language of their faith tradition.[13] This argument, however, reflects a fundamental misunderstanding of the chaplain's dual role. In the context of faith-group worship, the government has no legitimate interest in regulating the content of the chaplain's prayers. But official events are not faith-group worship. In official settings, the chaplain functions as a commissioned officer — in other words, an agent of the military — and thus speaks on behalf of the government. As we explained in chapter 4, constitutional law sharply distinguishes between wholly private speech, which merits constitutional protections, and official speech, which falls entirely within the government's discretion.[14] If the chaplain prays at an official event, the chaplain prays as the government's agent, and the content of the prayer is subject to government oversight.

At this point in the book, the statement that "the content of the prayer is subject to government oversight" should raise a few eyebrows. Based on

13. Chaplain James Klingenschmitt has provided the most prominent example of this claim. After being censured for improper conduct — including, he claims, prayer in the name of Jesus — Klingenschmitt was dismissed from the navy. He filed a lawsuit challenging his termination, but the suit was dismissed. *Klingenschmitt v. Winter,* 275 Fed. Appx. 12 (D.C. Cir. 2008). Representative Jones (R–N.C.) has attempted on several occasions to introduce legislation that would give chaplains the right to pray, at official events, "according to the traditions, expressions, and religious exercises" of their endorsing body. See 2014 National Defense Authorization Act, H.R. 1960, section 529, Protection of the Religious Freedom of Military Chaplains to Close a Prayer Outside of a Religious Service according to the Traditions, Expressions, and Religious Exercises of the Endorsing Faith Group. Congress did not include this provision in the act as passed.

14. Chapter 4 discusses this distinction between private and officially sponsored speech in the context of public schools. These questions can also arise, however, in contexts other than public schools, see, e.g., *Pleasant Grove City v. Summum,* 555 U.S. 460 (2009) (privately donated monument of Ten Commandments in public park is speech sponsored by government); *Salazar v. Buono,* 559 U.S. 700 (2010) (considering effect of transfer of land under a World War I memorial cross from the United States to private parties).

our understanding of nonestablishment, should the military bar all prayer, or at least faith-specific prayer, at official events? As we described in chapter 5, the law recognizes that ceremonial invocations have a well-settled historical provenance. Nonetheless, both *Marsh v. Chambers* and *Lee v. Weisman* demonstrate judicial sensitivity to the context and content of such prayers. Where the audience is compelled to attend, constitutional sensitivity is at its peak. Faith-specific prayer before a captive audience offends core nonestablishment principles, as well as the free exercise rights of those required to attend.

Where attendance is not mandatory, the government has much greater discretion with respect to the content of any particular invocation. As our discussion of the *Town of Greece* case shows, the nonestablishment principle still bars the government from systematically aligning itself with a particular religious identity. So even though a particular prayer that ends "in the name of Jesus" might raise no constitutional issues, a consistent pattern of such prayers might well violate nonestablishment norms.

Conscientious Objections of Chaplains

In the past few years, members of Congress have introduced legislation designed to grant chaplains and other service members broad religious accommodations for conduct or speech that conflicts with ordinary duties, unless military necessity trumps the accommodations.[15] The most prominent motive for these legislative proposals is the perception among some conservative groups that recent changes in the military threaten religious liberty, especially that of chaplains. The controversy over faith-specific prayer at official events has been part of this broader concern about chaplains' religious liberty. A mandatory accommodation for chaplains in that context would not produce a right to pray according to the chaplains' own faith, although it would give chaplains the right to be excused from offering official prayers.

The more prominent source for recent efforts at religious accommodations is the military's rapid and dramatic change regarding the status of gay and lesbian service members. In a few short years, the military has gone from a policy of don't ask, don't tell, to one that accepts openly gay and lesbian ser-

---

15. See 2013 National Defense Authorization Act, section 533, Protection of Rights of Conscience of Members of the Armed Forces and Chaplains of Such Members. Section 533 was not included in the act as passed.

vice members, to one that fully recognizes their legal marriages.[16] Chaplains opposed to these shifts in policy have expressed concern that the changes will force them to speak or act in ways that violate their religious conscience.[17]

To assess these concerns, we reiterate the chaplain's twofold role, as representative of a faith group and as agent of the military. With that distinction in mind, the concern most frequently raised is the one most easily addressed. As we explained earlier, the government may not compel a chaplain to perform any marriage ceremony or other religious service.[18] Such services belong wholly within the chaplain's role as faith-group representative.

Other duties, however, present a much more complicated interplay of these two roles. For example, consider a chaplain who is asked to lead a "marriage strengthening" workshop for military personnel and their spouses. Because of the recent legal developments, same-sex couples are eligible to participate in that workshop. Should a chaplain have the right to exclude same-sex couples? The answer depends on who is sponsoring the workshop. If the workshop is offered by the chaplain's faith community, then it falls within the ordinary norms governing faith-group activities. The chaplain may decide whom to serve, as well as which religious services he or she will offer. If, however, the military command sponsors the workshop as part of its care for service members' well-being, then the chaplain does not have the right to exclude any eligible participants.[19]

16. In late 2010, Congress enacted and the president signed the Don't Ask, Don't Tell Repeal Act, which permits persons who are openly gay or lesbian to serve in the U.S. armed forces. The repeal became fully effective in late 2011. Jim Garamone, American Forces Press Service, *"Don't Ask, Don't Tell" Repeal Certified by President Obama*, http://www.defense.gov/news/newsarticle.aspx?id=64780. Thereafter, in *United States v. Windsor*, 133 S. Ct. 2675 (2013), the Supreme Court held unconstitutional section 3 of the federal Defense of Marriage Act. The ruling in *Windsor* effectively obligates the federal government (including the armed forces) to recognize all same-sex marriages that are valid under state law.

17. See generally the Web site of the Chaplain Alliance for Religious Liberty, http://chaplainalliance.org/ (collecting various articles and news releases that articulate concerns about impact of the repeal of don't ask, don't tell).

18. See generally Ira C. Lupu and Robert W. Tuttle, *Same-Sex Family Equality and Religious Freedom*, 5 Nw. J. Law & Social Policy 274, 282-286 (2010) (constitutional right of clergy and religious communities to decide whether to marry any particular couple).

19. For example, the Air Force Chaplains Corps operates a program called MarriageCare, in which chaplains trained in family and marriage ministry offer a weekend retreat for eligible couples. Although led by chaplains, the program is open to couples from all religious traditions and those who profess no faith commitments. The program Web site states that "MarriageCare deals with spiritual issues while being respectful of all religious and/or spiritual beliefs." http://www.chaplaincorps.af.mil/news/chaplaincorpsprograms/marriagecare.asp.

Should the chaplain have a right to decline the commander's request to lead the government-sponsored marriage workshop? On the one hand, chaplains agree to serve in a pluralistic environment, which includes a diversity not only of faith perspectives but also of moral views. When chaplains are outside the faith-group context, they have a duty to serve all eligible personnel. Many of the chaplain's duties, such as advising a unit commander about a service member's request for a religious accommodation, do not implicate the chaplain's own status within a religious community. They belong fully to the chaplain's role as a government official, and the chaplain has no reasonable claim to be excused from performing those duties on behalf of a particular service member. On the other hand, some services — such as prayer at official events — do implicate the chaplain's status as a religious leader. If, by running the marriage workshop, the chaplain would be understood to be giving religious legitimacy to the relationships of those who participate, the chaplain has a reasonable basis for asking to be relieved of the duty.

Conclusion

The most determined critics of the military chaplaincy insist that the nonestablishment principle bars the government from maintaining such an institution. Its most ardent defenders argue that the free exercise rights of service members require the government to support the military chaplaincy. What these critics and defenders have in common is a tendency to see only half of the arrangements put in place by the religion clauses of the First Amendment. Their blinders obscure the larger genius of the Constitution's plan for the role of religion in the republic.

As this chapter demonstrates, the chaplaincy is neither a prohibited nor a mandatory institution. It exists as a matter of discretion. The chaplaincy's structure is neatly hemmed in by nonestablishment principles, which limit government control of religious experience; by the Free Exercise Clause, which empowers faith groups to choose their forms of worship and protects service members from involuntary religious experience; and by the constitutional boundaries on permissive accommodations of religion, which assure that the chaplaincy exists for all those — and only those — who need it.

The military chaplaincy vividly demonstrates that the government's limited jurisdiction does not create a state that is hostile to religion. Instead, the Constitution authorizes the government to show appropriate respect for the religious character of people. This respect is made concrete in practices both mandatory and permissive, like the chaplaincy, through which the government facilitates religious life.

But our analysis of the chaplaincy also shows the vital role of the limits that the nonestablishment principle imposes on the state. Those limits are especially important in the military, where officials face intense and understandable temptations to erase the distinction between a secular government and a religious people. The government can heighten its demand for loyalty by invoking a sacred meaning for military service. And the fear or suffering of loss can be assuaged through claims by officials about God's blessing, conferred on the nation and its ventures. Chaplains might provide that sense of meaning to service and sacrifice, but they do so only as representatives of the people, organized in communities of faith. In war, as in peace, the government itself must assert only secular authority, not divine approval, for its actions and its demands upon the people.

Authors' Note on *Town of Greece v. Galloway*

On May 5, 2014, a divided (5-4) Supreme Court announced its decision in *Town of Greece v. Galloway.*[1] Writing for the majority of five justices in most of his opinion, Justice Kennedy concluded that the town's prayer practices did not violate the Establishment Clause. Justice Kagan wrote the principal dissent for herself and three other justices. Several justices wrote separate opinions, emphasizing various aspects of the case.

The Supreme Court's decision in *Town of Greece* is notable for several reasons. First, no justice even mentioned the "endorsement" test, which had dominated discussion in the field of government-sponsored religious displays for thirty years — that is, from the moment Justice O'Connor introduced the endorsement concept in *Lynch* (1984) until she left the Court immediately after the Ten Commandments cases (2005). Although Justice Kagan's dissent in *Town of Greece* contained echoes of the test, the idea of "endorsement," with its accompanying baggage of reasonable and omniscient observers, appears to have come and gone with Justice Sandra Day O'Connor.

Second, everyone on the Court recognized the constitutional flaw in any test that would require courts to closely scrutinize particular prayers in order to determine whether they were "sectarian" or "nonsectarian." They likewise recognized the parallel constitutional problem of government officials specifying the precise content of prayers to be given by invited chaplains or others. As Justice Kennedy's opinion explicitly noted, any such official dissection of particular prayers — by judges in retrospect or by legislators in the process of invitation or review — violates the principle that civil government is constitutionally incompetent to decide religious questions or specify the content of

1. U.S. Supreme Court, No. 12-696 (May 5, 2014).

worship. The majority in *Town of Greece* appropriately cited *Hosanna-Tabor*, the ministerial exception case we discuss in chapter 2, to support this conclusion. Whether or not a policy or overall practice of legislative prayer violates the Establishment Clause, government violates that part of the First Amendment when it officially authors prayers or evaluates the theological content of prayers. After *Town of Greece*, if legislative bodies want to open sessions with prayer, they must choose the relevant prayer-giver, and then stand back and let that prayer-giver choose the content.

In addition to their agreement about the constitutional limits on parsing the content of prayers, and their shared rejection or avoidance of the "endorsement" test, all justices agreed that the Court's earlier decision in *Marsh v. Chambers* should control the outcome of *Town of Greece*. Although the justices agreed on those key points, they drew vastly different implications from them. Justice Kennedy's opinion treats legislative prayer as a practice largely immune from Establishment Clause scrutiny because the practice was accepted by the First Amendment's drafters and has continued since that time. Because of that provenance, Justice Kennedy would view as constitutionally troublesome only "a pattern of prayers that over time denigrate[s], proselytize[s], or betray[s] an impermissible government purpose."[2] Such a pattern, he suggested, would depart substantially from the practice upheld in *Marsh*.

From the perspective of the four dissenters (and the authors of this book), the majority's opinion ignored the key constitutional issue in the case — whether the town of Greece's policies and practices of legislative prayer represent a government asserting its own religious character. Instead of treating *Marsh v. Chambers* as a broad license for all forms of legislative prayer, the four dissenters closely scrutinized the town of Greece's practices and concluded that they did not share the features of the Nebraska legislative prayer practice key to the outcome in *Marsh*. Most importantly, the prayers challenged in *Town of Greece* cannot fairly be characterized as an accommodation of the legislators' religious needs. Instead, the chaplains directed the prayers at the assembled citizens, and invited them to participate in a reverential act. Thus, as argued in Justice Kagan's dissent, the town's prayer practices effectively aligned the body with a particular faith.[3] Put more simply, the board treated Christianity as the official faith of the town.

Of equal importance, Justice Breyer's separate dissent explains carefully

2. *Town of Greece v. Galloway*, Opinion of the Court, at 17 (slip opinion).
3. *Id.*, Kagan, J., joined by Breyer, Ginsburg, and Sotomayor, JJ, dissenting, at 12-18 (slip opinion).

how the town violated the Establishment Clause by failing to take reasonable steps to ensure that its prayer practices did not identify the town with a particular faith.[4] These simple measures include affirmative outreach to a variety of religious communities represented among the town's residents; publicity at board meetings and the town Web site of the opportunity for all residents to offer an invocation at a future meeting; disclaimers by board members that the prayer represents the town's religious voice; and general reminders to prayer-givers about the nature of the audience and the reasons why inclusive prayer would be wise and appreciated. Such efforts, and the diversity of prayers they are likely to invite, all would serve to disconnect the town's official character from the content of any particular prayer or series of prayers.

In the wake of *Town of Greece,* much will be made of Justice Kennedy's admonition that a governmental body may not intentionally discriminate against any particular faith tradition in selecting a prayer-giver from among the citizenry. If members of minority faiths seek the prayer-giving opportunity, this limitation on government discretion may indeed lead to the sort of diversity that the town of Greece sorely lacked. Indeed, some governmental bodies may abandon their prayer practices rather than permit invocations that express highly unpopular views. Proposed invocations by atheists, in particular, may generate sufficient controversy and hostility that governmental entities will opt to eliminate invocations altogether.

But *Town of Greece* includes no judicial command that governmental bodies allow citizens to have an opportunity to offer legislative invocations. In order to avoid any nondiscrimination requirement, the elected members of the official body may choose to rotate the prayer opportunity among themselves. Alternatively, officials may hire or appoint a chaplain, who will pray as he or she chooses at each or every meeting. Proving that the choice of chaplain itself was done on a religiously discriminatory basis may prove quite difficult. Indeed, in *Marsh v. Chambers,* the Presbyterian chaplain had held that position for eighteen years.[5] Either of these strategies, carefully pursued, would effectively eliminate the nondiscrimination approach to situations like that presented in the town of Greece.[6]

---

4. *Id.,* Breyer, J., dissenting, at 1-6 (slip opinion). See also Kagan, J., dissenting, at 18-19 (slip opinion).

5. *Marsh v. Chambers,* 463 U.S. 783, 785 (1983).

6. Another strategy left open for future cases involves demonstration that persons attending official gatherings have been coerced into participation in prayer. All the Justices agreed that coercion would be a constitutional violation, although Justices Thomas and Scalia would limit the category of unconstitutional coercion to the imposition of legal penalties for

Appendix

Town of Greece helps prune away from the law of nonestablishment the conceptually ineffective doctrine of endorsement. Offense and alienation are not the focus of the Establishment Clause. But *Town of Greece* does no better than earlier decisions in identifying the constitutionally relevant inquiry. The Establishment Clause forbids any and all units of government from asserting a religious character. By permitting the town to maintain a prayer practice that manifests such a character, the Court has invited other governmental bodies to do likewise. Some will be quick to accept such an invitation.[7]

<hr/>

refusing to participate. Thomas, J., joined by Scalia, J., concurring, at 5-8 (slip opinion). The other seven would not require such a formal showing of coercion. Justices Kennedy, Alito, and Roberts (the other three in the majority in *Town of Greece*), however, insisted that the record in this case did not contain sufficient evidence that anyone had been pressured or coerced. Kennedy, J., joined by Alito, J., and Roberts, C.J., at 18-23 (slip opinion). Because the case had not been originally argued or tried in the lower courts as a case about coercion, that omission from the record was no surprise. Litigation in other communities may produce such evidence of coercion, but finding and presenting such evidence will not be easy.

7. See Michelle Boorstein, "Following Supreme Court decision, Carroll [County] Commissioners Allowed to Pray — for Now," http://www.washingtonpost.com/local/following-supreme-court-decision-carroll-commissioners-allowed-to-pray--for-now/2014/05/06/d1244782 (describing lifting of temporary injunction against prayer by Carroll County Commissioners at official meetings, and quoting Roanoke County Supervisor Al Bedrosian as saying that "we are a Christian nation," and that County prayer policy should be made accordingly).

266

Index

Index